The KML Handbook

The KML Handbook

Geographic Visualization for the Web

Josie Wernecke

✦✦ Addison-Wesley

Upper Saddle River, NJ • Boston • Indianapolis • San Francisco
New York • Toronto • Montreal • London • Munich • Paris • Madrid
Capetown • Sydney • Tokyo • Singapore • Mexico City

The small images on the front and back covers (which also appear in the text) are from the following sources:

Front cover: Valery Hronusov and Ron Blakey (Chapter 7), Google Earth image (Chapter 8), United States Holocaust Memorial Museum (Chapter 1), Angel Tello (Chapter 3), Pamela Fox (Chapter 1)

Back cover: Alaska Volcano Observatory (Chapter 6), Stefan Geens (Chapter 5), Jerome Burg (Chapter 4), Peter Webley (Chapter 7), James Stafford (Chapter 7)

The publisher offers excellent discounts on this book when ordered in quantity for bulk purchases or special sales, which may include electronic versions and/or custom covers and content particular to your business, training goals, marketing focus, and branding interests. For more information, please contact:

U.S. Corporate and Government Sales
(800) 382-3419
corpsales@pearsontechgroup.com

For sales outside the United States please contact:

International Sales
international@pearsoned.com

Visit us on the Web: informit.com/aw

Library of Congress Cataloging-in-Publication Data
Wernecke, Josie.
  Geographic visualization for the Web / Josie Wernecke.
     p. cm.
  Includes bibliographical references.
  ISBN 0-321-52559-0 (pbk. : alk. paper)
  1. Geographic information systems. 2. Information visualization. 3. KML (Document markup language) I. Title.

G70.212.W455 2009
910.285—dc22   2008033499

ISBN-13:   978-0-321-52559-8
ISBN-10:   0-321-52559-0
Text printed in the United States on recycled paper at Courier in Kendallville, Indiana.
First printing, October 2008

For Byron

Contents

Chapter 4
Styles and Icons. 71

Chapter 5
Overlays 109

Foreword

If you have ever hiked a ridge or climbed an Alpine peak, you know that magic moment when your view rises above what's immediately around you to reveal the new and distant land beyond. This is my sense as I write this foreword. I look back at a decade-long climb to advance Earth browsing technology from an idea to a patent to a start-up business and finally into the everyday lives of hundreds of millions of people. I look ahead to those further peaks—the greater good that you and other KML developers work by building on what we have done. But most of all, I look inward to see how a decade of virtually exploring our planet has raised my own perception, tolerance, and respect for spaceship Earth and its crew.

Experience has vividly demonstrated that geographic browsing has the power of personal exploration—so much so that users of products Google Earth and Google Maps often remark after seeing their homes and locations of their lives that, as T. S. Eliot wrote in *Little Gidding*, they now "know the place for the first time."

World-spanning, detailed imagery and terrain make the geobrowsing experience real. Smooth motion and the freedom of exploration make it engaging. Brought together in a geobrowser, these attributes give the age-old complaint "if you were there, you would understand" a solution. You can now easily "go there" any time, using your personal computer or mobile phone, and when you "get there" you will see the relevant information in its natural geospatial context and have the ability to browse the area at will. For the first time, all people can know, feel, and understand in the deep ways that formerly only travel could teach.

This understanding is the ambition of the Open Geospatial Consortium's KML—to provide a popular, pervasive, and international standard for the "what" that is embedded in the "where" and "when" of Earth browsers. The chapters of this book detail many forms for this "what," including points on, above, or below the Earth or even in outer space, lines for roads, paths, and boundaries, filled and outlined regions, text, images, 3D objects like buildings and boats, and various mechanisms and encodings for sharing each of these.

Together these elements form a comprehensive markup language and publishing framework annotating the Earth and other planets with the unbounded diversity of humanity's information. This role is like the relationship between page-oriented web browsers and HTML, the difference being that a page browser without an HTML file is just a blank page, while an Earth browser without a KML file will still offer a richly detailed world to explore and enjoy—it will lack only the annotation information that would turn the planet into a storytelling mechanism.

If this idea of a planet lacking the critical annotations to make a point—say real-time traffic and weather, the locations of your bank's ATMs, the trend of sea temperature rise near coral reefs, the story of Shackleton's voyage, the details of every location mentioned in a Jane Austen novel or Shakespeare play, or the spread of the H5N1 virus—troubles you and moves you to action, then KML and this book are for you. For in that case, you are one who will use the power of geobrowsing and the geoweb to create the distant land we see beyond today's mountaintop, a land where information has the power to save our planet, reshape politics, educate people, and improve life. For your role in using the virtual world to change the real one, I salute you.

Michael T. Jones
Chief Technology Advocate
Google

Preface

"Learning to 'see geographically' means grasping an ever-changing world in an integrated way. It means getting to the heart of environmental and human problems. It involves balancing global and local understandings. It opens an opportunity to encompass themes vital to today's world: the working of the earth's natural systems, the increasingly problematic interaction between people and the physical environment, the nature of human social organisation with all its inequalities and struggles for power over people and nature."

From "Why Choose Geography?"
Geography Department, University of Liverpool

I took my only formal geography class in the eighth grade from Mr. Granger, and I loved it. I'm intrigued by the different graphical styles of maps and continue to be amazed by the variety of information that can be shown geographically. By luck, two years ago I was assigned to a project at Google called "KML," which has been as much fun as any work can be and as instructive as a year-long series of college seminars, lectures, and personal tutorials. **KML** stands for **Keyhole Markup Language** and is a simple, human-readable format originally used by Google Earth (and now by a host of other Earth browsers).

This book is an attempt to share the knowledge I've gained from the experts at Google. When I joined it, the KML team consisted of two engineers: Bent Hagemark and Michael Ashbridge ("Mash"). Bent and Mash's mission was to corral the existing KML into a formal XML schema, to create compelling examples that would represent good coding style, and to shepherd the language to its new and deserved status as an international standard. I was to create a website for KML and expand the existing documentation. I managed to complete that task, but it always felt as though I'd exposed only the tip of the iceberg. Well, here's The Iceberg.

The *KML Handbook* is also an effort to publicize some of the inspirational KML work by brilliant thinkers around the world—many of them technical experts in their own fields but completely new to XML, KML, and even to the basics of computer programming. They've discovered that KML brings raw numbers, arbitrary place names, and flat maps to life, and they've struggled and experimented to discover the hidden logic behind Google Earth's data format. I hope that, with this book at your side, there will be no more struggles.

Audience

This book is written for people who are curious about how to create customized presentations for an Earth browser such as Google Earth but have little or no experience with computer programming. It also contains information primarily of interest for "power users" who want to use the more advanced features of the language. The text suggests the level of complexity for each general topic, and the chapters follow a basic flow from relatively simple to more complex topics.

What You Should Know Before Reading This Book

This book assumes you are somewhat familiar with creating, storing, and loading files onto a computer and into a web browser and that you're connected to the Internet. Although it describes a few elements of HTML that are used in a placemark balloon, it does not attempt to provide an in-depth explanation of HTML. If you're new to HTML, you'll probably want to consult some additional resources on that subject. You do not need to know XML in order to use KML; this book teaches you the XML basics required to use KML.

If you want to set up a server to host KML files referenced in network links (Chapter 6), you'll also need to select a web server software package such as Apache or lighttpd and then install and configure the server according to the specific instructions for that product. Chapter 6 offers some basic information on this topic, but the details are best left to the individual product documentation.

What This Book Contains

Chapter 1, A Quick Tour, provides an overview of the many different uses of KML, ranging from simple sets of placemarks to elaborate blogs and websites that use KML to make attractive, informative presentations of geographic data. This chapter describes a simple "Hello, Earth" example that illustrates the basic parts of a KML file.

Chapter 2, Placemarks and Balloons, describes how to create custom icons and attractive balloon styles. It contains detailed information on how to specify colors in KML and how to create KMZ archives.

Chapter 3, Geometry, goes into detail on specifying coordinates and altitude modes and also explains concepts related to geometry such as tessellation and extrusion. It includes examples and explanations of all geometry elements, including Models. It also shows you how to add elements describing the author and source of a KML file.

Chapter 4, Styles and Icons, explains how to use shared styles and how to create all types of substyles: icon, label, line, polygon, balloon, and list substyles.

Chapter 5, Overlays, describes how to create screen, ground, and photo overlays. Other topics covered here include the special processing required to add very large (gigapixel) photos to a photo overlay and how to specify a viewpoint using the Camera element.

Chapter 6, Network Links, covers how to host KML files on a web server, where they can be refreshed periodically or processed by user-written scripts. It also introduces network link controls, which control certain aspects of the fetching network link.

Chapter 7, Dynamic KML, provides detailed examples of the Update feature, which allows you to create, modify, and delete elements in KML files that have been previously fetched by a network link. This chapter also describes the time elements, which allow you to animate geometry in a KML file.

Chapter 8, Dealing with Large Data Sets, contains important information on regions and custom data types. Regions are a powerful mechanism that allow you to control the conditions under which a given feature comes into view. If you're interested in creating a custom balloon-style template for use throughout a KML presentation, be sure to read the section Entity Replacement for Extended Data Elements.

Appendix A, KML Reference, is an alphabetical reference that contains a brief description of every element and type in the KML standard, with syntax sections for all complex elements. This appendix describes the basic structure of a KML file and conventions of the language.

Appendix B, Sky Data in KML, describes how to display astronomical data in an Earth browser. It includes the syntax for the "hint" used at the beginning of the KML file to alert the browser that the file contains sky data and also describes how to convert celestial coordinates for display in Google Earth and other Earth browsers.

Trying the Examples

The complete set of examples for *The KML Handbook* is available at informit.com/title/0321525590. Click the link for any example to launch Google Earth and view the presentation. Then use the copy-and-paste trick (Chapter 1) to view the KML code.

Formatting Conventions

Code examples are set in `Courier` font. Syntax sections for complex elements are also set in `Courier` font, and they have a shaded background that distinguishes them from the examples. Elements discussed in the chapter are set in **boldface type**.

 This special icon indicates that the code example can also be found online at informit.com/title/0321525590.

KML element names are set in the normal text font and enclosed in angled brackets (for example: <Placemark>, <NetworkLink>, <GroundOverlay>). For readability, element names also appear as simple lowercased words when no ambiguity results from this more casual usage (for example: placemark, network link, ground overlay).

Acknowledgments

It's been a privilege to work with members of the Google Earth team: intelligent, creative, and generous people. This book is the result of patient teaching, helpful criticism, and enthusiastic coaching from many people at Google.

At the very top of the list is Bent Hagemark. His easygoing, friendly demeanor and soft-spoken style belie a rigorously demanding technical intelligence of the highest caliber. He taught me most of what I know about KML, and he's been willing to read and reread my prose as many times as I've had the energy to write and rewrite it. Similarly, Michael Ashbridge has provided endless and cheerful assistance every time I've requested it, along with a great sense of humor. Mano Marks, who joined the KML team soon after me to support external developers, has promptly reviewed all drafts and helped me understand the needs of our audience. I would never have attempted this book, and I certainly could never have completed the project, without the support of Bent, Mash, and Mano.

Many thanks, too, to the members of the Google Earth team, especially John Rohlf, Francois Bailly, Brent Austin, Greg Coombe, Ryan Scranton, Peter Birch, Michael Weiss-Malik, Brian McClendon, and Michael T. Jones. I also appreciate the assistance of the Google Earth Outreach team, especially Rebecca Moore and Jenifer Foulkes, who helped me track down some great examples of KML in the wild.

One of the most delightful parts of this project was searching the web for interesting applications of KML technology. Special thanks to all of the KML authors who so graciously granted permission to include their code and examples. Although space here is limited, I'd like to highlight the creators of some of the key examples used in this book (in order of appearance): Pamela Fox; Mano Marks; John Bailey, Peter Webley, and the Alaska Volcano Observatory; the Jane Goodall Institute; the United States Holocaust Memorial Museum; Angel Tello; Jerome Burg; Brian Flood; Stefan Geens; Declan Butler; Valery Hronusov and Ron Blakey; James Stafford; Bent Hagemark; Michael Ashbridge; the David Rumsey Map Collection; and Antonio Rocha Graca.

Writing is hard work, and it helped to have the support and understanding of the Google EngDocs writing team. Special thanks to Tina Ornduff, who shared an office cubicle with me for the duration of this project and provided frequent encouragement. We often reminded ourselves of Anne Lamott's book, *Bird by Bird*, as we tackled our seemingly endless writing tasks.

Addison-Wesley recruited a dedicated group of reviewers: Warren Kelly, Stephen Kemp, Daniel McKinnon, Jennifer Minnick, and Bob Yewchuk. I appreciate your conscientiousness in promptly reading every chapter and sending me such helpful criticism. Thanks to my editor, Greg Doench, for keeping the faith when I fell behind schedule at the start of the project, and to Michelle Housley and Elizabeth Ryan for keeping us all on track.

And finally, hugs and a toast to my friends, especially Priscilla Hospers and Judy Coughlin, and my family: my sons Jeff and Evan, my daughter-in-law Caryn, my sister Ruth—you have all been patient and interested, and I needed your help. Lastly, and from the bottom of my heart, thanks to Byron for sharing this journey.

Chapter 1

A Quick Tour

After reading this chapter, you'll be able to do the following:

- Give a simple definition of KML in layman's terms.

- List four possible use cases for a KML presentation.

- Search for KML files on the web on a topic that interests you, and then view them with an Earth browser.

- Create a simple KML file and share it with your friends.

KML (Keyhole Markup Language) is an XML data format used to display information in a geographic context. Just as web browsers read and display HTML files, Earth browsers such as Google Earth read and display KML files. KML is a human-readable language composed of text and punctuation. It can be created and edited with a basic text editor, saved, and then viewed in an Earth browser. You don't need to be a technical wizard to master the basics of KML, and you'll find that this knowledge will enable you to create powerful presentations that paint your own geographic data and imagery over the global palette provided by many popular (and free) Earth browsers.

KML: An International Standard

As Michael T. Jones describes in his foreword to this book, KML was originally created in 2001 by a company called Keyhole as the data format for its Earth browser named Earth Viewer. Since that time, KML has evolved to its status as an international standard for presenting geographic information visually. Its official name is the *OpenGIS KML 2.2 Encoding Standard* (OGC KML), which is controlled by the Open Geospatial Consortium (www.opengeospatial.org/standards/kml/). At present, tens of millions of KML files are shared on the World Wide Web.

For consistency and simplicity, this book displays most KML examples using Google Earth, as shown in Figure 1-1. However, KML is now widely supported by a variety of applications, including Microsoft Virtual Earth, Microsoft WorldWide Telescope, NASA WorldWind, ESRI ArcGIS Explorer, Google Maps, Google Maps for mobile, Adobe PhotoShop, Autodesk AutoCAD, and Yahoo! Pipes. And the list of Earth browsers, mapping applications, and mobile devices that support KML is growing daily. Not all platforms support all features of KML 2.2, so be sure to test your work on the target system or software application if you have a special use in mind. There may be slight variations across browsers, but the KML basics are the same. KML is a 3D system: *Length*, *width*, and *depth* are the typical three dimensions in 3D, but in this context, it's *longitude*, *latitude*, and *altitude* that form the three dimensions. However, 2D mapping applications such as Google Maps and Google Maps for mobile also support a subset of KML.

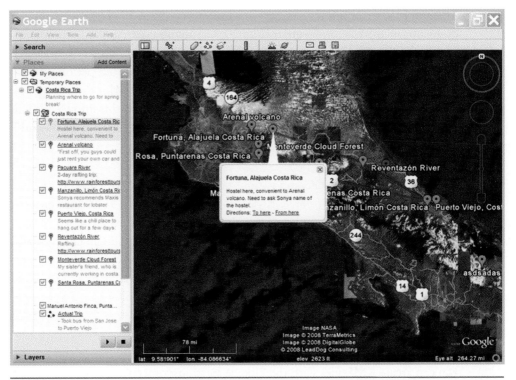

Figure 1-1 Share your experiences: your travels around town or around the world, places you've lived, photos you've taken. Blue icons indicate planned stops on a tour of Costa Rica. Balloons include travel tips and links to other trip resources. This file was originally created using Google's My Maps, a collaborative 2D mapping application, and was then imported into Google Earth. (KML created by Pamela Fox.)

Is the KML Specification Complete?

KML version 2.2 is complete, but the KML specification is evolving and will be expanded under control of the Open Geospatial Consortium (OGC). Version numbers for KML have a double numbering system in the form of *majorVersion.minorVersion*. KML versions that have the same major version are guaranteed to be compatible with each other. The official definition of the KML syntax is contained in the KML *schema*, a formal XML definition of the language (see www.opengeospatial.org/standards/kml/). KML 2.2, the current version, is guaranteed to be supported by the schema for KML 2.3 when it is developed. See Appendix A for more information on KML versioning.

The best place to check for progress on future versions of KML is the OCG website (www.opengeospatial.org/standards/kml/). Companies such as Google and Microsoft, which offer free Earth browsers, also provide documentation on KML. The website for this book (www.informit.com/title/9780321525598) is updated periodically to provide you with current information on recent developments in KML.

A Wealth of Resources

In addition to official OGC and various corporate websites, you'll want to check out the enthusiastic and informative KML blogging community. You'll find great tips, late-breaking news, and fabulous examples of using KML in the real world that will both educate and inspire you. Frank Taylor's long-running Google Earth Blog (www.gearthblog.com) and Stefan Geens' Ogle Earth (www.ogleearth.com) are two examples of blogs that offer a wealth of information on KML topics.

Creating and Sharing KML

You can create KML files with the Google Earth user interface, or you can use an XML or simple text editor to enter raw KML from scratch. KML files and their related images can be packaged up into KMZ archives so that all related image and model files are contained in one KMZ container (described in detail in Chapter 2). To share your KML and KMZ files, you can e-mail them as attachments, host them locally for sharing on a private home or corporate network, or host them publicly on a web server. Once you've properly configured your server and shared the web address of your KML files, anyone who's installed Google Earth (or other compatible application) can view the KML files you create.

Tell Your Story with KML

The KML community includes people with a broad range of interests and skills:

- Casual users create KML files to placemark their homes, to document journeys, and to plan cross-country hikes and cycling adventures.

- Students and teachers use KML to explore people, places, and events, both historical and current.

- Real estate professionals, architects, and city development agencies use KML to propose construction and visualize plans.

- Scientists use KML to provide detailed mappings of resources, models, and trends such as volcanic eruptions, weather patterns, earthquake activity, and mineral deposits (Figure 1-2).

- Organizations such as National Geographic, UNESCO, and the Smithsonian have all used KML to display their rich sets of global data.

You can use KML to add your own placemarks, geometry, annotations, and images on top of the base imagery of Google Earth. If you host the KML files on a server, you can

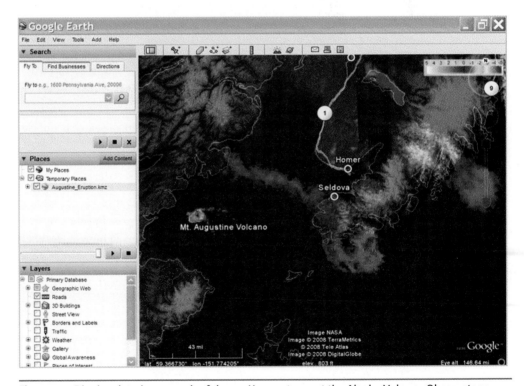

Figure 1-2 Display data in a meaningful way. Here, a team at the Alaska Volcano Observatory uses Google Earth to show an overlay of ash plumes created by an explosive eruption of Mt. Augustine Volcano. The colors represent temperature data. (Photo courtesy of John E. Bailey, Arctic Region Supercomputing Center, Fairbanks, Alaska.)

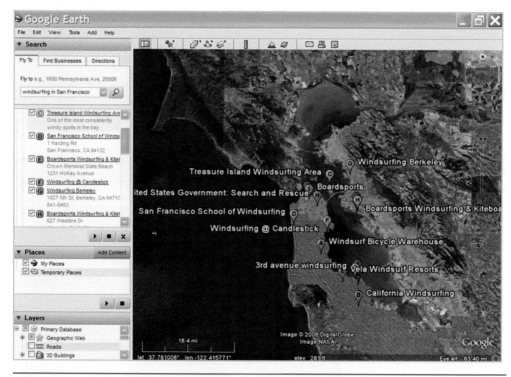

Figure 1-3 Search for information on a particular topic or place. Here, a search in Google Earth produces information on windsurfing spots near San Francisco.

even update your presentation on the user's system at regular intervals or whenever your data changes (see the discussion of network links in Chapter 6). Publicly hosted files are indexed by web search engines for easy access by all web users (Figure 1-3).

Personalizing your KML presentations is easy, through the use of custom styles for icons, information balloons, colors, lines, shapes, and labels. KML allows you to display features according to specific times within a given time range and to change the display according to the user's zoom level, with increasing levels of detail shown as the user flies in closer (Figure 1-4 and Figure 1-5).

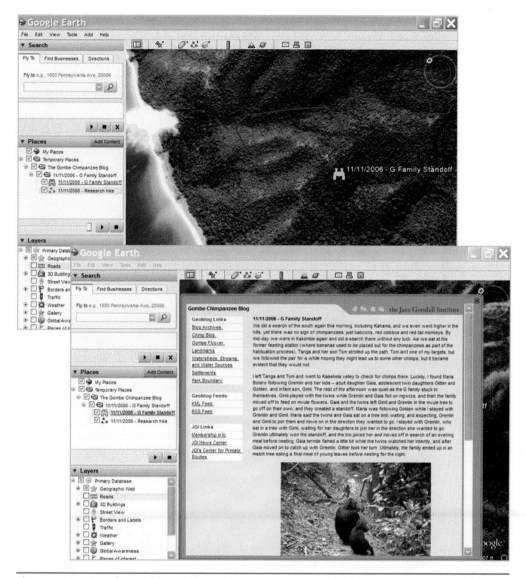

Figure 1-4 Explore the world . . . without leaving your armchair. Top image shows the path of a chimpanzee family studied by the Jane Goodall Institute in Gombe, Africa. Clicking the title opens the description balloon, which provides detailed information about the animals' behavior that day. (Images courtesy of the Jane Goodall Institute: http://gombeblog.janegoodall.org.)

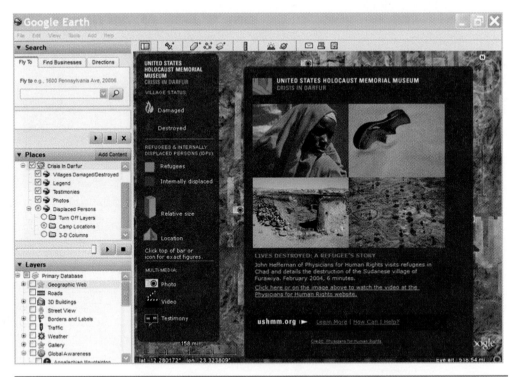

Figure 1-5 Deepen your understanding. Special projects like the United States Holocaust Memorial Museum's *Crisis in Darfur* initiative focus the world's attention on tragedies both personal and global by presenting photos, first-person narratives, and links to videos, all within a geographic context. (Image courtesy of United States Holocaust Memorial Museum: www.ushmm.org.)

Sky in KML

KML 2.2 supports presentation of astronomical as well as terrestrial data (as shown in Figure 1-6). When you include a special hint (`hint="target=sky"`) at the start of a KML file, the browser interprets the data in a different way and projects it onto a virtual celestial sphere that surrounds the Earth. In Sky mode, the Google Earth camera looks up at the heavens rather than down at the Earth. The main difference from the KML creator's point of view is that you need to perform some arithmetic to convert astronomical coordinates (*right ascension* and *declination*) into terrestrial coordinates (*longitude* and *latitude*). Everything else in KML works the same in both Sky and Earth modes.

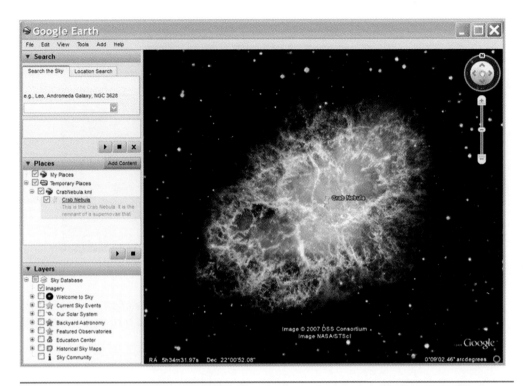

Figure 1-6 Travel through space. This KML file contains a placemark and balloon for a famous planetary nebula. To display sky data in an Earth browser, include the special KML hint, and convert astronomical coordinates to Earth coordinates (see Appendix B).

If you're primarily interested in using KML to show Sky data, read Appendix B, "Sky Data in KML," first.

"Hello, Earth"

A standard placemark in Google Earth uses a yellow pushpin icon to point to a particular spot on the Earth's surface. A placemark usually has a *name* that identifies the location. It's a good practice to include a *description* as well. The description is displayed by web search results and will help users decide if they want to view your KML files.

The following KML example creates a simple placemark with the name "Hello, Earth." The description provides additional information about this place (Figure 1-7).

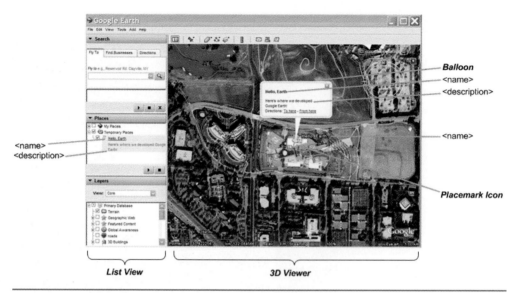

List View   **3D Viewer**

Figure 1-7 Anatomy of a placemark. You will usually create a *name* and a *description* for a place-mark. If you have a lot to say, description balloons provide related text, images, and links to other places on the web.

HelloEarth.kml

```
<?xml version="1.0" encoding="UTF-8"?>
<kml xmlns="http://www.opengis.net/kml/2.2">
  <Placemark>
    <name>Hello, Earth</name>
    <description>Here's where we developed Google Earth!</description>
    <Point>
      <coordinates>-122.084583,37.42227,0</coordinates>
    </Point>
  </Placemark>
</kml>
```

Viewing the Examples in This Book

To view this example in Google Earth, first download and install Google Earth. You can obtain a free copy of Google Earth from the Google website http://earth.google.com. A complete listing of examples is provided on this book's website at www.informit.com/title/9780321525598. Click the title of any example to view it in Google Earth.

Experiment!

If you'd like some hands-on experience, you can enter this example text into any basic text editor that saves text without adding any formatting information, such as Notepad. Save the file with a filename that ends in *.kml* and open the file in Google Earth on your computer. Once you've saved the file in this manner, you can also edit it. For example, try changing the <name>, save the file again, and then open it in Google Earth. Next, try modifying the values for the <coordinates> element, save the file, and watch where the new placemark appears.

The best way to learn KML is to experiment with sample files, changing values and viewing the results in your favorite Earth browser. If you make a mistake, you may not see anything in the browser, but that's your clue that something's amiss. Google Earth provides a feature for error checking that you may find helpful. (Select Options > General, and under the heading KML Error Handling, select Show Prompts for All Errors.) You can also use a KML validator to check your KML code. For example, see the KML validator by Galdos Systems at www. kmlvalidator.com.

Structure of a KML File

Every KML file begins with the two lines shown in this example.

```
<?xml version="1.0" encoding="UTF-8"?>
<kml xmlns="http://www.opengis.net/kml/2.2">
```

If you're creating a KML file from scratch, be sure to copy these two lines verbatim into the beginning of the file. A KML file can contain only one <kml> element. Don't forget the closing </kml> tag at the end of the file.

The file contains a <Placemark> element that has three children. The angled brackets < > indicate KML element names:

Children of <Placemark>

<name>	Label for the placemark.
<description>	Text (and optional images) providing additional information about the placemark. The <description> appears in the information *balloon*. This balloon pops up when the user clicks the placemark name in the Places panel or the placemark icon in the 3D viewer of Google Earth).
<Point>	Contains the <coordinates> element. The <coordinates> element contains values for the *longitude*, *latitude*, and *altitude* of the <Placemark>. See the section in Chapter 3 on "Coordinates" for more detail.

Figure 1-7 shows how the name and the description appear in both the 3D viewer and the Places panel of Google Earth.

Because KML is an XML data format, it has a consistent structure that observes certain patterns. An element begins with its name in angled brackets (<Placemark>). An element ends with an angled bracket and a slash preceding the element name (</Placemark>). The element's *value* is contained within these delimiters.

Definition of Simple/Complex Elements

In KML, any word contained in angled brackets < > is an *element*. When an element name begins with a capital letter, it is a *complex element,* which means that it can contain other elements. For example, in this code excerpt, <Point> is a complex element that *contains* the <coordinates> element:

```
<Point>
  <coordinates>-122.084583,37.42227,0</coordinates>
</Point>
```

Names of *simple elements* begin with a lowercase letter. Simple elements cannot contain other elements. A simple element contains only *character data* (in XML terms: letters, digits, and symbols that are not used for XML markup purposes). In the *HelloEarth.kml* example, <name>, <description>, and <coordinates> are examples of simple elements.

Complex elements are also called *parents* because they contain other elements. Simple elements are called *children*. In a KML file, the children are indented several spaces from their parent's position in the file, but this convention is simply for readability. The Earth browser does not pay attention to the different levels of indentation (white space).

General Rules in KML

Here are some general rules to keep in mind when authoring KML files:

- Case is significant. Each element name must be spelled exactly as shown in the KML 2.2 Reference, and with the same capitalization (see Appendix A).

- Order is significant. KML child elements must be listed in the same order as listed within their parent element in the KML 2.2 Reference. You can omit child elements, but you cannot rearrange them.

- Child elements can belong only to the allowed parent elements. Again, if you follow the ordering within the individual syntax sections in the KML 2.2 Reference, you'll be doing things correctly.

The Copy-and-Paste Trick

If you want to view the KML for a particular Google Earth folder or placemark, you can easily copy the feature from Google Earth and paste it into a text editor such as NotePad. (It's somewhat counterintuitive that you can copy a graphical feature from Google Earth's 3D viewer and, when you paste it into a text editor, it's converted to its corresponding KML textual format, but try it—it works!) Follow these steps to view the KML for a visible feature such as a Placemark, GroundOverlay (image laid on top of the basic Earth terrain), Polygon (shape), or LineString (path) in Google Earth.

1. In the 3D viewer (or Places panel) of Google Earth, place your cursor over the feature to highlight it.

2. Right-click and select Copy from the drop-down menu that appears.

3. Open a simple text editor and paste the contents of the clipboard; for example, by selecting Edit > Paste from the text editor menu.

   The KML for the selected feature appears in the text editor. (Be sure to use a text editor that does not add extra formatting or information to the text file.)

4. Save the file with a *.kml* extension in the filename (for example, *myHouseInPhila.kml*).

What's Next?

In the next chapter, you'll learn about two of the most basic KML elements, <Placemark> and <description>. Although you can create placemarks and balloon descriptions using an Earth browser graphical user interface, Chapter 2 explains how to modify the KML file to achieve custom effects and paves the way for you to efficiently create entire websites with a custom look and feel. The next chapter also explains how to package KML files into KMZ archives so that you can conveniently share them and post them on the web as one entity.

Chapter 2

Placemarks and Balloons

After reading this chapter, you'll be able to do the following:

- Create a placemark that uses HTML markup in a descriptive balloon.

- Add a custom icon to a placemark.

- Specify an explicit viewpoint for a placemark using the ‹LookAt› element.

- Create a set of placemarks and specify how to fly from one to the next.

X Marks the Spot

Use a <Placemark> element to mark a point on the Earth's surface. You can create a simple placemark—with a name, description, specific viewpoint, and location—with the user interface of an application such as Google Earth or Google Maps. This chapter takes you beyond the basics, so that you can create a KML file that adds special icons, more elaborate description balloons, and customized effects to your placemarks and tours.

In the "Hello, Earth" example in Chapter 1, you learned about the simple elements that make up a default balloon. You get this default balloon "for free"—that is, you don't explicitly create a "balloon" element. However, if you want to customize a balloon, you need to create a <BalloonStyle> element, which includes elements for customizing text color, background color, and text elements, as shown in the section "Changing the Background Color" later in this chapter.

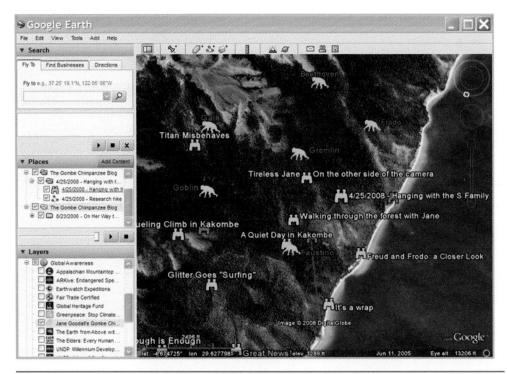

Figure 2-1 Placemarks with custom icons. This sample uses the binoculars icon for blog posts and the chimpanzee icon for profiles of individual animals. (Images courtesy of the Jane Goodall Institute: www.janegoodall.org/gombe-chimp-blog/.)

Customizing Your KML Presentation

An example of an informative and attractive style for KML balloons and placemarks is the Jane Goodall Institute blog, which describes firsthand observations of chimpanzee life in Gombe, Africa. Figure 2-1 shows placemarks and titles of various blog posts on this website (www.janegoodall.org/gombe-chimp-blog/). This site uses two custom icons. The chimpanzee icons link to profiles of individual chimpanzees, and the binoculars icons link to blog posts by naturalist Emily Wroblewski. Figure 2-2 shows the custom balloon style used by all the blog placemarks on this site. This balloon style uses an HTML table to position the two columns of text, as well as custom colors for text and the background. It also demonstrates use of an image link (to add the photograph) and hyperlinks to other web pages.

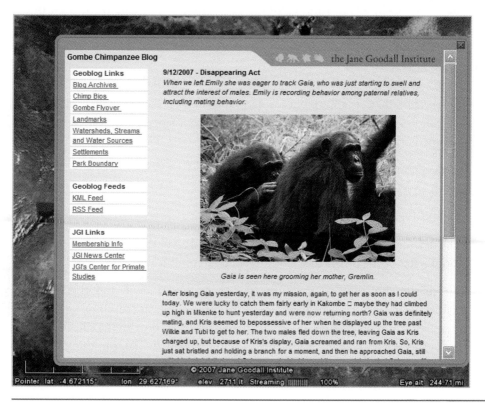

Figure 2-2 An attractive customized balloon style. This presentation by the Jane Goodall Institute uses a customized balloon style with a two-column layout, special fonts and background colors, hyperlinks, and images. (Used with permission of the Jane Goodall Institute; www.janegoodall.org.)

Placemarks with Points

What users commonly think of as a placemark in Google Earth is actually a <Placemark> element with a <Point> child in KML. A point placemark is the only way to draw an icon and label in the 3D view of Google Earth. By default, the icon is the familiar yellow pushpin. In KML, a <Placemark> can contain one or more Geometry elements, such as a <LineString>, <Polygon>, or <Model>. But only a <Placemark> with a <Point> has an icon and label. The icon indicates the position of the point.

The Geometry element in a <Placemark> is optional, but if you omit it, the balloon "floats" in the corner of the 3D view. In the Google Earth 3D view, a point placemark is the only object you can click or roll over. Other Geometry elements do not have an icon in the 3D view. You can, however, give any Geometry an icon by using a <MultiGeometry> element that contains both a <Point> and the other Geometry element. (See Chapter 3 for more information on Geometry and an example of this use.)

Default Balloon

This section dissects a simple placemark, focusing on how to make simple changes to the balloon and how to specify additional style elements. By default, a balloon in Google Earth includes the following elements:

- The <name>, in boldface type
- The placemark <description>
- Links for driving directions: *To here—From here*

The default balloon has a white background and a tail that is attached to the point coordinates of the placemark, if it includes a <Point> element.

The driving directions are useful for tours in areas with roads and in places where people drive cars or other vehicles. If your placemarks indicate camping spots in the Himalayas or jungle homes of chimpanzees, however, the driving directions are usually irrelevant. See the section "Omitting Driving Directions" later in this chapter for information on how to leave out this item. If a <Placemark> does not contain a <Point>, the driving directions are automatically omitted.

Modifying the Balloon

This section provides step-by-step instructions for modifying the balloon for a placemark.

Adding Text

The <description> element in <Placemark> supports a subset of HTML markup as described in the *KML 2.2 Reference* (see Appendix A). If you are using HTML, it's easiest if you include the HTML code inside CDATA brackets, as shown in the *SimpleTextBalloon.kml* example.

This technique hides the HTML from the KML parser. If you omit the CDATA tags, you'll need to escape angled brackets (which means to substitute special character sequences for HTML symbols). Without the CDATA tags, for example, you would type < instead of < and > instead of >. Instead of <p>, you would thus need to type <p>, which is much harder to type and read. Similar escape sequences must be used for any special HTML markup characters if you omit the CDATA tags.

SimpleTextBalloon.kml

```
<?xml version="1.0" encoding="UTF-8"?>
<kml xmlns="http://www.opengis.net/kml/2.2">
  <Placemark>
    <name>9/12/2007 - Disappearing Act</name>
    <description>
      <![CDATA[
        <p>After losing Gaia yesterday it was my mission to get her as
        soon as I could today. We were lucky to catch them fairly early
        in Kakombe.</p>

        <p>The two males fled down the tree, leaving Gaia as Kris
        charged up, but Gaia screamed and ran from Kris.</p>

        <p>Unfortunately, after they left the mvule tree, they headed to
        the waterfalls where they effortlesssly climbed up the vines and
        over the waterfall in a matter of seconds.</p>
      ]]>
    </description>
    <Point>
      <coordinates>18.615106,-4.841399,0</coordinates>
    </Point>
  </Placemark>
</kml>
```

Adding Space Between Paragraphs

The previous example shows how to use the HTML <p> paragraph element to add a line break and a space between paragraphs in a description. Close the paragraph with the </p> tag. For example:

```
<description>
  <![CDATA[
    <p>The two males fled down the tree, leaving Gaia as Kris charged
    up, but Gaia screamed and ran from Kris.</p>

    <p>Unfortunately, after they left the mvule tree, they headed to the
    waterfalls where they effortlesssly climbed up the vines and over
    the waterfall in a matter of seconds.</p>
  ]]>
</description>
```

To add a line break without the extra vertical space, use the tag <br />.

Adding Italic Type

To add italic type, enclose the italicized words with the HTML markup for italic: <em> and </em>, as shown here:

```
<description>
  <![CDATA[
    <p><em>After losing Gaia yesterday it was my mission to get her as
    soon as I could today. We were lucky to catch them fairly early in
    Kakombe.</em></p>
    <p>The two males fled down the tree, leaving Gaia as Kris charged
    up, but Gaia screamed and ran from Kris.</p>
    <p>Unfortunately, after they left the <em>mvule</em> tree, they
    headed to the waterfalls where they effortlesssly climbed up the
    vines and over the waterfall in a matter of seconds.</p>
  ]]>
</description>
```

Adding Boldface Type

To add boldface type, enclose the boldface words with the HTML markup for boldface: <b> and </b>, as shown here:

```
<description>
  <![CDATA[
    <b>The Jane Goodall Institute</b>
  ]]>
</description>
```

Adding Hyperlinks

Hyperlinks are references to other resources on the World Wide Web. Use standard HTML to add a hyperlink to the balloon. When the user clicks on this link, the target address (URL) opens in a new browser window. For example:

```
<description>
  <![CDATA[
    <a href="http://www.discoverchimpanzees.org">
    JGI's Center for Primate Studies</a>
  ]]>
</description>
```

The complete hyperlink is enclosed in the <a> and </a> tags. The href attribute of the opening <a> tag contains the URL of the link, in quotation marks. The value of the <a> tag (that is, the string between the beginning and end tags for this element) contains the text that is displayed in the description.

Adding Images

To add an image to the balloon, use the HTML <img> tag. For example:

```
<description>
  <![CDATA[
    <img src="janeGoodall.jpg" />
  ]]>
</description>
```

This example uses an image file that is located in the same directory as the KML file. The image reference can also be the URL of an image stored on the web (for example: http://someServer/someDirectory/myPhoto.jpg). Other supported image formats are *.png, .tif,* and *gif.*

Example

The *SimpleTextBalloon.kml* file shows the KML code for the sample description, with line breaks, italic and boldface text, a hyperlink, and an image:

SimpleTextBalloon.kml

```
<?xml version="1.0" encoding="UTF-8"?>
<kml xmlns="http://www.opengis.net/kml/2.2">
```

```
<Placemark>
  <name>9/12/2007 - Disappearing Act</name>
  <description>
    <![CDATA[
    <p><em>After losing Gaia yesterday it was my mission to get her as
    soon as I could today. We were lucky to catch them fairly early in
    Kakombe.</em></p>

    <p>The two males fled down the tree, leaving Gaia as Kris charged
    up, but Gaia screamed and ran from Kris.</p>

    <p>Unfortunately, after they left the <em>mvule</em> tree, they
    headed to the waterfalls where they effortlesssly climbed up the
    vines and over the waterfall in a matter of seconds.</p>
    <p>
    <a
    href="http://www.discoverchimpanzees.org">JGI's Center for Primate
    Studies</a></p>
    <br />
    <p align=center><img src="janeGoodall.jpg" /></p>
    <br />
    <b>The Jane Goodall Institute</b>
    ]]>
  </description>
  <Point>
    <coordinates>18.615106,-4.841399,0</coordinates>
  </Point>
</Placemark>
</kml>
```

Figure 2-3 shows this example displayed in Google Earth.

Simple Balloon Template

You can use the *BalloonTemplate.kml* file as a template for adding text, images, and links to a placemark balloon (Figure 2-4). Copy this text into a basic text editor such as Notepad (be sure it does not add any extra formatting). Then try substituting your own text, images, and links in this template. Save the file with a *.kml* extension in the file-name (for example, *MyFavoritePlacemark.kml*), and then open the file in Google Earth or any Earth browser that accepts KML files.

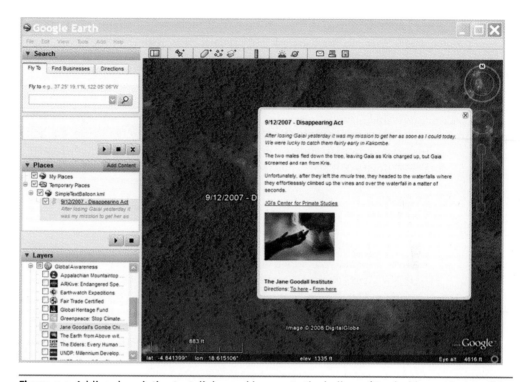

Figure 2-3 Adding descriptive text, links, and images to the balloon. (Used with permission of the Jane Goodall Institute; www.janegoodall.org.)

Figure 2-4 A simple template for modifying text and adding links and images.

In Google Earth, to reload the file and see your incremental changes to it, right-click the Placemark name in the list view and select Revert from the drop-down menu.

BalloonTemplate.kml

```
<?xml version="1.0" encoding="UTF-8"?>
<kml xmlns="http://www.opengis.net/kml/2.2">
<Document>
  <Placemark>
    <name>Placemark Name</name>
    <description>
      <![CDATA[
        Your first paragraph.
        <br/>

        Here is how you add a link:
        <p><a href="http://code.google.com/apis/kml">
          Substitute your own link name here.</a></p>

        <p>Here's the syntax to insert an image:
        <img src="http://code.google.com/images/code_sm.png"></p>

        <p><b>Boldface type example.</b></p>

        <p><em>Italic type example.</em></p>
      ]]>
    </description>
  </Placemark>
</Document>
</kml>
```

Changing the Background Color

To change the background color of the balloon, use the <BalloonStyle> element, which is always contained in a <Style> element. This example changes the background color to aqua:

```
<Style>
  <BalloonStyle>
    <bgColor>fff8fa00</bgColor>
  </BalloonStyle>
</Style>
```

Specifying Color Values

Color values in KML contain two parts: a *transparency* value and a *color* value that has *blue*, *green*, and *red* components. Currently, Google Earth ignores the transparency value for balloon backgrounds, so this discussion focuses on specifying the actual colors. See Chapter 5 for details on specifying transparency.

The range of values for any one color is 0 to 255, with 0 meaning "none of this color," and 255 meaning "complete saturation of this color."

In KML, colors are expressed in *hexadecimal notation* (base 16, which uses the digits *0* through *9* and then *a*, *b*, *c*, *d*, *e*, and *f* in its numerical notation). Each of the four components (transparency, blue, green, red) is expressed as two digits, in the following order: *aabbggrr*

where

> *aa* are the two digits specifying the transparency value (*a* stands for the alpha channel, which is often used in computer graphics to store the transparency component of a color). A value of 00 indicates completely transparent. A value of ff indicates completely opaque (no transparency).
>
> *bb* are the two digits specifying the blue color value.
>
> *gg* are the two digits specifying the green color value.
>
> *rr* are the two digits specifying the red color value.

In hexadecimal, 00 means "none of this color value," and ff means "full saturation of this color value."

Table 2-1 lists the basic colors.

Table 2-1 Specifying Hexadecimal Values for Color

Color Name	Hexadecimal Value in KML
Red (opaque)	ff0000ff
Green (opaque)	ff00ff00
Blue (opaque)	ffff0000
White (opaque)	ffffffff
Black (opaque)	ff000000

> **Note**
>
> HTML also uses the concept of red, green, and blue color components. However, the order in HTML is *RGB*, whereas the order in KML is *BGR*. You can search for "HTML colors" on the web to find tables of HTML hexadecimal color values. If

you reorder the RGB components to BGR, you can use them in KML files. Another difference between HTML and KML color specification is that KML does not recognize the standard color names ("red," "white," "pink," etc.) that can be used in place of numerical values in HTML.

Table 2-2 lists a sample set of KML colors.

Table 2.2 Specifying Hexadecimal Values for Color

Color Name	Hexadecimal Value in KML (all values are opaque)
Aqua	ff00ffff
Cornflower Blue	ffed9564
DarkBlue	ff8b0000
DarkGreen	ff006400
GreenYellow	ff2fffad
DarkMagenta	ff8b008b
DeepPink	ff9314ff
FireBrick	ff2222b2
DarkOrange	ff008cff
Olive	ff008080
Tan	ffccffff

For example, to specify a balloon with a background color of tan, the KML code is as follows:

```
<Style>
  <BalloonStyle>
    <bgColor>ffccffff</bgColor>
  </BalloonStyle>
</Style>
```

Using the Google Earth Color Selector

The Google Earth user interface includes a Color Selector that allows you to choose colors for lines and polygon outlines and fills. Although the user interface does not allow you to specify the color for a balloon background, you can use the Color Selector to identify the desired color, as described in the following steps. Then you can add a <bgColor> element to the KML file with this color as its value.

1. Create a Polygon in Google Earth. Right-click to select Properties; then go to the Style/Color tab and click the Color square to bring up the Color Selector.

2. Use the Color Selector tool to choose a color. Suppose you select a vibrant yellow with values of Red:255, Green:255, and Blue:127.

3. Use the copy-and-paste trick to copy the colored polygon into a simple text editor such as Notepad.

4. You can now view the hexadecimal value for the color you've created. In this example, you'll see these lines of KML code:

```
<PolyStyle>
    <color>ff7fffff</color>
</PolyStyle>
```

To use this yellow color as the background color of a balloon, specify it as the value for the <bgColor> element, as follows:

```
<Style>
 <BalloonStyle>
   <bgColor>ff7fffff</bgColor>
 </BalloonStyle>
</Style>
```

Inline Styles

Chapter 4 describes the Style element in detail and shows you how to define a *shared style*. For now, just include the <Style> element as an *inline* element within the <Placemark> element, as shown in *SimpleTextBalloonWithStyle.kml*. This example also includes a KML comment, which begins with <!-- and ends with -->. A comment adds information to the file that is not displayed in the Earth browser.

SimpleTextBalloonWithStyle.kml

```
<?xml version="1.0" encoding="UTF-8"?>
<kml xmlns="http://www.opengis.net/kml/2.2">
  <Document>
  <Placemark>
    <name>9/12/2007 - Disappearing Act</name>
    <description>
      <![CDATA[
        <em>After losing Gaia yesterday it was my mission to get her as
        soon as I could today. We were lucky to catch them fairly early
        in Kakombe.</em>
        <p>
        <b>The Jane Goodall Institute</b>
      ]]>
    </description>
```

```
      <Style>
        <BalloonStyle>
          <bgColor>ff669999</bgColor>        <!-- default=ffffffff -->
        </BalloonStyle>
      </Style>
      <Point>
        <coordinates>18.615106,-4.841399,0</coordinates>
      </Point>
    </Placemark>
    </Document>
</kml>
```

In KML, the order of child elements within the parent element must be maintained. In the <Placemark> element, for example, the <Style> element is always placed after the <description>.

Changing the Text Color

Changing the color of the text inside a balloon is similar to specifying the color of the background. Use the <textColor> element of <BalloonStyle> to change the text color. The color is specified in the same way as the background color: specify four hexadecimal values for the *alpha*, *blue*, *green*, and *red* color components. For example, to specify navy blue text and a putty background:

```
<Style>
  <BalloonStyle>
    <bgColor>ff669999</bgColor>
    <textColor>ff660000</textColor>
  </BalloonStyle>
</Style>
```

Omitting Driving Directions

To include the *To here/From here* driving directions in a balloon, you can include the following line anywhere in the <text> child element of <BalloonStyle>:

```
$[geDirections]
```

To omit the driving directions from a balloon, include a text element with *entities* for the <name> and <description> elements. The entities are easy to spot because they begin with a $ sign, with the element name enclosed in square brackets:

```
<Style>
  <BalloonStyle>
    <text>
      <![CDATA[
        $[name]
        <p>
        $[description]
      ]]>
    </text>
  </BalloonStyle>
</Style>
```

The entity acts as a placeholder for the actual values defined in the <Placemark> element. Thus, in this example, $[name] is replaced with "9/12/2007 - Disappearing Act" and $[description] is replaced with the text that begins "After losing Gaia yesterday . . . ."

Adding a Custom Icon

To add a custom icon, use the <IconStyle> element to specify the custom image to use as an icon. You can specify one of the standard Google Earth icons located on the web, or you can specify your own image. If you supply your own image, be sure to include the image in the KMZ archive, or post it on a web server so that other users can load the icon with your KML file.

> **Tip**
>
> To use a standard Google Earth icon, go to the Edit Placemark dialog in Google Earth and click the yellow pushpin icon. This action brings up the standard icon palette In Google Earth. When you click an icon in this palette, its URL is displayed at the top of the dialog box. You can specify this URL as the value of <href> in the <IconStyle> element.

Here is an example of using the <IconStyle> element to add the binoculars icon shown in the Jane Goodall website blog. The image file is stored in the same location as the KML file that references it, so it does not need the full path specification.

```
<IconStyle>
  <Icon>
    <href>binoculars1.png</href>
  </Icon>
</IconStyle>
```

If the icon image file is stored on a remote server, you need to specify the full URL in the <href> element. Here is an example:

```
<IconStyle>
  <Icon>
    <href>http://www.janegoodall.org/news/gombe-
      blog/assets/binoculars1.png
    </href>
  </Icon>
</IconStyle>
```

Advanced Balloon Template

The *AdvancedTemplate.kml* file is a template you can use to begin adding text, images, links, custom colors, and custom icons to a placemark balloon. Copy this text into a basic text editor and try substituting your own text, colors, and links in this template. Save the file with a *.kml* extension in the filename—for example, *MyFavoritePlacemark.kml*—then open the file in Google Earth or any Earth browser that accepts KML files.

In Google Earth, to reload the file and see your incremental changes to it, right-click the placemark name in the list view and select Revert from the drop-down menu.

AdvancedTemplate.kml

```
<?xml version="1.0" encoding="UTF-8"?>
<kml xmlns="http://www.opengis.net/kml/2.2">
<Document>
  <Placemark>
    <name>Placemark Name</name>
    <description>
      <![CDATA[
        Your first paragraph.
        </br>

        Here is how you add a link:
        <a href="http://code.google.com/apis/kml">
          Substitute your own link name here.</a>

        <p>
        Here's the syntax to insert an image:
          <img src="http://code.google.com/images/code_sm.png">
        </p>
```

```
          <p>
            <b>Boldface type example.</b>
          </p>

          <p>
            <em>Italic type example.</em>
          </p>
        ]]>
      </description>
      <Style>
        <IconStyle>
          <Icon>
            <href>binoculars1.png</href>
          </Icon>
        </IconStyle>
        <BalloonStyle>
          <bgColor>ff669999</bgColor>      <!-- default=ffffffff -->
          <textColor>ff660000</textColor>  <!-- default=ff000000 -->
          <text>                    <!-- eliminates the driving directions -->
            <![CDATA[
            $[name]
            <p>
            $[description]
            ]]>
          </text>
        </BalloonStyle>
      </Style>
      <Point>
        <coordinates>...</coordinates>
      </Point>
    </Placemark>
  </Document>
</kml>
```

Specifying a Viewpoint

When the user double-clicks a placemark, Google Earth automatically zooms to a view directly over the placemark. You can control the initial view of the placemark by specifying a <LookAt> or <Camera> element that defines the exact viewpoint for the point of interest. This section describes how to specify a <LookAt> element for a placemark.

Once you've created a set of placemarks, you can fly to each in succession, as shown in the section "Flying to a Placemark" later in this chapter. See Chapter 5, "Overlays," for more information on cameras.

LookAt Element

The <LookAt> element describes a viewpoint using a point on the Earth's surface as a reference. Here is the syntax for this element:

```
<LookAt id="ID">
   <longitude>0.0</longitude>
   <latitude>0.0</latitude>
   <altitude>0.0</altitude>
   <heading>0.0</heading>
   <tilt>0.0</tilt>
   <range>0.0</range>
   <altitudeMode>clampToGround</altitudeMode>
</LookAt>
```

In the syntax sections of this book, default values are listed for each simple element. For more detailed syntax information on KML elements, see Appendix A, which includes information on the type of each element. If the element is an enumerated value, the appendix also lists all of the defined enum values. (In <LookAt>, the <altitudeMode> element contains enumerated values.) The syntax sections in Appendix A use comments to enclose the type information for each element value.

The child elements for <LookAt> are as follows:

<longitude>
> Longitude of the point the viewpoint is looking at. Angular distance in degrees, relative to the Prime Meridian. Values west of the Meridian range from −180 degrees to 0 degrees. Values east of the Meridian range from 0 degrees to 180 degrees.

<latitude>
> Latitude of the point the viewpoint is looking at. Degrees north or south of the Equator (0 degrees). Values range from −90 degrees to 90 degrees.

<altitude>
> Distance from the Earth's surface, in meters. See <altitudeMode> for how this value is interpreted.

<heading>

Direction (that is, North, South, East, West), in degrees. Default = 0 (North). Values range from 0 degrees to 360 degrees, with 90 degrees = East, 180 degrees = South, 270 degrees = West. This value can also be specified in negative degrees (counterclockwise from 0).

<tilt>

Angle between the direction of the LookAt position and the normal surface of the Earth (see Figure 2-5). Values range from 0 degrees to 180 degrees. Values for <tilt> cannot be negative. A <tilt> value of 0 degrees indicates viewing from directly above, looking straight down. A <tilt> value of 90 degrees indicates viewing along the horizon.

<range>

Distance in meters from the point specified by <longitude>, <latitude>, and <altitude> to the LookAt position (see Figure 2-5).

<altitudeMode>

Specifies how the <altitude> specified for the LookAt point is interpreted. Possible values are as follows:

`clampToGround` (default)

Indicates to ignore the <altitude> specification and place the LookAt position on the ground.

`relativeToGround`

Interprets the <altitude> as a value in meters above the ground.

`absolute`

Interprets the <altitude> as a value in meters above sea level.

Figure 2-5 shows how these parameters relate to the position of a virtual camera that defines the viewpoint.

Tip

The easiest way to create a ‹LookAt› element with the desired values is to use the Snapshot View feature of Google Earth. Select the Feature in the Google Earth 3D viewer, and then fly around, tilt, or rotate until you're satisfied with the view. Right-click the Feature and select Snapshot View. Use the copy-and-paste trick described in Chapter 1 to view the ‹LookAt› values in a text editor.

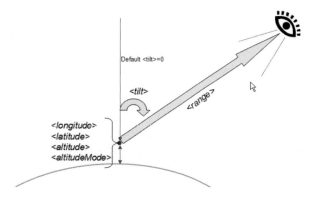

Figure 2-5 Parameters for the ‹LookAt› element.

Troubleshooting

If you explicitly specify a viewpoint for a placemark, Google Earth observes your viewpoint, even if the placemark containing the <LookAt> or <Camera> element is not visible. Test your KML code to be sure the viewpoint achieves the results you desire. If you've specified a <LookAt> and your placemark suddenly disappears from view, it's possible you need to adjust the parameters in your <LookAt> element.

Here is an example of using the <LookAt> element to specify a viewpoint for the Disappearing Act placemark:

```
<LookAt>
  <longitude>18.615083</longitude>
  <latitude>-4.841518</latitude>
  <altitude>0</altitude>
  <range>8969.164821</range>
  <tilt>57.480205</tilt>
  <heading>11.022992</heading>
</LookAt>
```

Figure 2-6 shows this placemark viewed with this <LookAt> element. The <LookAt> element is added to the placemark element immediately after <description>.

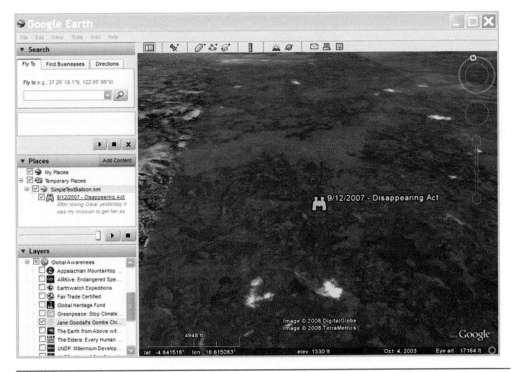

Figure 2-6 Adding a <LookAt> element and a custom icon to a <Placemark>.

Flying to a Placemark in Google Earth

Use a <Folder> element to group multiple placemarks. A <Folder>, like a <Placemark>, has <name> and <description> elements, which appear in the list view. In Google Earth, you can tour the placemarks in a folder by clicking the folder and selecting the triangular Play button in the list view. If you specify viewpoints for the placemarks, Google Earth automatically flies to the specified viewpoint for each placemark. The *GroupingPlacemarks.kml* file shows a <Folder> that contains four <Placemark> elements, each with a viewpoint specified by a <LookAt> element.

GroupingPlacemarks.kml

```
<?xml version="1.0" encoding="UTF-8"?>
<kml xmlns="http://www.opengis.net/kml/2.2">
  <Folder>
```

```
<name>Flying to a Placemark</name>
<open>1</open>
<Placemark id="home">
  <name>My First Placemark</name>
  <description>This is the beginning of the journey.</description>
  <LookAt>
    <longitude>18.595265</longitude>
    <latitude>-4.809265</latitude>
    <altitude>0</altitude>
    <range>13962.113122</range>
    <tilt>52.8432160</tilt>
    <heading>-146.759920</heading>
  </LookAt>
  <Style>
    <IconStyle>
      <Icon>
        <href>binoculars1.png</href>
      </Icon>
    </IconStyle>
   </Style>
  <Point>
    <coordinates>18.615106,-4.841399,0</coordinates>
  </Point>
</Placemark>
<Placemark id="lunch">
  <name>My Second Placemark</name>
  <description>
    <![CDATA[
      This is the second stop on the tour.
      <a href="#journeyEnd;balloonFlyto">
      Click here</a> to go to the end of the tour.
    ]]>
  </description>
  <LookAt>
    <longitude>18.598893</longitude>
    <latitude>-4.833605</latitude>
    <altitude>0</altitude>
    <range>11566.909708</range>
    <tilt>52.843802</tilt>
    <heading>-111.390223</heading>
  </LookAt>
  <Style>
    <IconStyle>
      <Icon>
```

```
      <href>binoculars1.png</href>
    </Icon>
   </IconStyle>
  </Style>
 <Point>
   <coordinates>18.605812,-4.856031,0</coordinates>
 </Point>
</Placemark>
<Placemark id="rest">
  <name>My Third Placemark</name>
  <description>
   <![CDATA[
    Moving right along ... <a href="#lunch;balloonFlyto">
    Click here</a> to return
    to the lunch spot.
   ]]></description>
  <LookAt>
    <longitude>18.579639</longitude>
    <latitude>-4.8470967</latitude>
    <altitude>0</altitude>
    <range>7431.249174</range>
    <tilt>52.843246</tilt>
    <heading>-79.190397</heading>
  </LookAt>
  <Style>
   <IconStyle>
    <Icon>
      <href>binoculars1.png</href>
    </Icon>
   </IconStyle>
  <Style>
  <Point>
    <coordinates>18.59093,-4.863163,0</coordinates>
  </Point>
</Placemark>
<Placemark id="journeyEnd">
  <name>My Fourth Placemark</name>
  <description>This is the last stop.</description>
  <LookAt>
    <longitude>18.566320</longitude>
    <latitude>-4.721962</latitude>
    <altitude>0</altitude>
    <range>18890.906055</range>
    <tilt>52.843308</tilt>
```

```
      <heading>-9.004620</heading>
    </LookAt>
    <Style>
      <IconStyle>
        <Icon>
          <href>binoculars1.png</href>
        </Icon>
      </IconStyle>
    </Style>
    <Point>
      <coordinates>18.575425,-4.755368,0</coordinates>
    </Point>
  </Placemark>
  </Folder>
</kml>
```

Flying to a New Placemark

Notice in the previous example how each <Placemark> element has an ID assigned to it. The *id* attribute is a unique identification of a KML element within a KML file. Once you assign an ID to an element, you can reference that element, both within the file and from other KML files. To reference an element defined in the current file, precede the ID with a # sign, as shown in the previous example. To reference an element defined in another file, include the complete filename. For example:

```
http://myserver.com/TourOfFrenchChateaux.kml#PalaisRoyale
```

Feature Anchors

The FlyTo behavior associated with hyperlinks in Google Earth can be further specified by appending one of the following three strings to the URL:

`;flyto` Fly to the placemark.

`;balloon` Open the placemark's balloon but do not fly to the placemark.

`;balloonFlyto` Open the placemark's balloon and fly to the placemark.

The *GroupingPlacemarks.kml* example uses the `balloonFlyto` specification in the second and third placemarks.

Other Children of Placemark

Other commonly used child elements of <Placemark> include the following:

- <visibility> specifies whether the 3D view draws the placemark when it is first shown in Google Earth. A value of 1 specifies to draw the placemark (and places a check in its checkbox in the list view). A value of 0 specifies not to draw the placemark (and leaves the checkbox empty in the list view). In the Google Earth list view, the user can click the checkbox to toggle its value.

- <Snippet> is a short description of the placemark that is used in the list view under the placemark name. You can specify the maximum number of lines displayed. If no snippet is provided, the first two lines of the <description> are used in the list view. In contrast to the <description> element, the <Snippet> does not support HTML markup. To prevent the <description> from appearing in the list view, include an empty snippet element in the <Placemark>: <Snippet/>

Syntax for <Placemark>

Here is the complete list of the child elements for <Placemark>. This sections lists all the child elements you can add to a <Placemark> element. The child elements discussed in this chapter are listed in boldface type. See Appendix A for a complete description of all elements.

```
<Placemark id="ID">
  <!-- inherited from Feature element -->
  <name>...</name>
  <visibility>1</visibility>
  <open>0</open>
  <atom:author>...<atom:author>
  <atom:link />
  <address>...</address>
  <xal:AddressDetails>...</xal:AddressDetails>
  <phoneNumber>...</phoneNumber>
  <Snippet maxLines="2">...</snippet>
  <description>...</description>
  <AbstractView>...</AbstractView>
  <TimePrimitive>...</TimePrimitive>
  <styleUrl>...</styleUrl>
  <StyleSelector>...</StyleSelector>
  <Region>...</Region>
  <ExtendedData>...</ExtendedData>
  <!-- specific to Placemark element -->
  <Geometry>...</Geometry>
</Placemark>
```

Related Feature Elements

A *Feature* is an abstract element, which means it is never actually used in a KML file. *Abstract elements* are an efficient way to define elements that have many behaviors in common. Figure 2-7 also shows that Feature itself is derived from another base element, Object. Any element derived from Object can have an *id* attribute assigned to it. Identifiers are useful in creating links to placemarks, as shown in this chapter. They are also used to update element values after a KML file has been loaded (see Chapter 7, "Dynamic KML").

The <Placemark> element belongs to a family of elements, all of which are derived from the base element, Feature. The Feature element provides a set of children that are inherited by all of its descendants. Figure 2-7 shows the elements derived from Feature.

These elements all have a set of children in common, and they each have certain children that are unique to them and give them their distinctive behavior. Review the syntax for the <Placemark> element to see the elements common to all elements derived from Feature. (See "Syntax for <Placemark>" earlier in the chapter.)

The behavior of the child elements depends on the context in which it is used. For example, the <open> element specifies whether a <Document>, <Folder>, or <NetworkLink> is open (1) or closed (0) when the feature is first opened. When it is included in any other feature—for example, a <Placemark>—the <open> element is ignored.

Packaging Up KML Files into KMZ Archives

Many KML presentations include additional images, models, and textures that reside in separate files. For example, you might create a custom placemark icon, and your information balloons may include photographs taken at the location of each placemark. If

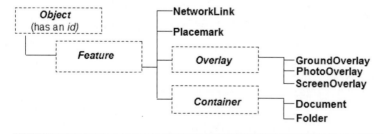

Figure 2-7 Feature element and its derived elements.

you want to share a KML file, perhaps by e-mailing it to a friend, you need to ensure that these auxiliary files are packaged up and included along with the main file.

A *KMZ archive* is a collection of files used to create a single KML presentation. This archive includes all the local files that are referenced in the *.kml* file. A KMZ archive is a self-contained package that does not need to be hosted on a network server and can easily be e-mailed and stored as a single unit. In addition, the data in a KMZ archive is compressed, so the archive is smaller than the original collection of files. Google Earth can read *.kml* and *.kmz* files directly, and it can also save files as KMZ archives.

By default, when Google Earth creates a KMZ archive, it names the main KML file *doc.kml* file. The local files it references are compressed into an archive using the ZIP file format. You can create ZIP archives using the Windows Explorer or Mac Finder directly. In general, you simply select the contents of the folder that contains the main KML file and then select an option such as *"WinZip > Add to Zip file ..."* Many applications can also produce this format. WinZip on Windows systems, Stuffit on Macintosh systems, and zip on Linux or Macintosh systems are popular applications that can read and write the ZIP format.

> **Note**
>
> In a KMZ archive, only the first (that is, the "top-level") KML file is loaded. This KML file (named *doc.kml* by default) can reference other KML files (for example, in a ‹NetworkLink› element, described in Chapter 6, "Network Links."

After you have created the *.zip* file, change the file extension to *.kmz* (for example, you would rename *myHawaiiTrip.zip* to *myHawaiiTrip.kmz)*. A KMZ archive can be loaded directly into Google Earth without first extracting it.

Recommended File Structure

This section describes the recommended practice for organizing the hierarchy of files that are referenced by a KML file. If your main file is greater than about 10 Kbytes, compress it into a KMZ archive even if it does not reference external files. *Always* create a KMZ archive if your main file references other files (images, textures, models). General guidelines for creating a KMZ archive are as follows:

1. Create a folder with a descriptive name for the archive.

2. Add the main KML file to the folder and name the file *doc.kml*.

3. Create a subfolder for the images (if any). Give this subdirectory a descriptive name (for example, *images/*).

4. Add the image files to the *images/* subfolder.

5. Create subfolders for other types of supporting files (for example, *models/*, *textures/*, *overlays/*). You can use any descriptive name for these subfolders.

6. Add the files to each subfolder.

7. Be sure your *doc.kml* file uses *relative* references to the subelements. For example, if your *doc.kml* file refers to an image in the *images/* subfolder, the ground overlay reference to the JPEG files would look like this:

```
<href>images/etnaErupting.jpg</href>
```

8. Before you zip up your KMZ archive, make sure the links work by loading the *doc.kml* file into Google Earth (double-click it).

9. If all the links load successfully, select the contents of the archive folder and zip them up.

10. Change the file extension from *.zip* to *.kmz*.

Similarly, if you want to examine the files contained in a KMZ archive, you can change the suffix from *.kmz* to *.zip* and then unzip the archive. To view the KMZ archive in Google Earth, just double-click the file (no need to extract it first).

> **Tip**
>
> The *.kmz* extension is used for the name of the KMZ archive itself. Do not use the *.kmz* extension in the name of a folder inside the KMZ archive.

Examples

The *MtEtna.kmz* sample illustrates the structure of a simple KMZ archive. It has a main *doc.kml* file and one supporting image for the ground overlay (*etnaErupting.jpg*), which is added to the *images/* folder (Figure 2-8).

Figure 2-9 shows a more complex KMZ archive that illustrates the use of this same organization for a larger collection of files.

> **Tip**
>
> For pathnames of folders and subfolders, use the forward slash on all systems (even Windows)—for example: *images/people/SamSpade.jpg*. (On Windows systems, Google Earth converts the slashes as necessary.) Do not include absolute, local pathnames such as C:\. Shorthand for relative path references (such as ".." for "go up one directory") can be used in file specifications.

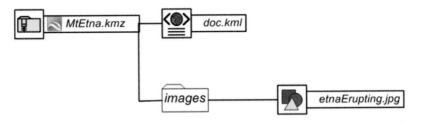

Figure 2-8 Structure of a simple KMZ archive. Name the top-level (root) KML file doc.kml. Put supporting files in subfolders.

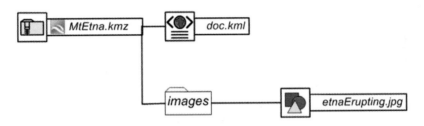

Figure 2-9 Organizing a collection of files in a KMZ archive. Create your own subfolders with descriptive names as a way to organize your files. Be sure the *doc.kml* file uses relative references to these files.

What's Next?

In the next chapter, you will learn about a new family of elements, derived from the abstract Geometry element. You'll also examine the <coordinate> element in more detail and learn how to specify additional parameters for geometric shapes, including tessellation, extrusion, and altitude mode.

Chapter 3

Geometry

After reading this chapter, you'll be able to do the following:

- Create a path and specify its width and color.

- Create a polygon and specify its color and transparency.

- Explain what line tessellation is and why you would use it.

- Add a simple model to a KML file.

- Add elements to a KML file with information about the author and web source of the file.

Chapter Overview

As you've already seen, a <Placemark> can contain a <Point> that defines its geographic location. This chapter describes how a Placemark can contain any member of the Geometry family of elements, or a combination of the following elements:

- <Point>
- <LineString>
- <LinearRing>
- <Polygon>
- <MultiGeometry>
- <Model>

A Geometry element defines the fundamental shape of the object associated with a <Placemark>. In the case of a <Point>, <LineString>, <LinearRing>, or <Polygon>, the *coordinates* of the Geometry define its shape. The shape of a <Model> is defined by a set of coordinates contained in an external file. Other elements that affect the shape are the following:

- <altitudeMode> Indicates how to interpret the altitude
- <extrude> Specifies whether to extend the shape to the ground
- <tessellate> Specifies whether long line strings should be subdivided into smaller segments so that they can follow the curvature of the Earth

You can also define *styles* for a shape—*line styles* for shapes composed of lines and *poly styles* for polygons (filled shapes with three or more sides). This chapter goes into each of these subjects in more detail.

Coordinates: A Closer Look

The <Point> element contains one child element, <coordinates>, which specifies the *longitude*, *latitude*, and *altitude* of a position on the Earth. Here are the coordinates for a point that is 300 meters above the south end of the Golden Gate Bridge:

```
<Point>
  <coordinates>-122.478,37.8107,300</coordinates>
</Point>
```

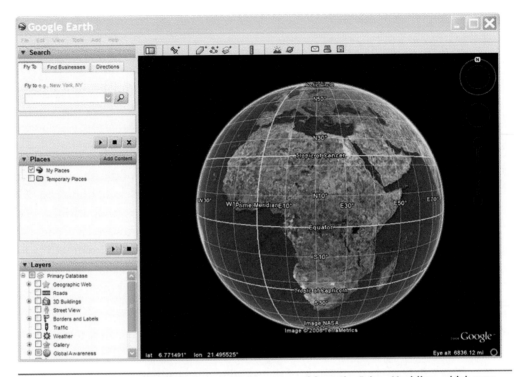

Figure 3-1 Longitude and latitude. Longitude is measured from the Prime Meridian, which runs through Greenwich, England. Latitude is measured from the Equator.

The three values within the <coordinates> element are separated by commas (without spaces). They are sometimes referred to as a *tuple*. Figure 3-1 shows longitudes and latitudes in Google Earth.

> **Note**
>
> In Google Earth, the *longitude* value is specified first, followed by the *latitude* value. In many other geographic systems, the latitude value is placed first.

Longitude

Longitude lines run from North to South, with 0 degrees longitude set at the Prime Meridian, an arbitrary reference point of longitude that runs through Greenwich, England. Longitude values range from 0 degrees to 180 degrees traveling East of the Prime Meridian, and from 0 degrees to −180 degrees traveling West of the Prime Meridian.

Latitude

Latitude lines run from East to West, with 0 degrees latitude set at the Equator. Latitude values range from 0 degrees to 90 degrees from the Equator to the North Pole, and from 0 degrees to −90 degrees from the Equator to the South Pole. In KML, fractional values for longitude and latitude are expressed as decimal values.

Altitude and Altitude Mode

The *altitude* value, which is optional, specifies the location of the point in meters above sea level. Altitudes can be specified in a number of elements (<coordinates>; <Camera>; <LookAt>; Geometry elements such as <Point>, <LineString>, <LinearRing>, <Polygon>, <MultiGeometry>, and <Model>; <GroundOverlay>; <PhotoOverlay>, and <Region>). An altitude specification is always interpreted according to the current setting for <altitudeMode>. The default value for <altitudeMode> is clampToGround, which indicates to ignore altitude specifications. If you want the geobrowser to take altitude values into account, specify either of the following values:

- relativeToGround sets the altitude of the coordinates relative to the actual ground elevation at a particular location.

- absolute sets the altitude of the coordinates according to distance above sea level, regardless of the elevation of the terrain at the particular location.

For example, consider a point with an <altitude> of 160 meters, where the terrain itself has an altitude of 40 meters. If <altitudeMode> equals absolute, the altitude is set to 160 meters (that is, to the value of <altitude>). This point is 120 meters above the current ground level. But if <altitudeMode> is relativeToGround, the actual altitude is set relative to this current elevation, which in this case would be 40 meters + 160 meters, or 200 meters. In this case, the point is 160 meters above ground level, as shown in Figure 3-2.

Line Strings

A <LineString> is a collection of two or more coordinate values. Each coordinate in the series is connected to the next coordinate by a line segment. Line strings are commonly thought of as *paths*. Figure 3-3 shows a mapping of tectonic plates in California, created by the U.S. Geological Survey, which uses <LineString> and <LineStyle> elements to mark the boundaries between the plates.

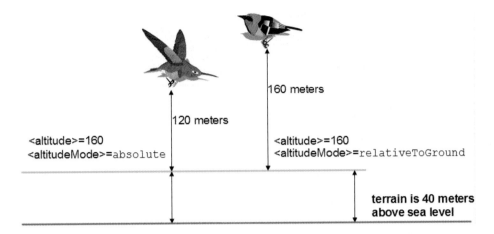

160 meters

120 meters

<altitude>=160
<altitudeMode>=absolute

<altitude>=160
<altitudeMode>=relativeToGround

**terrain is 40 meters
above sea level**

Figure 3-2 Altitude values are always affected by the value for <altitudeMode>. (Models created by Henry Wilton; from Google 3D Warehouse.)

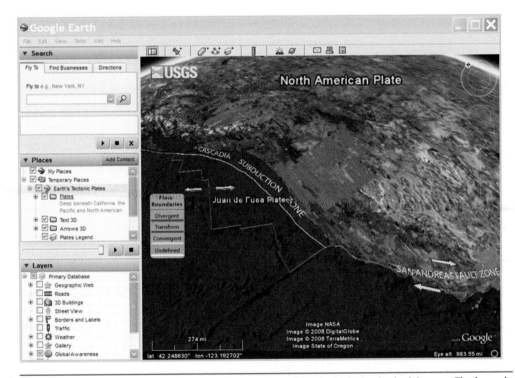

Figure 3-3 Map of tectonic plates in California, created by the U.S. Geological Survey. The boundaries between the plates are marked by line strings in different colors. The legend and logo are screen overlays (see Chapter 5). (http://earthquake.usgs.gov/regional/nca/virtualtour/kml/Earths_Tectonic_Plates.kmz)

The *SimpleLineString.kml* example contains the KML code to create some of the line segments that form the boundary of the Juan de Fuca Plate off the coast of Oregon and Washington.

SimpleLineString.kml

```
<?xml version="1.0" encoding="UTF-8"?>
<kml xmlns="http://www.opengis.net/kml/2.2">
  <Document>
    <name>Tectonic Plates</name>
    <Placemark>
      <name>Juan de Fuca Plate</name>
      <LineString>
        <coordinates>
          -130.597293,50.678292,0
          -129.733457,50.190606,0
          -130.509877,49.387208,0
          -128.801553,48.669761,0
          -129.156745,47.858658,0
          -128.717835,47.739997,0
        </coordinates>
      </LineString>
    </Placemark>
  </Document>
</kml>
```

Tessellating a Line String

Without tessellation, a line string is formed by drawing a line from one coordinate to the next. If the coordinates are reasonably close together, the line segments will usually be visible from most angles. However, if the coordinates are far apart, the straight line connecting them may travel through the surface of the earth, and some parts of the line may not be visible.

To prevent this effect, specify 1 (equals TRUE, or "yes") for the <tessellate> element, as shown in *TessellatedLineString.kml*.

TessellatedLineString.kml

```
<?xml version="1.0" encoding="UTF-8"?>
<kml xmlns="http://www.opengis.net/kml/2.2">
  <Document>
```

```
     <name>Tessellated Line String</name>
     <Placemark>
       <name>Imaginary Plate</name>
       <LineString>
         <tessellate>1</tessellate>
         <coordinates>
           -123.597293,50.678292,0
           -121.717835,47.739997,0
         </coordinates>
       </LineString>
     </Placemark>
   </Document>
</kml>
```

Try substituting a value of 0 (equals FALSE, or "no") for <tessellate>, save the file, and reload it into Google Earth. Experiment by viewing this line string from different angles and watching how the middle part goes underground when it's not tessellated. For tessellation to take effect, the value of <altitudeMode> must be clampToGround.

Extruding a Line String

When a Geometry element is *extruded*, it is extended to the ground. If it's already on the ground, it can't be extended, so this element has no effect in the case of the default <altitudeMode>, which is clampToGround.

When a line string is extruded, each coordinate is extended toward the center of the Earth's sphere. Figure 3-4 shows a simple extruded line string. The *ExtrudedLineString.kml* example shows the KML code for this extruded line string. Notice that each coordinate tuple contains an altitude value, and the <altitudeMode> is now relativeToGround.

ExtrudedLineString.kml

```
<?xml version="1.0" encoding="UTF-8"?>
<kml xmlns="http://www.opengis.net/kml/2.2">
  <Document>
    <name>Extruded LineString</name>
    <Placemark>
      <name>Extruded LineString</name>
      <LineString>
      <extrude>1</extrude>
      <tessellate>1</tessellate>
      <altitudeMode>relativeToGround</altitudeMode>
```

```
    <coordinates>
        -130.597293,50.678292,2800
        -129.733457,50.190606,2800
        -130.509877,49.387208,2800
        -128.801553,48.669761,2800
        -129.156745,47.858658,2800
        -128.717835,47.739997,2800
    </coordinates>
   </LineString>
  </Placemark>
 </Document>
</kml>
```

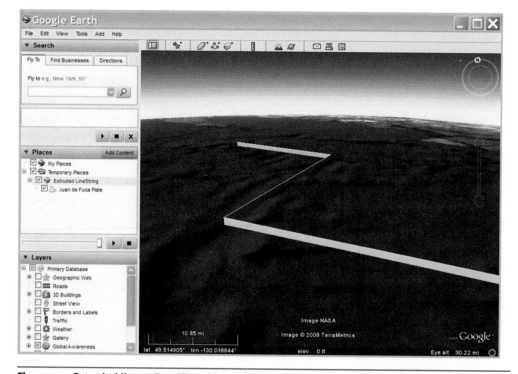

Figure 3-4 Extruded line string. The <altitudeMode> value must be *relativeToGround* or *absolute* for extrusion to take effect.

Experimenting with AltitudeMode

Try copying the *LineStringWithAltitude.kml* file to your system and experiment by changing the values for <altitudeMode> to see the effect of the three possible values for this element: clampToGround (the default), absolute, and relativeToGround.

LineStringWithAltitude.kml

```xml
<?xml version="1.0" encoding="UTF-8"?>
<kml xmlns="http://www.opengis.net/kml/2.2">
  <Document>
    <name>KML Handbook: Ch. 3</name>
    <Placemark>
      <name>Pink Path With Altitude</name>
      <Style>
        <LineStyle>
          <color>ffff55ff</color>
          <width>5</width>
        </LineStyle>
      </Style>
      <LineString>
        <tessellate>1</tessellate>
        <altitudeMode>relativeToGround</altitudeMode>
        <coordinates>
          -65.255616,-22.813902,3000
          .
          .
          .
          -64.6413,-22.712729,3000 </coordinates>
      </LineString>
    </Placemark>
  </Document>
</kml>
```

Google Maps

Because Google Maps is a 2D mapping application, it ignores the <altitude> and <altitudeMode> elements in a KML file. Similarly, <tessellate> and <extrude> are not used in a 2D context. Figure 3-5 shows the same file, *LineStringWithAltitude.kml*, as it appears in the Satellite mode of Google Maps.

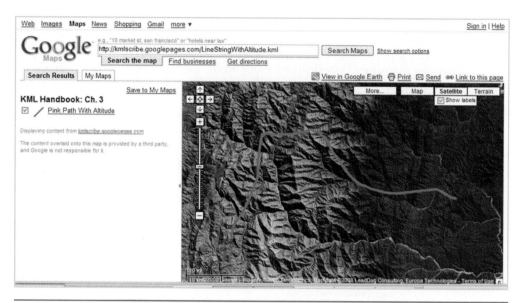

Figure 3-5 LineString shown in Google Maps. Some elements, such as ‹altitude› and ‹altitudeMode›, are not used in this 2D context.

LineStyle

The *LineStringWithAltitude.kml* example also illustrates how you can use the ‹LineStyle› element to change the color and width of a path, as shown here:

```
<Style>
  <LineStyle>
    <color>ffff55ff</color>   <!-- bright pink -->
    <width>5</width>          <!-- 5 pixels wide -->
  </LineStyle>
</Style>
```

The line *color* is specified in the same way the background and text colors in the ‹BalloonStyle› element are specified (see the detailed section in Chapter 2 on "Changing the Background Color"). Color and transparency (alpha) values are expressed as hexadecimal values from 00 to ff for each of the four components: *alpha, blue, green,* and *red*. The order of expression is *aabbggrr*, where *aa*=alpha; *bb*=blue; *gg*=green; and *rr*=red. See Chapter 5, "Overlays," for a detailed discussion of transparency values.

The line *width* is a floating point value that specifies the width of the line in pixels.

The <LineStyle> element is a child of <Style>, which can contain other style elements, such as the <BalloonStyle> element shown in Chapter 2. This example shows how to specify <Style> as an *inline* child of a Feature. Chapter 4 shows how to specify *shared styles*, which can be referenced by multiple Features in a KML file.

Polygons

Polygons are closed shapes formed by three or more line segments. The faces of a polygon can be filled with color. Figure 3-6 shows how the U.S. Geological Survey's Hawaiian Volcano Observatory uses colored polygons to designate lava-flow hazard zones on the island of Hawaii.

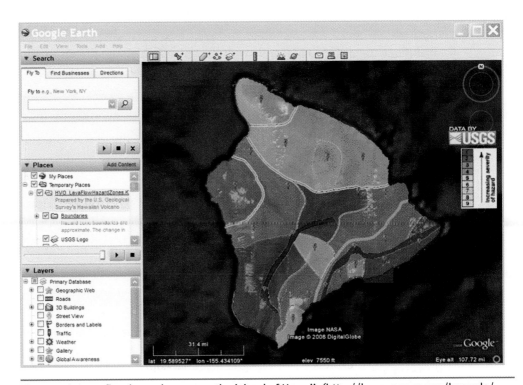

Figure 3-6 Lava-flow hazard zones on the island of Hawaii. (http://hvo.wr.usgs.gov/hazards/lavazones/HVO_LavaFlowHazardZones.kmz)

Simple Polygon

A simple polygon has one *outer boundary*, which is a set of coordinates that begins and ends with the same coordinate point (to form the closed loop). The <coordinates> element is a child of the <LinearRing> element. The basic structure for a simple polygon that consists of one outer boundary is as follows:

```
<Polygon>
   <outerBoundaryIs>
    <LinearRing>
      <coordinates>...</coordinates>            <!-- lon,lat[,alt] -->
    </LinearRing>
  </outerBoundaryIs>
</Polygon>
```

The *SimplePolygon.kml* example shows how one of the polygons in Figure 3-6 is constructed. It includes the following important elements:

<description>

Includes a standard HTML table with four rows (which use the <tr> tag) and two columns (which use the <td> tag).

<Style>

Includes a <LineStyle> element that specifies white lines for the outline of the polygon and a <PolyStyle> element that specifies light aqua for the fill color of the polygon face.

<Polygon>

Contains the <outerBoundaryIs>, <LinearRing>, and <coordinates> elements that define the Geometry for the Placemark.

Notice, too, that Polygons, like LineStrings, have <extrude> and <tessellate> elements.

SimplePolygon.kml

```
<?xml version="1.0" encoding="UTF-8"?>
<kml xmlns="http://www.opengis.net/kml/2.2">
<Document>
  <name>KML Handbook: Chapter 3</name>
  <Placemark>
    <name>Simple Polygon</name>
    <description>
      <![CDATA[
        <br><br><br>
```

```
            <table border="1" padding="0">
            <tr><td>ZONE</td><td>3</td></tr>
            <tr><td>pct_covered_since_1800</td><td>1-5%</td></tr>
            <tr><td>pct_covered_in_750_yrs</td><td>15-75%</td></tr>
            <tr><td>Explanation</td>
                <td>Areas gradationally less hazardous than Zone 2 because of
                greater distance from recently active vents and/or
                because the topography makes it less likely that flows will
                cover these areas.
                </td>
            </tr>
        ]]>
    </description>
    <Style>
      <LineStyle>
        <color>ff000000</color>
      </LineStyle>
      <PolyStyle>
        <color>f7ebffd5</color>
      </PolyStyle>
    </Style>
    <Polygon>
      <extrude>1</extrude>
      <tessellate>1</tessellate>
      <outerBoundaryIs>
        <LinearRing>
          <coordinates>
            -155.087713,19.728869,0          <!-- first coordinate -->
            .
            .
            .
            -155.098943,19.7239,0
            -155.101018,19.722097,0
            -155.087713,19.728869,0          <!-- last coordinate is same
                                                  as the first -->
          </coordinates>
        </LinearRing>
      </outerBoundaryIs>
    </Polygon>
  </Placemark>
</Document>
</kml>
```

PolyStyle

The Simple Polygon example shows using the <PolyStyle> element to color the faces of a Polygon. It also includes a <LineStyle> element to color the lines that form the outer boundary of the Polygon. The syntax for <PolyStyle> is as follows:

```
<PolyStyle>
  <color>ffffffff</color>
  <colorMode>normal</colorMode>
  <fill>1</fill>
  <outline>1</outline>
</PolyStyle>
```

The child elements of <PolyStyle> are defined as follows:

<color>

Specifies the color for polygons, polygon extrusions, and line extrusions.

<colorMode>

Can be either normal or random. A value of random applies a random linear scale to the base <color>. For truly random colors, apply specify white (00ffffff) for <color>. The default is normal. (See the section "Advanced Example" in Chapter 4 for an example of using this element.)

<fill>

Specifies whether to fill the polygon with color. 1=fill, 0=do not fill.

<outline>

Specifies whether to outline the polygon. 1=outline, 0=do not outline. Because they are *lines*, Polygon outlines use the current LineStyle.

Figure 3-7 illustrates how, when a Polygon is extruded and <outline> has a value of 1, the boundary and the lines that connect each coordinate point to the ground use the <LineStyle> color (in this case, ff000000, or black).

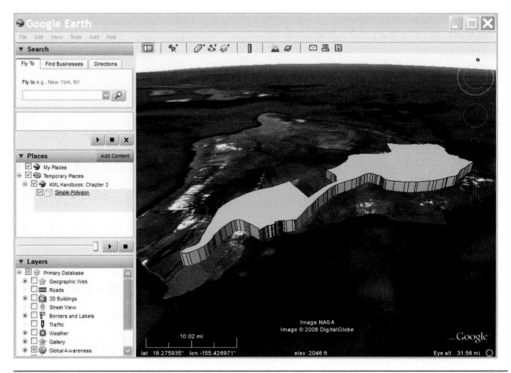

Figure 3-7 A simple polygon with one outer boundary. This polygon is *extruded*, which means its outer boundary is extended to the ground.

Polygons with Holes

Use an *inner boundary* element to define a hole inside a polygon. A polygon can contain multiple inner boundaries. The basic structure of a <Polygon> element with a hole is as follows:

```
<Polygon>
  <outerBoundaryIs>
    <LinearRing>
      <coordinates>...</coordinates>         <!-- lon,lat[,alt] -->
    </LinearRing>
  </outerBoundaryIs>
  <innerBoundaryIs>
    <LinearRing>
      <coordinates>...</coordinates>         <!-- lon,lat[,alt] -->
    </LinearRing>
  </innerBoundaryIs>
</Polygon>
```

The same rules apply to an inner boundary as to an outer boundary—namely that the first and last coordinates must be the same. The placemark's <Style> elements apply to all elements of the <Polygon>. If an inner boundary is *outside* an outer boundary, the "inner" boundary is displayed as a separate polygon. Google Maps treats all inner boundaries as separate polygons, but it shows the polygons within the same placemark in the left panel.

Example

Figure 3-8 shows an example of a polygon with two inner boundaries that create holes in the polygon. Each inner boundary is a <LinearRing>, with its first and last coordinates the same. The *PolygonWithInnerAndOuterBoundaries.kml* file creates this polygon.

PolygonWithInnerAndOuterBoundaries.kml

```
<?xml version="1.0" encoding="UTF-8"?>
<kml xmlns="http://www.opengis.net/kml/2.2">
    <Placemark>
      <name>Polygon with 2 holes</name>
      <Polygon>
        <outerBoundaryIs>
          <LinearRing>
            <coordinates>
              -122.431938278749,37.8019857095478,0
              -122.431873068102,37.8016611830403,0
              -122.431497938539,37.8017138829201,0
              -122.431564485129,37.8020299537248,0
              -122.431938278749,37.8019857095478,0
            </coordinates>
          </LinearRing>
        </outerBoundaryIs>
        <innerBoundaryIs>
          <LinearRing>
            <coordinates>
              -122.431886016065,37.8019318219595,0
              -122.431842117396,37.8017208533219,0
              -122.431719499379,37.8017366044116,0
              -122.431763224388,37.8019475540673,0
              -122.431886016065,37.8019318219595,0
            </coordinates>
          </LinearRing>
        </innerBoundaryIs>
```

```
                <innerBoundaryIs>
                  <LinearRing>
                    <coordinates>
                        -122.431713379578,37.8019536360684,0
                        -122.431671885143,37.8017428837353,0
                        -122.431549296352,37.8017586463012,0
                        -122.431592641627,37.8019684859395,0
                        -122.431713379578,37.8019536360684,0
                    </coordinates>
                  </LinearRing>
                </innerBoundaryIs>
              </Polygon>
            </Placemark>
        </kml>
```

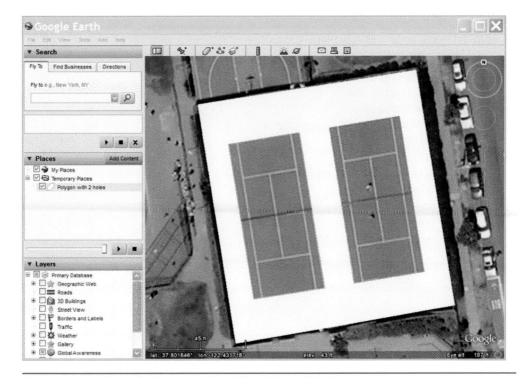

Figure 3-8 Inner boundaries are used to define holes within Polygons.

MultiGeometry

The <MultiGeometry> element is a container for zero or more Geometry elements. If you want to add an icon to a polygon, you need to use a <MultiGeometry> element. In this case, add both a <Point> and a <Polygon> to a <MultiGeometry> element in the <Placemark>. When a <MultiGeometry> element contains both a <Polygon> and a <Point>, you get all the features of the point placemark described in Chapter 2. The user can now click the icon and open the balloon associated with the point and polygon, as shown in the *MultiGeometry.kml* example.

MultiGeometry.kml

```
<?xml version="1.0" encoding="UTF-8"?>
<kml xmlns="http://www.opengis.net/kml/2.2">
  <Placemark>
    <name>Adelaide</name>
    <description>This polygon shows the boundaries of a city.
    </description>
    <Style>
      <LineStyle>
        <color>ff000000</color>
      </LineStyle>
      <PolyStyle>
        <color>7f9f7fe0</color>
      </PolyStyle>
    </Style>
    <MultiGeometry>
      <Point>
        <coordinates>138.600000,-34.910000</coordinates>
      </Point>
      <Polygon>
        <outerBoundaryIs>
          <LinearRing>
            <coordinates>
                138.64,-34.93 138.64,-34.94 138.63,-34.94 138.62,-34.94
                138.62,-34.95 138.62,-34.96 138.63,-34.96 138.62,-34.96
                138.61,-34.97 138.60,-34.97 138.59,-34.97 138.58,-34.97
                138.57,-34.97 138.57,-34.96 138.57,-34.95 138.57,-34.95
                138.57,-34.94 138.57,-34.93 138.57,-34.92 138.57,-34.92
                138.57,-34.91 138.56,-34.91 138.56,-34.90 138.57,-34.90
                138.57,-34.90 138.57,-34.89 138.57,-34.89 138.57,-34.89
                138.56,-34.88 138.56,-34.88 138.56,-34.88 138.56,-34.88
                138.57,-34.88 138.58,-34.87 138.58,-34.87 138.58,-34.86
                138.58,-34.85 138.58,-34.85 138.60,-34.85 138.61,-34.85
```

```
                138.63,-34.85 138.63,-34.85 138.64,-34.86 138.64,-34.87
                138.64,-34.87 138.63,-34.87 138.63,-34.88 138.62,-34.88
                138.62,-34.88 138.62,-34.89 138.62,-34.89 138.62,-34.89
                138.63,-34.89 138.63,-34.90 138.64,-34.90 138.64,-34.90
                138.64,-34.91 138.64,-34.91 138.64,-34.92 138.64,-34.92
                138.64,-34.93 138.64,-34.93
            </coordinates>
          </LinearRing>
        </outerBoundaryIs>
      </Polygon>
    </MultiGeometry>
  </Placemark>
</kml>
```

This MultiGeometry is shown in Figure 3-9. The icon looks and functions as though it's associated with the polygon, but it is actually part of a simple point placemark. To see the effect of the <Point> element, edit this example and comment out the <Point> element using `<!--` to begin the comment and `-->` to end the comment. Reload the example in Google Earth and notice how the icon and label disappear.

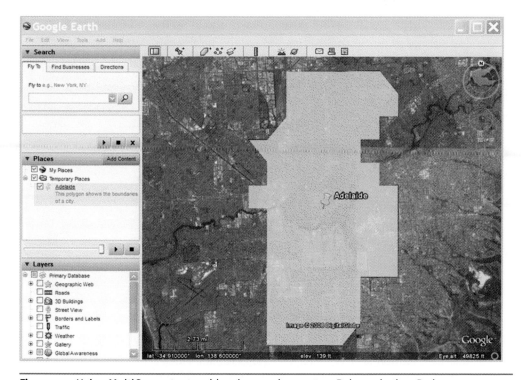

Figure 3-9 Using MultiGeometry to add an icon and name to a Polygon in the 3D view.

Models

To import a 3D model into Google Earth, use the <Model> element to specify the external file that contains the model. The <Model> element is used just as any other Geometry element in KML—as the child of <Placemark> or <MultiGeometry>. In KML, you can import 3D models—such as buildings, bridges, monuments, and statues—in the COLLADA interchange file format. Models are defined independently of Google Earth in their own coordinate space, using applications such as Google SketchUp, Autodesk 3D Studio Max, Maya, or Softimage XSI. When a 3D model is imported into Google Earth, it is positioned, rotated, and scaled to fit into the Earth coordinate system. Models already loaded into Google Earth can be repositioned and resized using the <Update> element (see Chapter 7, "Dynamic KML").

Figure 3-10 shows an example of a model of King Tutankhamon's tomb, complete with stone textures and frescoes of baboons painted on the sides of the burial chamber. The

Figure 3-10 Model of King Tutankhamon's tomb, with realistic textures and a series of viewpoints that allow the user to move through the series of underground chambers. (Model created by Angel Tello. http://bbs.keyhole.com/ubb/download.php?Number=408502. Used by permission.)

coordinates that define the polygons that make up this model are contained in the COLLADA file, identified by its *.dae* suffix. This model was created using Google SketchUp, a 3D modeling program. The COLLADA file references a set of external texture files, which are JPEG images that are mapped onto the polygons that make up the model. The KML file containing the <Model> element, the COLLADA file, and all the supporting texture files are compressed into one KMZ archive so that they can be e-mailed and downloaded as one simple package (see Chapter 2, "Placemarks and Balloons").

The COLLADA file that contains the model's geometry is specified in the <Link> element as follows:

```
<Link>
   <href>KingTutsTomb3D.kmz/files/SUPreview2.dae</href>
</Link>
```

The complete syntax for <Model> is as follows:

```
<Model id="ID">
  <altitudeMode>clampToGround</altitudeMode>
  <Location>
    <longitude>0.0</longitude>
    <latitude>0.0</latitude>
    <altitude>0.0</altitude>
  </Location>
  <Orientation>
    <heading>0.0</heading>
    <tilt>0.0</tilt>
    <roll>0.0</roll>
  </Orientation>
  <Scale>
    <x>1.0</x>
    <y>1.0</y>
    <z>1.0</z>
  </Scale>
  <Link>...</Link> <!-- includes the href to the Model file -->
  <ResourceMap>
    <Alias>
      <targetHref>...</targetHref>
      <sourceHref>...</sourceHref>
    </Alias>
  </ResourceMap>
</Model>
```

The major elements and related concepts are described in the following sections:

<Location>
> Specifies the initial placement of the model on Earth.

<Orientation>
> Specifies how to the rotate the model on Earth so that is is oriented properly.

<Scale>
> Specifies how to resize the model in Earth.

<ResourceMap>
> Specifies the correspondence between the texture references in the original
> COLLADA file and the location of the texture files in the KMZ archive.

Location

The <Location> element includes the standard specifications you're already familiar
with for <longitude>, <latitude>, and <altitude>. As always, <altitude> is affected by
<altitudeMode>, which is the first child of <Model>. The origin of the model's coordinate system (0,0,0) is placed at this location.

Orientation

Figure 3-11 shows the orientation of these axes for a typical model. In this case, the $+x$
axis points to the right, the $+y$ axis points to the front and is oriented North, and the $+z$
axis points up. (This is the usual convention for modeling, but it is not a requirement.)

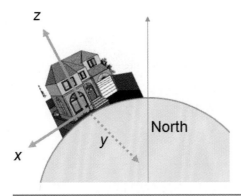

Figure 3-11 Orientation of a typical model. (Model created by Michael Massicotte; from Google 3D Warehouse.)

Rotating in 3D

After the model is placed at the specified Location, it is rotated in 3D. The order in which the rotations are applied to a model is as follows:

1. <roll>
2. <tilt>
3. <heading>

Figure 3-12 shows the effects of <heading>, <tilt>, and <roll>, which are as follows:

<heading>
> Specifies the rotation about the z axis, which is the equivalent of azimuth (compass direction). A rotation of 0 equals North, 90 degrees equals East, 180 degrees equals South, and 270 degrees equals West.

<tilt>
> Specifies rotation about the x axis. A positive rotation is clockwise, when you are looking down the x axis toward the origin. Values are in degrees, from 0 to 180.

<roll>
> Specifies rotation about the y axis. A positive rotation is clockwise, when you are looking down the y axis toward the origin. Values are in degrees, from 0 to +/-180.

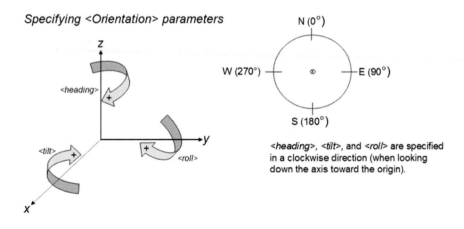

Figure 3-12 Rotations about the *x, y,* and *z* axes.

Scale

The <Scale> values for <x>, <y>, and <z> specify how much to stretch or shrink the model in each of three directions. Scaling by 1 leaves the extent of the model unchanged in that direction. Scaling by .5 makes the model half as large in the specified direction. Scaling by 2 makes it twice as big in the specified direction. The scale factor is applied in the model's coordinate space. If the model is created in an external application, you may need to scale the model up or down so that it fits "naturally" into the Earth browser's coordinate system. The necessary scale will be different in each case, and you'll need to experiment a bit to achieve the correct effect.

Resource Map

The original COLLADA model file contains references to the textures used by the model. The <ResourceMap> element provides a mapping between the original locations of the files and their new locations in the KML or KMZ file that contains the Model and its textures. This way you can move and rename texture files without having to update the original COLLADA file that references those textures.

The Resource Map contains one or more <Alias> elements that map a texture file path from the original COLLADA file path (the *source* path) to the new KML/KMZ file path (the *target* path).

<Alias> contains a mapping from a <sourceHref> to a <targetHref>, as follows:

<targetHref>
> Specifies the texture file to be fetched by Google Earth. This reference can be a relative reference to an image file within the *.kmz* archive, or it can be an absolute reference to the file (for example, a URL).

<sourceHref>
> Is the path specified for the texture file in the COLLADA *.dae* file.

Often, the COLLADA file uses relative references, and the <targetHref> simply mimics the <sourceHref>.

The following example of a resource map shows how Google Earth automatically fills in the <ResourceMap> element with the proper mappings when you save a KMZ archive to your desktop. This excerpt is from the King Tutankhamon model shown in Figure 3-10, which uses 16 textures and images to achieve its realistic effect (see *KingTut.kmz*).

```
.
.
.
<ResourceMap>
  <Alias>
    <targetHref>
      C:/Documents and Settings/username/Local Settings/Temp/
      408502-Tutankhamon&apos;stomb3D.kmz/files/Material1.jpg
    </targetHref>
    <sourceHref>
      ../images/Material1.jpg
    </sourceHref>
  </Alias>
  <Alias>
    <targetHref>
      C:/Documents and Settings/username/Local Settings/Temp/
      408502-Tutankhamon&apos;stomb3D.kmz/files/
      Material1Stone_Brushed_Khaki_big.jpg
    </targetHref>
    <sourceHref>
      ../images/Material1Stone_Brushed_Khaki_big.jpg
    </sourceHref>
  </Alias>
  <Alias>
    <targetHref>
      C:/Documents and Settings/username/Local Settings/Temp/
      408502-Tutankhamon&apos;stomb3D.kmz/files/
      Material1Stone_Brushed_Khaki_big1noCulling.jpg
    </targetHref>
    <sourceHref>
      ../images/Material1Stone_Brushed_Khaki_big1noCulling.jpg
    </sourceHref>
  </Alias>
  .
  .
  .
</ResourceMap>
  .
  .
  .
```

Including Author and Source Information

It's a good practice to include information about the author and address of the web page where users can find your KML files. Including this information in the KML file itself ensures that proper attribution for the file will be maintained even if the KML file or archive is distributed on its own. This information is displayed in geo search results, both in Earth browsers such as Google Earth and in other applications such as Google Maps.

Google Earth uses the *author, name*, and *link* elements exactly as they are defined in the Atom Syndication Format. The complete specification is found at http://atompub.org. Here is an example of using these attribution elements in a KML file:

```
<kml xmlns="http://www.opengis.net/kml/2.2"
     xmlns:atom="http://www.w3.org/2005/Atom">
  <Document>
    <atom:author>
      <atom:name>Angel Tello</atom:name>
    </atom:author>
    <atom:link
      href="http://bbs.keyhole.com/ubb/download.php?Number=408502" />
    .
    .
    .
  </Document>
</kml>
```

If you use these elements, your KML file must reference the Atom namespace. Include this line inside the <kml> element, immediately after the declaration of the KML namespace:

```
<kml xmlns="http://www.opengis.net/kml/2.2"
     xmlns:atom="http://www.w3.org/2005/Atom">
    .
    .
    .
</kml>
```

What's Next?

The next chapter builds on what you've already learned about styling balloons, lines, and polygons. It introduces the concept of *shared styles,* a powerful mechanism for developing uniform presentation styles that can be easily applied to a large set of features. You'll also learn about styles for icons and labels.

Chapter 4

Styles and Icons

After reading this chapter, you'll be able to do the following:

- List the six elements that define substyles for a KML feature.

- Create a shared style that makes all polygons the same color.

- Determine "who wins" when both a shared style and an inline style specify different values for the same SubStyle element.

- Create a simple custom ‹BalloonStyle›.

- Create a ‹StyleMap› that affects the appearance of an icon when the user mouses over it.

Chapter Overview

Styles allow you to define a custom treatment for icons, lines, polygons, balloons, and list view entries. You can create a special style for all the lines, balloons, labels, and polygons in your presentation, or you can create multiple styles to convey different types of information and meaning. In KML, features and geometries are specified *along with* their styles. KML does not employ styling mechanisms such as Cascading Style Sheets (CSS) and Styled Label Descriptor (SLD), which separate content from style. See the section "Defining Styles Externally" later in the chapter for more information on this topic.

A *Style* is actually a collection of the following *substyles*:

- <IconStyle>
- <LabelStyle>
- <LineStyle>
- <PolyStyle>
- <BalloonStyle>
- <ListStyle>

This chapter describes each of the substyles and provides an example of its use. You've already been introduced to <BalloonStyle> and <IconStyle> in Chapter 2, and <LineStyle> and <PolyStyle> in Chapter 3, so those sections are presented here mainly as review. Following the discussion of the six style building blocks, this chapter covers the key concepts related to styles:

- Use of *inline styles* versus *shared styles,* which are an efficient way to apply one style to many Features
- How inline style values can *override* shared (and default) style values
- Different ways to specify a <styleUrl>
- *Style maps*, which define how Google Earth responds when the user mouses over a point placemark

Travels through Literature

Jerome Burg has developed a creative curriculum for teaching literature using Google Earth called *Google Lit Trips* (http://googlelittrips.com). Designed primarily for grades kindergarten through twelve, this program traces the paths of such famous travels as

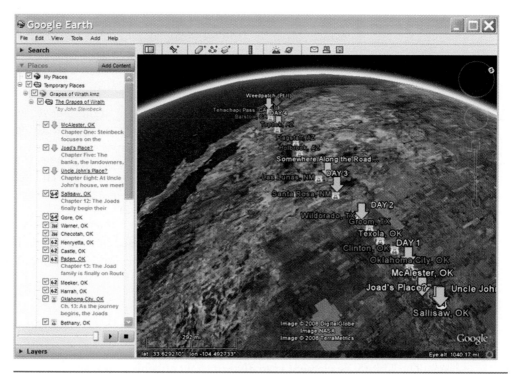

Figure 4-1 Google Lit Trips allow students to trace the travels and hardships of the Joad family as it journeys to California in Steinbeck's *Grapes of Wrath*. Detailed balloon descriptions and links to outside resources enrich the understanding of this novel. (http://googlelittrips.com)

Homer's *Odyssey*, Virgil's *Aeneid*, Voltaire's *Candide*, Steinbeck's *Grapes of Wrath*, and Joyce's *Portrait of the Artist as a Young Man*. Balloons filled with related facts, images, and links along the trip's route make each piece of literature come alive as we all resume our seats in the virtual classroom. See Figure 4-1 for the summary view of the Joads' journey in a *Grapes of Wrath* Lit Trip.

Building Blocks for Styles

A substyle element is always contained in a <Style> element, which can contain 0 or 1 of each of the substyle elements. The first half of this chapter covers the syntax of each substyle and provides a simple code example of each. Here is the syntax for the <Style> element itself:

```
<Style id="ID">
  <IconStyle>...</IconStyle>
  <LabelStyle>...</LabelStyle>
  <LineStyle>...</LineStyle>
  <PolyStyle>...</PolyStyle>
  <BalloonStyle>...</BalloonStyle>
  <ListStyle>...</ListStyle>
</Style>
```

When you create a style, you don't need to include all the substyle elements. If a given substyle is not specified, the default values for its elements are used. The child elements of <Style> must be added in the order shown above in the syntax section.

A <Style> element can be included as a child of any Feature element (see "Related Feature Elements" in Chapter 2). When a <Style> element is used in this manner, it is called an *inline style*. See the section "Shared Versus Inline Styles" later in this chapter for information on other ways to use the <Style> element.

Element Tree for Styles

Figure 4-2 shows the portion of the KML element tree that contains the substyle classes. The ColorStyle element is an *abstract* element, which means that it is never actually used in a KML file. It provides the set of color-related elements that are used by all four style elements listed to the right in Figure 4-2. <LineStyle>, <PolyStyle>, <IconStyle>, and <LabelStyle> all inherit the following elements from ColorStyle:

- <color>
- <colorMode>

In the element tree, elements to the right are said to be *derived from* elements to their left.

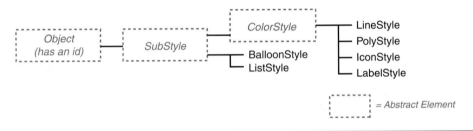

Figure 4-2 Substyle element hierarchy.

The four ColorStyle elements are covered here first.

LineStyle

The <LineStyle> element allows you to specify the color and width of the lines that compose *line strings* (paths), the *outlines* of polygons, and the extruded lines of points. Here is the syntax for this element:

```
<LineStyle id="ID">
  <color>ffffffff</color>
  <colorMode>normal</colorMode>
  <width>1.0</width>
</LineStyle>
```

See Chapter 2 for details on how to specify the <color> and <width> elements of <LineStyle>.

Random Color

The <colorMode> element can be either `normal` (the default) or `random`. When <colorMode> is `normal`, the line color is as specified in the <color> element. Specifying `random` for <colorMode>, as its name suggests, allows the Earth browser to arbitrarily choose a different color value each time the KML file is loaded into the Earth browser. For a truly random set of opaque colors, specify white (ffffffff) for the base <color>. The PolyStyle example in this chapter includes an example of specifying random color. For additional details on color randomization, see Appendix A, <ColorStyle>.

Example

The Lit Trips example uses a LineStyle element to specify orange for the color of the Joads' path and a value of 3 pixels for the line width, as shown in Figure 4-3. The *LineStyle.kml* example shows the KML code illustrating this simple <LineStyle>.

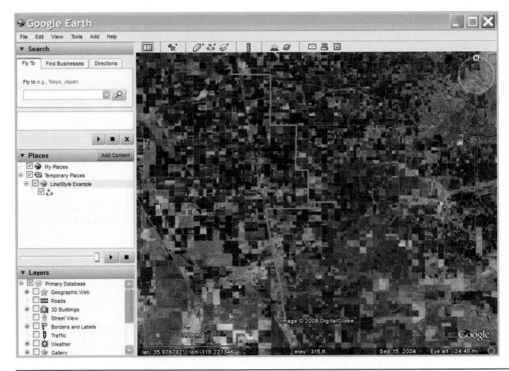

Figure 4-3 Applying a ‹LineStyle› with an orange color and a width of 3 pixels.

LineStyle.kml

```
<?xml version="1.0" encoding="UTF-8"?>
<kml xmlns="http://www.opengis.net/kml/2.2">
<Document>
  <Placemark>
    <Style>
      <LineStyle>
        <color>ff0080ff</color>
        <width>3</width>
      </LineStyle>
    </Style>
    <LineString>
      <tessellate>1</tessellate>
      <coordinates>
        -119.039568,35.351234,0
        -119.039393,35.362090,0
        -119.039826,35.363108,0
        -119.043660,35.372132,0
```

```
       .
       .
       .
      -119.347536,36.130671,0
    </coordinates>
   </LineString>
  </Placemark>
 </Document>
</kml>
```

PolyStyle

The PolyStyle element allows you to specify the color for the faces of a Polygon. Poly-Style has child elements that specify whether to fill the Polygon with color and whether to outline the Polygon. When <outline> is 1, the color value specified in LineStyle is used for the Polygon outlines.

A Note about Boolean Values

A *Boolean value* is defined as a value that can be either true or false. KML uses 1 or true to indicate TRUE (or "yes") for Boolean values, and 0 or false to indicate FALSE (or "no") for these values. The <PolyStyle> elements <fill> and <outline> are examples of Boolean values.

Here is the syntax for this element:

```
<PolyStyle id="ID">
   <color>ffffffff</color>
   <colorMode>normal</colorMode>
   <fill>1</fill>
   <outline>1</outline>
</PolyStyle>
```

Default Values

The syntax sections in this book list default values for all elements. If you omit an element, the Earth browser simply uses the default value.

Example

The *PolyStyle.kml* example shows the state of Oklahoma, formed by a polygon that uses an outline color of orange and a random <colorMode>. Note that the color of a polygon's outline is determined by the <color> in the <LineStyle> element. Figure 4-4 shows one example of this randomly colored polygon.

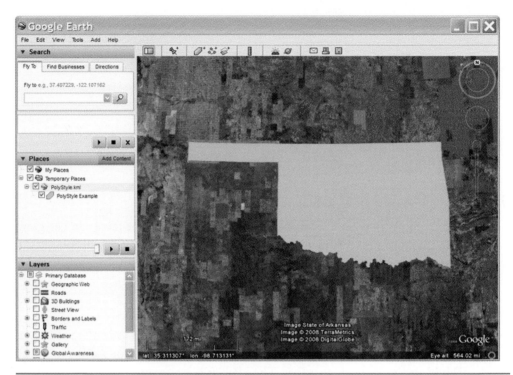

Figure 4-4 Example of a ‹Polygon› with a random fill color.

PolyStyle.kml

```
<?xml version="1.0" encoding="UTF-8"?>
<kml xmlns="http://www.opengis.net/kml/2.2">
<Document>
  <Placemark>
    <Style>
      <LineStyle>
        <color>ff0080ff</color>   <!-- orange -->
        <width>3</width>
      </LineStyle>
      <PolyStyle>
        <colorMode>random</colorMode>
      </PolyStyle>
    </Style>
    <Polygon>
      <outerBoundaryIs>
        <LinearRing>
```

```
        <coordinates>
          -94.4393221493475,34.9291508772006,0
          -94.4285520120899,35.40054626950861,0
          -94.46848521103671,35.6410882624306,0
          -94.48593482605899,35.7603104941298,0
          -94.5424172738563,36.10683580389291,0
          -94.55311361988042,36.1645252110653,0
          -94.4393221493475,34.9291508772006,0
          .
          .
          .

        </coordinates>
      </LinearRing>
    </outerBoundaryIs>
  </Polygon>
 </Placemark>
</Document>
</kml>
```

IconStyle

The IconStyle element specifies how icons for point placemarks are drawn. The <Icon> element specifies the image file to use for the icon. This <href> element can be a local file or an HTTP address of the image file. Here is the syntax for this element:

```
<IconStyle id="ID">
  <color>ffffffff</color>
  <colorMode>normal</colorMode>
  <scale>1.0</scale>
  <heading>0.0</heading>
  <Icon>
    <href>...</href>
  </Icon>
  <hotSpot x="0.5"  y="0.5"
    xunits="fraction" yunits="fraction"/>
</IconStyle>
```

The child elements of <IconStyle> are defined as follows:

<color>

The color specified here (in the form *aabbggrr*, where *aa*=alpha/transparency, *bb*=blue, *gg*=green, and *rr*=red) is blended with the color of the image specified in the <href> child element of <Icon>.

<colorMode>

Can be either `normal` or `random`. A value of `normal` specifies to blend the <color> specified in <IconStyle> with the icon's color. A value of `random` specifies to blend an arbitrarily selected color with the icon color. The default is `normal`.

<scale>

Resizes the icon. The icon image (specified in the <href> child element of <Icon>) is multiplied by this scale factor in both the *x* (horizontal) and *y* (vertical) directions. A <scale> of 1, the default, leaves the icon size unchanged.

<heading>

Specifies a clockwise rotation of the icon, where 0 equals North (no rotation), 90 equals East, 180 equals South (or upside-down), and 270 equals West. Figure 4-5 illustrates these heading values.

<Icon>

   <href>

Specifies the image to be used for the custom icon. Here, the <Icon> element has one child: <href>, which specifies an HTTP address or a local file specification for the icon image. A local file can reside on disk or can be part of the KMZ archive. File specifications can be absolute or relative. In most cases, you'll use a relative reference so that the icon and the KML file can be packaged into a KMZ archive and e-mailed or moved to a different server without changing any path specifications. Use absolute references if you are maintaining a standard icon repository that rarely changes.

<hotSpot x="0.5" y="0.5" xunits="fraction" yunits="fraction" />

The <hotSpot> element identifies the location on the icon that is to be anchored to the ground (or tether) at the location specified in the placemark's

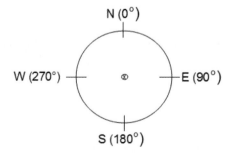

Figure 4-5 Values for the <heading> element are specified clockwise, with 0 equal to North.

<Point>. By default, the center of the icon is "pinned" to the point. In some cases—for example, where the icon is an arrowhead—you want a different part of the icon to be tied to the point (for example, the tip of the arrow). As the user tilts and rotates the view, the icon will "stand up and twirl" around its <hotSpot>.

The <hotSpot> can be specified in one of three ways: as a *pixel location*, as a *fraction* of the icon image, or as an *inset* from the upper-right edge of the icon image. For starters, the example in this chapter uses the pixel location technique. (See Appendix A, <IconStyle>, for details on the other techniques.)

Notice that the <hotSpot> element includes name/value pairs inside the element tag. In XML these entities are called *attributes*. Their values are surrounded by quotation marks. You'll notice that the entire <hotSpot> element is contained in one self-closing tag; for example:

```
<hotSpot x="5" y="9" xunits="pixels" yunits="pixels" />
```

This notation is the same as the following:

```
<hotSpot x="5" y="9" xunits="pixels" yunits="pixels"></hotSpot>
```

Icon HotSpot

Here is a simple example that demonstrates the use of an icon hotspot. The following KML code specifies a custom icon. This icon belongs to the custom icon palette provided by Google Earth, which is hosted on http://maps.google.com and is available through the Google Earth user interface. The icon is scaled up (that is, made larger) by a factor of 1.2:

```
<IconStyle>
  <scale>1.2</scale>
  <Icon>
    <href>http://maps.google.com/mapfiles/kml/shapes/arrow.png</href>
  </Icon>
</IconStyle>
```

The image on the left in Figure 4-6 shows this custom arrow icon with default placement, which centers the icon over the placemark's point. To make the tip of the arrow align with the point, you need to specify the arrow tip as the hotspot. Here is one way to specify this hotspot:

```
<IconStyle>
  <scale>1.2</scale>
  <Icon>
    <href>http://maps.google.com/mapfiles/kml/shapes/arrow.png</href>
```

```
  </Icon>
  <hotSpot x="32" y="1" xunits="pixels" yunits="pixels"/>
</IconStyle>
```

The image on the right in Figure 4-6 shows this adjustment, and the arrow tip now aligns nicely with the placemark's point.

Most browsers and photo applications list the pixel dimensions when they display an image. For example, Mozilla Firefox includes the pixel data in the banner for the displayed image, as shown in Figure 4-7.

As shown in Figure 4-8, the coordinate system for icon pixels has its origin (0,0) in the lower-left corner of the image. The x distance is measured in pixels counting to the right along the x axis. The y distance is measured in pixels counting up along the y axis.

Example

The Google Lit Trips example includes several examples of custom icons: an arrow icon and an icon for historic Route 66, as shown in Figure 4-9. The *IconStyle.kml* example shows the KML code that creates these two placemarks and icons, each with a different style.

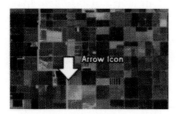 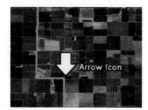

Figure 4-6 Custom icon using default placement (left image) and placement using <hotSpot> (right image).

Figure 4-7 Mozilla Firefox displays the image and lists its size (64x64 pixels) in the browser banner.

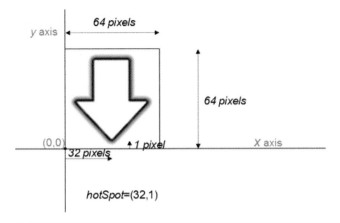

Figure 4-8 Specifying the icon hotspot in pixels. Origin of the x/y coordinate system is at the lower-left corner of the image.

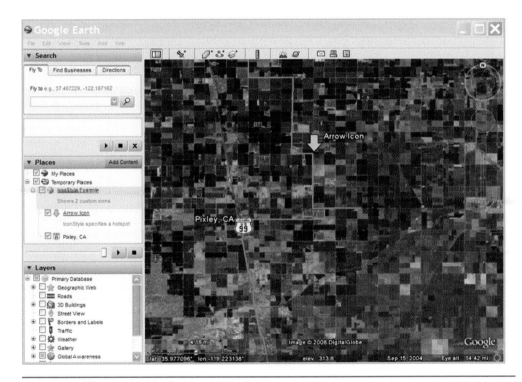

Figure 4-9 Inline <IconStyle> for two custom icons.

```xml
<?xml version="1.0" encoding="UTF-8"?>
<kml xmlns="http://www.opengis.net/kml/2.2">
<Document>
  <name>IconStyle Example 2</name>
  <open>1</open>
  <description>Shows 2 custom icons.</description>
  <Placemark>
    <name>Arrow Icon</name>
    <description>IconStyle specifies a hotspot.</description>
    <Style>
      <IconStyle>
        <color>ff66ccff</color>
        <scale>1.2</scale>
        <Icon>
          <href>http://maps.google.com/mapfiles/kml/shapes/arrow.png
          </href>
        </Icon>
        <hotSpot x="32" y="1" xunits="pixels" yunits="pixels"/>
      </IconStyle>
    </Style>
    <Point>
      <coordinates>-119.232195,36.016021,0</coordinates>
    </Point>
  </Placemark>
  <Placemark>
    <name>Pixley, CA</name>
    <Style>
      <IconStyle>
        <scale>1.2</scale>
        <Icon>
          <href>http://www.gbcnet.com/ushighways/logos/99_old_shield.gif
          </href>
        </Icon>
      </IconStyle>
      <LineStyle>
        <color>ff0080ff</color>
        <width>3</width>
      </LineStyle>
      <PolyStyle>
        <colorMode>random</colorMode>
      </PolyStyle>
    </Style>
```

```
            <MultiGeometry>
              <LineString>
                .
                .
                .
              </LineString>
              <Polygon>
                .
                .
                .
              </Polygon>
              <Point>
                <coordinates>-119.290316,35.967076,0
                </coordinates>
              </Point>
            </MultiGeometry>
          </Placemark>
      </Document>
  </kml>
```

LabelStyle

The <LabelStyle> element specifies how the <name> of a Feature is drawn in the 3D view. You can specify a custom color, color mode, and scale for the label (name).

```
<LabelStyle id="ID">
  <color>ffffffff</color>
  <colorMode>normal</colorMode>
  <scale>1.0</scale>
</LabelStyle>
```

The child elements of <LabelStyle> are defined as follows:

<color>

Color of the label (specified in the form *aabbggrr*, where *aa*=alpha/transparency, *bb*=blue, *gg*=green, and *rr*=red). Default color is opaque white (ffffffff).

<colorMode>

Can be either normal or random. A value of normal specifies to use the specified <color>. A value of random specifies to use an arbitrarily selected color. The default is normal.

\<scale\>

> The default label is multiplied by this scale factor. A \<scale\> of 1, the default, leaves the label size unchanged.

The *LabelStyle.kml* example makes the label green and slightly larger than the default size. Figure 4-10 shows this label.

LabelStyle.kml

```xml
<?xml version="1.0" encoding="UTF-8"?>
<kml xmlns="http://www.opengis.net/kml/2.2">
  <Document>
    <name>Label Style Example</name>
    <Placemark>
      <name>Topock, AZ</name>
        <open>1</open>
        <LookAt>
          <longitude>-114.486391</longitude>
          <latitude>34.718331</latitude>
          <altitude>0</altitude>
          <heading>9.723522844174414e-015</heading>
          <tilt>3.066389237480416e-012</tilt>
          <range>9489.366703</range>
        </LookAt>
        <Style>
        <IconStyle>
          <scale>1.2</scale>
          <Icon>
          <href>http://www.gbcnet.com/ushighways/logos/99_old_shield.gif
          </href>
          </Icon>
        </IconStyle>
        <LabelStyle>
          <color>ff00ffaa</color>
          <scale>1.2</scale>
        </LabelStyle>
        </Style>
        <Point>
          <coordinates>-114.486391,34.718331,0
          </coordinates>
        </Point>
    </Placemark>
  </Document>
</kml>
```

Figure 4-10 Using ‹LabelStyle› to color and scale the placemark's label. The ‹name› element is used for the label text in the 3D view.

BalloonStyle

Although balloons are commonly associated with placemarks, recall that they can be associated with any KML *Feature* (<Document>, <Folder>, <NetworkLink>, <ScreenOverlay>, <GroundOverlay>, and <PhotoOverlay>; see "Related Feature Elements" in Chapter 2). Chapter 2 introduced the <BalloonStyle> element, which has the following syntax:

```
<BalloonStyle id="ID">
  <bgColor>ffffffff</bgColor>
  <textColor>ff000000</textColor>
  <text>...</text>
  <displayMode>default</displayMode>
</BalloonStyle>
```

The child elements of <BalloonStyle> are defined as follows:

<bgColor>

Background color of the balloon (specified in the form *aabbggrr*, where *aa*=alpha/transparency, *bb*=blue, *gg*=green, and *rr*=red). Default color is opaque white (ffffffff).

<textColor>

Color of the text inside the balloon (specified in the form *aabbggrr*, where *aa*=alpha/transparency, *bb*=blue, *gg*=green, and *rr*=red). Default text color is black (ff000000).

<text>

Text to display in the balloon.

You can add entities to the <text> tag using the following format to refer to a child element of Feature: `$[name]`, `$[description]`, `$[address]`, `$[id]`, `$[snippet]`. Google Earth looks in the current Feature for the corresponding string entity and substitutes that information in the balloon. Entities are very useful in shared styles (see "Shared Versus Inline Styles" later in the chapter).

To include *To here—From here* driving directions in the balloon, use the `$[geDirections]` tag. To prevent the driving directions links from appearing in a balloon, include the <text> element with some content, or with $[description], to substitute the <description> specified in the Feature.

If no <text> element is specified, Google Earth draws the default balloon, which includes the following:

- <name>, as specified in the Feature
- <description>, as specified in the Feature
- The standard *To here—From here* driving direction headings
- On a white background, with a balloon tail attached to the point coordinates of the Feature (if specified)

<displayMode>

Can be either `default` or `hide`. If <displayMode> is `default`, the information supplied in <text> is used in the balloon. If <displayMode> is `hide`, no balloon is displayed. In Google Earth, clicking the list view icon for a placemark whose balloon's <displayMode> is `hide` causes Google Earth to fly to the placemark.

The *BalloonStyle.kml* example adds a <BalloonStyle> element to a <Folder>. Clicking the folder name in the list view opens the balloon. The <BalloonStyle> makes the background color of the balloon tan and the text brown. It uses entities as placeholders for the <name> and <description> specified in the individual Feature. Figure 4-11 shows this example in Google Earth.

BalloonStyle.kml

```xml
<?xml version="1.0" encoding="UTF-8"?>
<kml xmlns="http://www.opengis.net/kml/2.2">
  <Document>
    <name>Google Lit Trips by Jerome Burg</name>
    <open>1</open>
    <Style id="tan_balloon_style">
      <BalloonStyle id="ID">
        <bgColor>ff87d1ec</bgColor>    <!-- balloon background is tan -->
        <textColor>ff0055aa</textColor> <!-- text is brown -->
      <text>
    <!-- picks up name and description from the individual Feature -->
        <![CDATA[
          $[name]
          $[description]
        ]]>
      </text>
    </BalloonStyle>
  </Style>
  <Folder>
    <name>The Grapes of Wrath</name>
    <description><![CDATA[<i>by John Steinbeck</i>
      <p><center>
      <img src="http://nmxs-images.forbesautos.com/streamer/advice/
        toptens/cars_literature/grapes_wrath2?WID=225
      "><br></center>
      <B>First Published: </b>The Viking Press, 1939
      <p>
      <B>Read more about </b><a href="http://nobelprize.org/
        nobel_prizes/literature/laureates/1962/steinbeck-bio.html">
      John Steinbeck</a>
      <p>
      <i>The Grapes of Wrath</i> by John Steinbeck has been burned,
      banned, and a best seller.
      Explore this <a href="http://www.npr.org/programs/morning/
        features/patc/grapesofwrath/">
      National Public Broadcast website</a> to hear interviews, songs,
      and see clips about this history-making novel.
      <p>
```

```
    <a href="http://books.google.com/books?q=Books+by+John+
      Steinbeck&ots=dpyZMKB6wY&sa=X&oi=print&ct=title">
    Other books by John Steinbeck</a>
    <center><hr>
    <font style="font-size: 10pt" >A Google Certified Teacher
      Literature Project<br>Visit us at<br>
    http://www.GoogleLitTrips.com</font></center>]]></description>
  <LookAt>
    <longitude>-104.492732</longitude>
    <latitude>33.629209</latitude>
    <altitude>0</altitude>
    <heading>-58.258961</heading>
    <tilt>38.106572</tilt>
    <range>2005783.422867</range>
  </LookAt>
  <styleUrl>#tan_balloon_style</styleUrl>
  </Folder>
  </Document>
</kml>
```

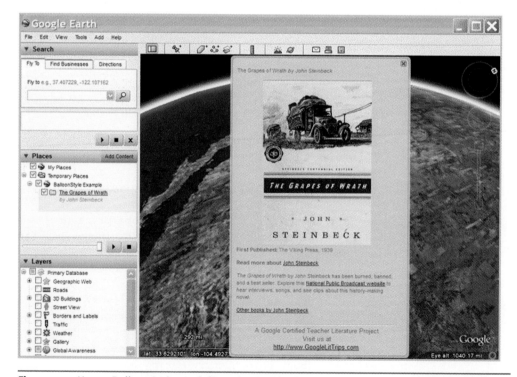

Figure 4-11 Use a ‹BalloonStyle› to define a background color, text color, text elements, and balloon layout that can be shared by multiple Features.

For more information on balloon templates, see Chapter 8, "Dealing with Large Data Sets." You can define your own data elements in KML and then reference those elements as $ entities in the <text> element of <BalloonStyle> in the same way that you reference the built-in KML entities. See the example of the <Data> element in Chapter 8.

ListStyle

This element specifies how Feature elements are displayed in the list view. In Google Earth, the list view is shown in the Places panel of the left navigation bar and includes the items shown in Figure 4-12.

```
<ListStyle id="ID">
  <listItemType>check</listItemType>
  <bgColor>ffffffff</bgColor>
  <ItemIcon>
    <state>open</state>
    <href>...</href>
  </ItemIcon>
  <maxSnippetLines>2</maxSnippetLines>
</ListStyle>
```

The child elements of <ListStyle> are defined as follows:

<listItemType>

Specifies how a Feature is displayed in the list view. Choices are as follows:

check (default)   (applies to any Feature)

Specifies that the Feature's visibility is tied to the state of the checkbox. Checked equals visible; unchecked equals hidden.

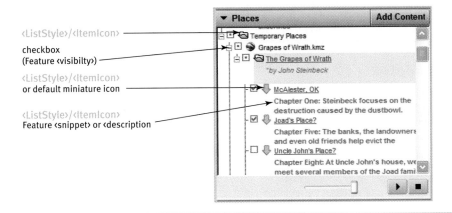

Figure 4-12 List view of Google Earth.

`radioFolder`   (applies only to a Document or Folder)

Specifies that only one of the Container's children can be visible at a time.

`checkHideChildren`   (applies only to a Document or Folder)

Specifies to hide the Container's children in the list view and to include a check-box for the parent Container only. Checking the box makes all the children of this Container visible. This value is useful for network links (see Chapter 6) that contain many network links as children.

`checkOffOnly`   (applies to any Feature)

Specifies that the user can turn off all the child elements using the Container's checkbox but cannot turn them all on at the same time. Each child element needs to be turned on separately by the user. This setting is useful for folders containing large amounts of data and for large network link hierarchies (see Chapter 6).

\<bgColor\>

Background color for the snippet in the list view.

\<ItemIcon\>

By default, the icon used in the 3D view of the Earth browser is also used in the list view. The \<ItemIcon\> element allows you to specify a special icon in the list view.

\<state\>

Specifies the current state of a folder or network link that is loaded from an external source on the web. Possible values are `open`, `closed`, `error`, `fetching0`, `fetching1`, and `fetching2`. These values can be combined by inserting a space between two values (no comma).

\<href\>

Specifies the URL of the icon image to be used in the list view for the Feature. See the discussion of absolute and relative references in the "Icon Style" section earlier in this chapter.

\<maxSnippetLines\>

Specifies the maximum numbers of lines to display for the snippet in the list view.

The *ListStyle.kml* example adds a \<Style\> named "lit_trips_style" to a \<Folder\> and its six \<Placemarks\>. Figure 4-13 shows this example in Google Earth. Try loading this sample code into Google Earth. Then open the example in a simple text editor and modify it, specifying each of the different possible values for \<listItemType\>. Each time you change the example, save it; then right-click the folder name in Google Earth and

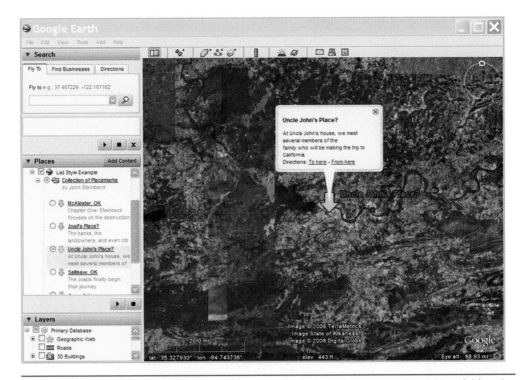

Figure 4-13 Using a ‹ListStyle› element to create radio buttons for placemarks within a folder, the user can select only one placemark at a time. The ‹ListStyle› also adds a yellow background to the snippets of the Features in the list view.

click Revert. Watch how the different values for <listItemType> affect how the placemarks appear in the list view.

> **Note**
>
> For the sake of brevity, this ‹ListStyle› example uses a *shared style*. Using an inline style would have added 120 lines to the program, so we provided a preview of this important technique. See the next section for more information on creating and using shared styles.

ListStyle.kml

```xml
<?xml version="1.0" encoding="UTF-8"?>
<kml xmlns="http://www.opengis.net/kml/2.2">
  <Document>
    <name>List Style Example</name>
```

```xml
<Style id="lit_trips_style">
  <IconStyle>
    <color>ff66ccff</color>
    <scale>1.4</scale>
    <Icon>
      <href>http://maps.google.com/mapfiles/kml/shapes/arrow.png
      </href>
    </Icon>
    <hotSpot x="32" y="1" xunits="pixels" yunits="pixels"/>
  </IconStyle>
  <LabelStyle>
    <color>ff0080ff</color>
  </LabelStyle>
  <ListStyle>
    <listItemType>radioFolder</listItemType>
    <!-- experiment with the other list item types: checkOffOnly, -->
    <!-- checkHideChildren, and check -->
    <bgColor>ffb0fffc</bgColor> <!-- background color for snippet -->
  </ListStyle>
</Style>
<Folder>
  <name>Collection of Placemarks</name>
  <description><![CDATA[<i>by John Steinbeck</i>
  <center>
  <img src="http://nmxs-images.forbesautos.com/streamer/advice/
   toptens/cars_literature/grapes_wrath2?WID=225"><br></center>
  <B>First Published: </b>The Viking Press, 1939]]>
  </description>
  <styleUrl>#lit_trips_style</styleUrl>
  <Placemark>
    <name>McAlester, OK</name>
    <description>Chapter One: Steinbeck focuses on the destruction
      caused by the dustbowl.
    </description>
    <styleUrl>#lit_trips_style</styleUrl>
    <Point>
      <coordinates>-95.769443,34.933332,0
      </coordinates>
    </Point>
  </Placemark>
  <Placemark>
    <name>Joad's Place?</name>
    <description>The banks, the landowners, and even old friends
      help evict the farmers.</description>
    <styleUrl>#lit_trips_style</styleUrl>
```

```
      <Point>
        <coordinates>-94.861783,35.26326,0
        </coordinates>
      </Point>
    </Placemark>
    <Placemark>
      <name>Uncle John's Place?</name>
      <description>At Uncle John's house, we meet several members of
         the family who will be making the trip to California.
      </description>
      <styleUrl>#lit_trips_style</styleUrl>
      <Point>
        <coordinates>-94.725316,35.314922,0
        </coordinates>
      </Point>
    </Placemark>
    <Placemark>
      <name>Sallisaw, OK</name>
      <description>The Joads finally begin their journey.</description>
      <styleUrl>#lit_trips_style</styleUrl>
      <Point>
        <coordinates>-94.787638,35.459897,0
        </coordinates>
      </Point>
    </Placemark>
    <Placemark>
      <name>Gore, OK</name>
      <styleUrl>#lit_trips_style</styleUrl>
      <Point>
        <coordinates>-95.116942,35.529166,0
        </coordinates>
      </Point>
    </Placemark>
    <Placemark>
      <name>Warner, OK</name>
      <styleUrl>#lit_trips_style</styleUrl>
      <Point>
        <coordinates>-95.300951,35.4937,0
        </coordinates>
      </Point>
    </Placemark>
  </Folder>
 </Document>
</kml>
```

Shared versus Inline Styles

The styles you've created up to this point have mostly been *inline styles*—that is, they are specified inside the Feature that uses them. This section describes a powerful way to define styles that can be *shared* by multiple Features, in the same file or in other files, both local and remote. This is an efficient technique and is a recommended practice.

Documents

A <Document> is a container for Features and shared styles. You can add any number of <Style> elements to a <Document>. (Do not put shared styles inside a Folder.) To share a <Style> among multiple Features, follow these steps:

1. Define all styles in a <Document>. Assign a unique id to each <Style>.

2. Within a given Feature, reference the id of the <Style> using a <styleUrl> element.

The id must be unique within a given KML file. For readability, try to use descriptive strings for ids.

The *SharedStyles.kml* example shows defining a <Style> named "blue_arrow" that specifies a blue arrow, red label, orange lines that are 3 pixels wide, and balloons with light blue backgrounds. This <Style> is defined within a <Document> and then referenced by two placemarks:

SharedStyles.kml

```
<?xml version="1.0" encoding="UTF-8"?>
<kml xmlns="http://www.opengis.net/kml/2.2">
  <Document>
    <name>Shared Style Example</name>
    <Style id="blue_arrow">
      <IconStyle>
        <color>ffff0000</color>
        <scale>1.4</scale>
        <Icon>
          <href>http://maps.google.com/mapfiles/kml/shapes/arrow.png
          </href>
        </Icon>
        <hotSpot x="32" y="1" xunits="pixels" yunits="pixels"/>
      </IconStyle>
      <LabelStyle>
        <color>ff0000ff</color>
```

```
        </LabelStyle>
        <LineStyle>
          <color>ff0080ff</color>
          <width>3</width>
        </LineStyle>
        <BalloonStyle>
          <bgColor>fffff8ce</bgColor>
        </BalloonStyle>
      </Style>
      <Placemark>
        <name>Placemark 1</name>
        <styleUrl>#blue_arrow</styleUrl>
        <Point>
          <coordinates>-119.232195,36.016021,0</coordinates>
        </Point>
      </Placemark>
      <Placemark>
        <name>Placemark 2</name>
        <styleUrl>#blue_arrow</styleUrl>
        <MultiGeometry>
          .
          .
          .
          <Point>
            <coordinates>-119.290316,35.967076,0
            </coordinates>
          </Point>
        </MultiGeometry>
      </Placemark>
    </Document>
</kml>
```

In addition to enhancing performance, shared styles make a file more readable and shorter since styles are defined one time, no matter how many Features reference them.

How to Specify a Style URL

If the <Style> is defined in the same file, precede the Style id with a # sign, as shown in this example:

```
<styleUrl>#blue_arrow</styleUrl>
```

If the Style is defined in an external file, use a full URL along with the # referencing (for the Style `id`). For example:

```
<styleUrl>http://server.com/fancyStylesFile.kml#clubs</styleUrl>
```

or

```
<styleUrl>http://server.com/fancyStylesFile.kmz#clubs</styleUrl>
```

to refer to a Style with the `id` of "clubs" that is defined in a file named *fancyStylesFile.kml* (or an archive named *fancyStylesFile.kmz*) that resides on a server named *server.com*. Note that this allows you to host styles that someone else can refer to in their files that are hosted on a different site. However, unlike CSS, you cannot impose a style on a Feature within a given KML file from a different, external file. (The original file must contain the reference to the external file.)

Another example is

```
<styleUrl>sportsclubs.kml#favorites</styleUrl>
```

to refer to a Style with the `id` of "favorites" that is defined in a local file in the same directory named *sportsclubs.kml*.

Caveat

If a style is to be applied to a document, the <Document> itself must include a <styleUrl> even if the <Style> is a direct child of <Document>.

```
<Document>
  <Style id="myPrettyDocument">
    <ListStyle> ... </ListStyle>
  </Style>
  <styleUrl>#myPrettyDocument</styleUrl>
  ...
</Document>
```

Overriding Style Values

What happens when a substyle is specified both in a shared style and in an inline style? Who wins? As you might guess, the inline substyle overrides the shared style. In the following example, the shared style ("blue_arrow") specifies an <IconStyle> with a blue arrow and a red label. The <Placemark> adds this style in its <styleUrl> element, but it then adds its own <IconStyle>/<color> element (green), which overrides the <IconStyle>/<color> value in the shared style (see Figure 4-14).

Overriding Styles Example

```xml
<?xml version="1.0" encoding="UTF-8"?>
<kml xmlns="http://www.opengis.net/kml/2.2">
  <Document>
    <name>Overriding Style Values</name>
    <Style id="blue_arrow">
      <IconStyle>
        <color>ffff0000</color>          <!-- blue -->
        <Icon>
          <href>http://maps.google.com/mapfiles/kml/shapes/arrow.png
          </href>
        </Icon>
        <hotSpot x="32" y="1" xunits="pixels" yunits="pixels"/>
      </IconStyle>
      <LabelStyle>
        <color>ff0000ff</color>          <!-- red -->
      </LabelStyle>
    </Style>
    <Placemark>
      <name>Placemark 1</name>
      <styleUrl>#blue_arrow</styleUrl>
      <Style>
        <IconStyle>
          <color>ff00ff00</color>          <!-- green -->
        </IconStyle>
      </Style>
      <Point>
        <coordinates>-119.232195,36.016021,0</coordinates>
      </Point>
    </Placemark>
  </Document>
</kml>
```

Figure 4-14 The green color of the inline <IconStyle> element overrides the blue color specified in the shared style. Since there are no inline styles to override them, the arrow icon and the red label specified in the shared style remain in effect.

Style Maps for Rollover Behavior

Have you noticed how an icon changes size or reveals the label text when you mouse over it in the 3D view of Google Earth? That's a style map at work. A <StyleMap> element specifies two styles: `normal` and `highlight`. The `highlight` style is triggered whenever the user places the mouse over a point placemark that includes that <StyleMap>. The `normal` style is in effect at all other times. To create a <StyleMap>, follow these steps:

1. Create the **normal** <Style>. Be sure to assign an `id` to it (for example, *normalState*).

2. Create the **highlight** <Style>. Be sure to assign an `id` to it (for example, *highlightState*).

3. Create the <StyleMap> element. In the <StyleMap>, reference *normalState* in the <StyleMap>/<key> for `normal`. Reference *highlightState* in the <StyleMap>/<key> for `highlight`.

Here is how this <StyleMap> would look:

```
<StyleMap id="styleMapExample">
  <Pair>
    <key>normal</key>
    <styleUrl>#normalState</styleUrl>
  </Pair>
  <Pair>
    <key>highlight</key>
    <styleUrl>#highlightState</styleUrl>
  </Pair>
</StyleMap>
```

Since you have defined an `id` for this <StyleMap>, you can reference it in multiple <styleUrl> elements as a *shared style*. In effect, using a <StyleMap> adds two levels of references within a KML file. When you read through a KML file that contains <StyleMap> elements, you need to find where the <StyleMap> for a particular `id` is created. Then you have to read back through the file to find where the styles for the normal and highlight `id` references were created, as shown in Figure 4-15.

The styles created for the `normal` and `highlight` states can be composed of any (or all) of the six substyles discussed in the first half of this chapter. All style elements are composed in the same way, whether they are used in a <StyleMap>, as inline elements within a Feature, or as shared styles among multiple Features.

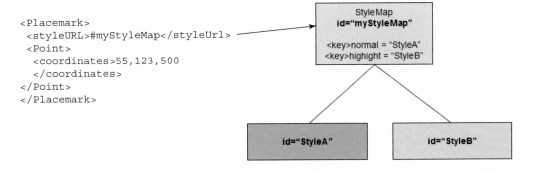

```
<Placemark>
 <styleURL>#myStyleMap</styleUrl>
 <Point>
  <coordinates>55,123,500
  </coordinates>
 </Point>
</Placemark>
```

StyleMap
id="myStyleMap"

<key>normal = "StyleA"
<key>highlight = "StyleB"

id="StyleA"

id="StyleB"

Figure 4-15 A <StyleMap> provides two key/value pairs that specify one Style for the "normal" state and another Style for "highlighted" state. The rollover behavior is triggered by the icon in a point placemark.

Syntax for <StyleMap>

Here is the syntax for the <StyleMap> element:

```
<StyleMap id="ID">
   <Pair id="ID">
     <key>normal</key>
         <!-- kml:styleStateEnum:  normal or highlight -->
     <styleUrl>...</styleUrl> or <Style>...</Style>
   </Pair>
</StyleMap>
```

> **NOTE**
>
> According to the KML Specification, <StyleMap> can be contained in any Feature. In the current release of Google Earth (Release 4.3), however, a <StyleMap> element is triggered only when the user mouses over the icon of a point placemark (or the icon of a photo overlay, described in Chapter 5, "Overlays"). This discussion focuses on the current behavior and usage of this element.

The Power of the Point

A <StyleMap> takes effect only when it is used in a placemark that contains a point element. The placemark can contain other geometry as well, in which case the point and other geometry would be added to a <MultiGeometry> element (see the section "Advanced Example: Additional Ways to Use a Style Map" later in the chapter).

The <styleUrl> elements within a <StyleMap> are referenced as any other <styleUrl>, as described in the previous section, "How to Specify a Style URL."

Simple Example

Here is a simple example that uses a StyleMap ("my_arrow_style") to add behavior to the arrow icon and label shown earlier in this chapter. When the user mouses over the arrow icon, the arrow turns blue and the label turns red. In this example, both Placemarks share the same StyleMap. Figure 4-16 shows how the icon style changes when the user mouses over the icon labeled "Arrow Icon."

StyleMap Example

```xml
<?xml version="1.0" encoding="UTF-8"?>
<kml xmlns="http://www.opengis.net/kml/2.2">
<Document>
  <name>Style Map Example</name>
  <open>1</open>
    <Style id="highlight_arrow">
    <IconStyle>
      <color>ffff0000</color>
      <scale>1.4</scale>
      <Icon>
        <href>http://maps.google.com/mapfiles/kml/shapes/arrow.png
        </href>
      </Icon>
      <hotSpot x="32" y="1" xunits="pixels" yunits="pixels"/>
    </IconStyle>
    <LabelStyle>
      <color>ff0000ff</color>
    </LabelStyle>
    <LineStyle>
      <color>ff95eaff</color>
    </LineStyle>
  </Style>
  <Style id="normal_arrow">
    <IconStyle>
      <color>ffffcdc0</color>
      <scale>1.2</scale>
      <Icon>
        <href>http://maps.google.com/mapfiles/kml/shapes/arrow.png
        </href>
      </Icon>
```

```
            <hotSpot x="32" y="1" xunits="pixels" yunits="pixels"/>
          </IconStyle>
          <LineStyle>
            <color>ff95eaff</color>
            <width>4</width>
          </LineStyle>
        </Style>
        <StyleMap id="my_arrow_style">
          <Pair>
            <key>normal</key>
            <styleUrl>#normal_arrow</styleUrl>
          </Pair>
          <Pair>
            <key>highlight</key>
            <styleUrl>#highlight_arrow</styleUrl>
          </Pair>
        </StyleMap>
        <Placemark>
          <name>Arrow Icon</name>
            <styleUrl>#my_arrow_style</styleUrl>
          <Point>
            <coordinates>-119.232195463845,36.01602191169524,0</coordinates>
          </Point>
        </Placemark>
        <Placemark>
          <name>Pixley, CA</name>
          <styleUrl>#my_arrow_style</styleUrl>
          <MultiGeometry>
            <LineString>
              <tessellate>1</tessellate>
              <coordinates>
                -119.0395685387087,35.35123494106257,0
                -119.0393930554139,35.36209022954709,0
                -119.0398267514389,35.36310863448006,0
              </coordinates>
            </LineString>
            <Point>
              <coordinates>-119.2903164748038,35.96707634646665,0
              </coordinates>
            </Point>
          </MultiGeometry>
        </Placemark>
      </Document>
    </kml>
```

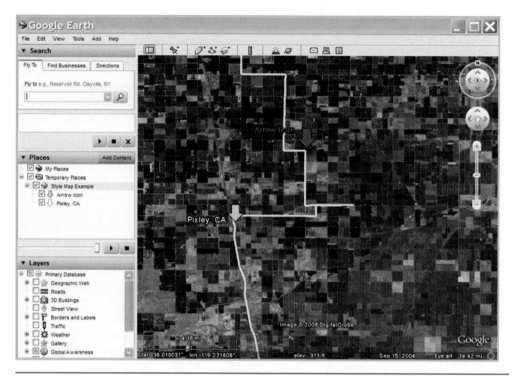

Figure 4-16 Using a style map to create custom icons that change color when the user mouses over them.

Advanced Example: Additional Ways to Use a Style Map

Although you cannot add highlight behavior directly to a Polygon, you can simulate this behavior by creating a Placemark that contains both a Point and a Polygon in a MultiGeometry element, as shown in the following example. Figure 4-17 shows the highlighted polygon and icon for one of the Placemarks. The <colorMode> for the highlighted Polygon is random, so the example will look different each time you load the file. The <color> for the normal Polygon is transparent, so the state is not shown until the user moves the mouse over the icon. Note again that the rollover behavior is triggered by the Point Placemark, but it can affect the other Geometry elements in that Placemark.

Using a Style Map to Trigger Styles for Geometry

```
<?xml version="1.0" encoding="UTF-8"?>
<kml xmlns="http://www.opengis.net/kml/2.2">
```

```
<Document>
  <Style id="normal_state">
    <IconStyle>
      <Icon>
        <href>http://maps.google.com/mapfiles/kml/shapes/flag.png</href>
      </Icon>
      <hotSpot x="0.5" y="0" xunits="fraction" yunits="fraction"/>
    </IconStyle>
    <LineStyle>
      <color>00000000</color>
    </LineStyle>
    <PolyStyle>
      <color>00000000</color>
    </PolyStyle>
  </Style>
  <Style id="selected_state">
    <IconStyle>
      <Icon>
        <href>http://maps.google.com/mapfiles/kml/shapes/flag.png</href>
      </Icon>
      <hotSpot x="0.5" y="0" xunits="fraction" yunits="fraction"/>
    </IconStyle>
    <LineStyle>
      <color>ff00ffff</color>
      <width>4</width>
    </LineStyle>
    <PolyStyle>
      <colorMode>random</colorMode>
    </PolyStyle>
  </Style>
  <StyleMap id="highlight_the_state">
    <Pair>
    <key>normal</key>
      <styleUrl>#normal_state</styleUrl>
      </Pair>
    <Pair>
    <key>highlight</key>
      <styleUrl>#selected_state</styleUrl>
      </Pair>
  </StyleMap>
  <Placemark>
    <name>Oklahoma City</name>
    <styleUrl>#highlight_the_state</styleUrl>
    <MultiGeometry>
```

```
<Polygon>
  <outerBoundaryIs>
    <LinearRing>
      <coordinates>
        -94.4393221493475,34.9291508772006,0
        -94.4285520120899,35.40054626950861,0
        -94.46848521103671,35.6410882624306,0
          .
          .
          .
        -94.4393221493475,34.9291508772006,0 </coordinates>
    </LinearRing>
  </outerBoundaryIs>
</Polygon>
<!-- try commenting out the point and watch what happens
     to the rollover behavior -->
<Point>
  <coordinates>-97.52033000000002,35.47204,0</coordinates>
</Point>
</MultiGeometry>
  </Placemark>
</Document>
</kml>
```

Figure 4-17 In the Earth browser, moving the mouse over an icon triggers the "highlight" ‹Style›
within a ‹StyleMap›. A ‹Point› element is required to activate this behavior. This example simulates highlight behavior for a ‹Polygon› by including the ‹Polygon› in a ‹MultiGeometry› element
that contains a ‹Point›. Left image is "normal" Style, and right image is "highlight" Style.

Using a Style Map to Simplify the Display

You can use the <StyleMap> element to simplify a crowded display of placemarks by setting the <scale> child of <LabelStyle> to 0 for normal state and 1 for highlight state. These settings have the effect of hiding the label until the user mouses over the placemark icon.

You can also use a style map to present very different information depending on whether the user's mouse is currently over the placemark icon. For example, the normal state could display a simple icon, while the highlight state displays a set of multiple icons that represent pertinent data.

Defining Styles Externally

Although KML does not support many aspects of CSS, it does allow you to define all styles in an external KML file and then refer to them explicity from other KML files. The KML file containing the styles can be hosted on a different computer from the KML file that contains the Features that reference the styles in a <styleUrl> element. This separation of content from style is often a useful way to share styles and update them. The individual Feature element contains the explicit reference to its (externally defined) <Style>.

What's Next?

In Chapter 5, you get to look under the hood to see how screen overlays, ground overlays, and photo overlays can be created and manipulated in KML. Adding overlays to Google Earth gives you the power to add your own layers of imagery to Google Earth, presenting data in a vivid geographic context.

Chapter 5

Overlays

After reading this chapter, you'll be able to do the following:

- Search the web for an interesting aerial view of the Earth, a historical map, or a topographical map and add the image as a ground overlay to a KML file.

- Create a screen overlay from a corporate logo and display it in the top-right corner of the Google Earth screen.

- Explain how a ‹LatLonBox› is used in a ‹GroundOverlay› element.

- Add one of your photos to Google Earth in a ‹PhotoOverlay› element.

- Create a ‹Camera› element that views your house or school from an interesting viewpoint.

Chapter Overview

This chapter explains how to create the three different types of overlays:

- Ground overlays
- Screen overlays
- Photo overlays

The chapter begins by describing each type of overlay and typical uses for it. Then it explains basic concepts that apply to all three types of overlays. These concepts include the following:

- Color (described in detail in Chapter 2)
- Transparency (described in detail in this chapter)
- Draw order
- Icons

In Chapter 2, you learned how to specify a viewpoint using the <LookAt> element. Here you learn about the other AbstractView element, the <Camera>. Either a <LookAt> or a <Camera> element can be used to specify the viewpoint for any Overlay (or Feature).

Once we've covered these basics that are common to all overlays, we'll explore each type of overlay in detail. The syntax and concepts related to creating and modifying ground, screen, and photo overlays are described, with examples and diagrams to illustrate the process.

What Is an Overlay?

An *overlay* is an image that is added on top of the basic Google Earth satellite imagery. There are three different kinds of KML overlays:

- *Ground overlays* are images that are draped onto the terrain of Google Earth or added at a specified altitude above the Earth's surface. Whether on or above the Earth's surface, a ground overlay follows the curvature of the Earth. This added imagery can be high-resolution satellite imagery of the Earth, imagery showing weather patterns above the Earth, 2D maps that have been saved as images, or polygons and other annotations saved as images. Most Earth browsers support a wide variety of formats for ground overlays, including BMP, DDS, GIF, JPG, PGM, 32-bit PNG, PPM,

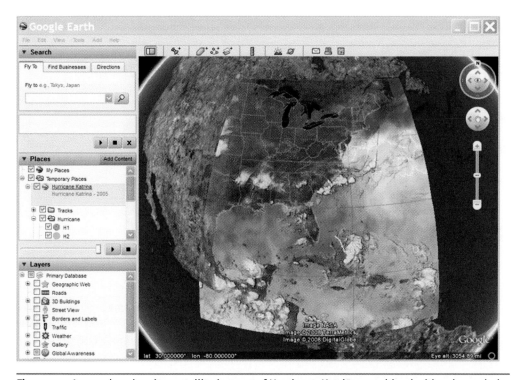

Figure 5-1 An overlay showing satellite images of Hurricane Katrina, combined with color-coded sea-surface temperatures. (KML by Brian Flood, www.spatialdatalogic.com/CS/blogs/brian_flood/archive/2006/09/22/Google-Earth-Time-Sample-_2D00_-Animation-Part-2.aspx. Used with permission.)

TGA, and TIFF. The ground overlay shown in Figure 5-1 shows satellite imagery of Hurricane Katrina combined with color-coded temperatures of the sea surface (part of a KML animation created by Brian Flood).

- *Screen overlays* are 2D images that appear to be "glued" onto the screen. Logos, credits, and map legends are often added to an Earth browser as screen overlays. Figure 5-2 shows a screen overlay used to credit the image source.

- *Photo overlays* are photographs added to Google Earth at specified locations. Photo overlays can be rectangular (appearing as billboards on the Earth's surface), cylindrical, or spherical. The user can "fly into" a photo overlay to explore portions of it in detail and then exit to browse the basic imagery of the Earth browser. This feature supports the addition of very large panoramic images that are preprocessed into

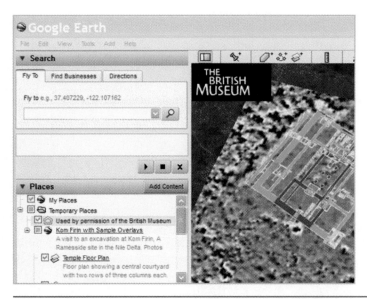

Figure 5-2 A screen overlay can be used to credit the source of the imagery (here, the British Museum). This example uses a ‹ListStyle› element to display a custom icon in the list view (see ‹ScreenOverlay› example in this chapter).

multiple layers for efficient browsing. Figure 5-3 shows a photographic tour of an archaeological dig by a team from the British Museum in Kom Firin, Egypt (www.britishmuseum.org/research/research_projects/kom_firin/introduction.aspx). This KML presentation, created by Stefan Geens, author of the Ogle Earth blog, forms the basis of the examples used in this chapter.

Tools for Creating Overlays

This chapter explains the KML details of the three overlay elements. In many cases, you will use a software tool to create the overlays and will not need to edit the KML file itself. Google Earth itself provides a user interface for adding ground and photo overlays to its base imagery. For screen overlays, and in cases in which you want to create programmatic interfaces between your imagery and the KML overlay, you will need to be familiar with the information presented in this chapter.

Figure 5-3 A creative blending of several different techniques that help users visualize an archaeological dig at Kom Firin, a Ramesside temple complex in the Nile Delta. The background image is a cylindrical photo overlay that the Google Earth user can "fly into" and explore in detail. The thumbnail images are Placemark icons with associated balloons and links to a photo website. (Images courtesy of Stefan Geens, www.ogleearth.com/2007/11/the_kom_firin_d.html.)

Basic Concepts

Overlays, like Placemarks, are derived from the Feature element, as shown in Figure 5-4. The Feature element provides a set of children that are inherited by all of its descendants.

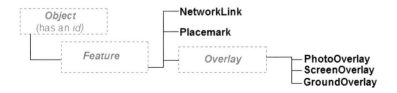

Figure 5-4 Overlay element and its derived elements.

This means that all three Overlay elements (GroundOverlay, PhotoOverlay, and ScreenOverlay) have names, descriptions, snippets, and balloons, for example.

Syntax for ‹Overlay›

The following shaded box lists the complete syntax for the Overlay element, which includes all the children of Feature as well as the three child elements of Overlay.

```
<!-- Overlay  -->
  <!-- inherited from Feature element -->
  <name>...</name>
  <visibility>1</visibility>
  <open>0</open>
  <atom:author>...<atom:author>
  <atom:link />
  <address>...</address>
  <xal:AddressDetails>...</xal:AddressDetails>
  <phoneNumber>...</phoneNumber>
  <Snippet maxLines="2">...</Snippet>
  <description>...</description>
  <AbstractView>...</AbstractView>
  <TimePrimitive>...</TimePrimitive>
  <styleUrl>...</styleUrl>
  <StyleSelector>...</StyleSelector>
  <Region>...</Region>
  <ExtendedData>...</ExtendedData>
  <!-- specific to Overlay -->
  <color>ffffffff</color>
  <drawOrder>0</drawOrder>
  <Icon>
     <href>...</href>
     <refreshMode>onChange</refreshMode>
     <refreshInterval>4.0</refreshInterval>
     <viewRefreshMode>never</viewRefreshMode>
     <viewRefreshTime>4</viewRefreshTime>
     <viewBoundScale>1</viewBoundScale>
     <viewFormat>...</viewFormat>
     <httpQuery>...</httpQuery>
  </Icon>
 <!-- /Overlay -->
```

The following child elements are common to all overlays:

- Color (and transparency)
- Draw order
- Icon (in this case, the *image* used for the overlay)

Color and Transparency for Overlays

The <color> value specifies the *transparency* of the overlay image as well as an optional *color* that is to be blended with the image. As explained in detail in Chapter 2, color and transparency (alpha) values are expressed as hexadecimal values. The range of values for any one color is 0 to 255. In hexadecimal, this is 00 to ff for each of the four components: alpha, blue, green, and red. The order of expression is *aabbggrr*, where *aa*=alpha; *bb*=blue; *gg*=green; and *rr*=red.

> **Note**
>
> This is the same <color> element that you have already seen in the <IconStyle>, <LineStyle>, <LabelStyle>, and <PolyStyle> elements.

Table 5-1 lists hexadecimal values for varying percentages of transparency. The hexadecimal value listed is used as the first two numbers in the <color> element.

For example, to specify an overlay image that is 30 percent transparent, you would include this element in <GroundOverlay>:

```
<color>43000000</color>
```

The image must be in a format that supports transparency (for example, PNG or GIF) for this transparency value to be used.

Table 5-1 Specifying Hexadecimal Values for Transparency

Percentage of Transparency	Hexadecimal Value
0	00
10	19
20	33
25	40
30	43
40	66
50	7F
60	99
75	BF
80	CC
90	E5
100	FF

Draw Order

The <drawOrder> element determines the stacking order for images that overlap. Images with high numbers are drawn on top of images with lower numbers.

Icons: Specifying and Refreshing the Overlay Image

The <href> child of <Icon> specifies which image file to use as the overlay. The image file can be on a local file system or on a web server. For example, this code specifies an image file located in the same directory as the KML file:

```
<href>clouds.jpg</href>
```

This code specifies an image file located on a remote server named "WeatherStation.com":

```
<href>http://WeatherStation.com/clouds.jpg</href>
```

If the <href> element is omitted or empty, a rectangle is drawn using the color and size defined by the overlay.

<Icon> also includes elements for specifying the conditions under which the overlay image should be reloaded (refreshed). Basically, you can specify to reload the image according to the following:

- Refresh whenever any of the <Icon> parameters change.
- Refresh image according to a specified time interval.
- Refresh when the expiration time is reached.
- Refresh when the user's view changes.

The <Icon> element in an Overlay has the same children as the <Link> element in <NetworkLink>. See Chapter 6, Network Links, for more information on refreshes based on view or time.

Another Way to Specify the Viewpoint: Camera

In Chapter 2, you learned how to use the <LookAt> element to describe the viewpoint for a given Feature or NetworkLinkControl. This section introduces the other AbstractView element: the <Camera>. An Overlay, like any Feature, can contain an AbstractView that specifies a viewpoint for it. The AbstractView can be either a <LookAt> or a <Camera> element.

Differences between <Camera> and <LookAt>

The <LookAt> and <Camera> elements are both used to specify the viewpoint for a Feature or <NetworkLinkControl>. They differ in two ways:

- <LookAt> defines the viewpoint relative to the position of the scene that is being viewed, whereas <Camera> defines the viewpoint in terms of the eye point for a virtual camera that is viewing the scene.

- <Camera> provides full six-degrees-of-freedom control, which allows you to position the camera in space and then rotate it around the *x*, *y*, and *z* axes (described later in this section). With a <Camera> element, you can position the viewpoint so that you're looking above the horizon into the sky.

Syntax for <Camera>

The <Camera> element describes the position and viewing direction of a virtual "camera" that is viewing the Feature or the contents of a <NetworkLinkControl>. The camera position is defined by <longitude>, <latitude>, <altitude>, and <altitudeMode>. The viewing direction of the camera is defined by <heading>, <tilt>, and <roll>.

```
<Camera id="ID">
    <longitude>0.0</longitude>
    <latitude>0.0</latitude>
    <altitude>0.0</altitude>
    <heading>0.0</heading>
    <tilt>0.0</tilt>
    <roll>0.0</roll>
    <altitudeMode>clampToGround</altitudeMode>
</Camera>
```

The child elements for <Camera> are as follows:

<longitude>

Longitude of the virtual camera (eye point). Angular distance in degrees, relative to the Prime Meridian. Values west of the Meridian range from −180 degrees to 0 degrees. Values east of the Meridian range from 0 degrees to 180 degrees.

<latitude>

Latitude of the virtual camera (eye point). Degrees north or south of the Equator (0 degrees). Values range from −90 degrees to 90 degrees.

<altitude>

Distance from the Earth's surface, in meters. See <altitudeMode> for how this value is interpreted.

<heading>

Direction (that is, North, South, East, West), in degrees. Default=0 (North). Values range from 0 degrees to 360 degrees, with 90 degrees = East, 180 degrees = South, 270 degrees = West. This value can also be specified in negative degrees (counterclockwise from 0).

<tilt>

Rotation, in degrees, of the camera around the x axis. A value of 0 indicates that the view is aimed straight down toward the Earth (the most common case). A value of 90 degrees for <tilt> indicates that the view is aimed toward the horizon. Values greater than 90 degrees indicate that the view is pointed up into the sky. Values for <tilt> range from 0 to +180 degrees.

<roll>

Rotation, in degrees, of the camera around the z axis. Values range from −180 degrees to +180 degrees.

<altitudeMode>

Specifies how the <altitude> specified for the Camera point is interpreted. Possible values are as follows:

`clampToGround` (default)
Indicates to ignore the <altitude> specification and place the Camera position on the ground.

`relativeToGround`
Interprets the <altitude> as a value in meters above the ground.

`absolute`
Interprets the <altitude> as a value in meters above sea level.

Initial Position of the Camera

Figure 5-5 shows the initial orientation of the camera, with the x, y, and z axes, as follows:

- The x axis points toward the right of the camera and is called the *right vector* in 3D graphics.

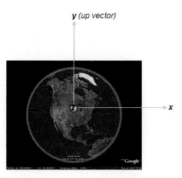

Figure 5-5 Default orientation of the virtual camera.

- The *y* axis defines the "up" direction relative to the screen and is called the *up vector*.
- The *z* axis points from the center of the screen toward the eye point. The camera looks down the -*z* axis, which is called the *view vector*.

The order of rotation is important. By default, the camera is looking straight down the −*z* axis toward the Earth. The order of rotations is as follows:

1. <heading>   Rotate around the *z* axis (the look-at vector).

2. <tilt>   Rotate around the *x* axis.

3. <roll>   Rotate around the (new) *z* axis (the new look-at vector).

Note that each time a rotation is applied, two of the camera axes change their orientation.

Here are a few examples of rotations.

Figure 5-6 (left) shows a <Camera> placed directly above the Pyramids in Egypt. Figure 5-6 (right) shows the effect of changing the <heading> value to 90 degrees, which points the Camera's up vector toward the East.

Figure 5-7 (left) changes the <tilt> value to 75 degrees, which points the Camera up toward the horizon. Figure 5-7 (right) changes the <roll> value to 30 degrees, which tilts the view (probably a less commonly desired effect).

CameraRotations.kml illustrates how different camera rotations affect the view. See also Figures 5-6 and 5-7, which show the effects of these rotations.

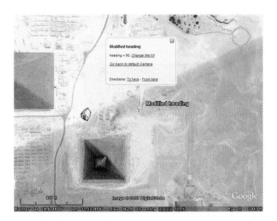

Figure 5-6 Left image shows default Camera position, looking straight down. Right image shows changing the <heading> value to 90.

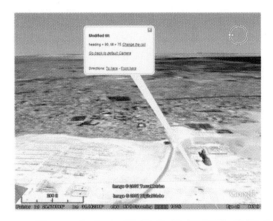

Figure 5-7 Left image shows changing the <tilt> value to 75. Right image shows changing the <roll> value to 30.

CameraRotations.kml

```
<?xml version="1.0" encoding="UTF-8"?>
<kml xmlns="http://www.opengis.net/kml/2.2">
  <Document>
    <name>Camera Rotations</name>
    <Camera>                                <!-- initial camera view -->
      <longitude>31.132959</longitude>
```

```
      <latitude>29.976565</latitude>
      <altitude>1000</altitude>
      <heading>0</heading>
      <tilt>0</tilt>
      <roll>0</roll>
      <altitudeMode>relativeToGround</altitudeMode>
  </Camera>
<Placemark id="defaultCamera">
    <name>Default Camera</name>
    <description>
      <![CDATA[
        Default camera orientation.
      <a href="#changeHeading;balloonFlyto">
                <em>Change the heading<em></a>
      <p>
     ]]>
    </description>
    <Camera>
      <longitude>31.132959</longitude>
      <latitude>29.976565</latitude>
      <altitude>1000</altitude>
      <heading>0</heading>
      <tilt>0</tilt>
      <roll>0</roll>
      <altitudeMode>relativeToGround</altitudeMode>
    </Camera>
    <Point>
      <coordinates>31.1324,29.9739,0</coordinates>
    </Point>
</Placemark>

<Placemark id="changeHeading">
    <name>Modified heading</name>
    <description>
      <![CDATA[
      heading = 90; <a href="#changeTilt;balloonFlyto">
      <em>Change the tilt</em></a>
      <p>
      <a href="#defaultCamera;balloonFlyto">
      <em>Go back to default Camera</em></a>
      <p>
      ]]>
    </description>
```

```
<Camera>
  <longitude>31.132959</longitude>
  <latitude>29.9746</latitude>
  <altitude>1000</altitude>
  <heading>90</heading>
  <tilt>0</tilt>
  <roll>0</roll>
  <altitudeMode>relativeToGround</altitudeMode>
</Camera>
<Point>
  <coordinates>31.133,29.9746,0</coordinates>
</Point>
</Placemark>
<Placemark id="changeTilt">
  <name>Modified tilt</name>
  .
  .
  .
  <Camera>
    <longitude>31.132959</longitude>
    <latitude>29.976565</latitude>
    <altitude>200</altitude>
    <heading>90</heading>
    <tilt>75</tilt>
    <roll>0</roll>
    <altitudeMode>relativeToGround</altitudeMode>
  </Camera>
  <Point>
    <coordinates>31.1337,29.9754,0</coordinates>
  </Point>
</Placemark>
<Placemark id="changeRoll">
  .
  .
  .
  <Camera>
    <longitude>31.132959</longitude>
    <latitude>29.976565</latitude>
    <altitude>200</altitude>
    <heading>90</heading>
    <tilt>75</tilt>
    <roll>30</roll>
    <altitudeMode>relativeToGround</altitudeMode>
```

```
      </Camera>
      <Point>
        <coordinates>31.1343,29.976,0</coordinates>
      </Point>
    </Placemark>
  </Document>
</kml>
```

See the PhotoOverlay section later in this chapter for an example of a <Camera> being used to define the view for a PhotoOverlay.

Ground Overlay

Ground overlays are most commonly created using a tool such as the Google Earth user interface, but you can also create them directly in KML if you know the coordinates of the image boundaries, as described in the following section. In Google Earth, ground overlays are called "image overlays."

Syntax for <GroundOverlay>

The syntax for the <GroundOverlay> element is as follows (see the section Syntax for <Overlay> earlier this chapter, and Appendix A for the elements inherited from Feature and Overlay):

```
<GroundOverlay id="ID">
  <!-- elements inherited from Feature -->
  .
  .
  .
  <!-- elements inherited from Overlay -->
  .
  .
  .
  <!-- elements specific to GroundOverlay -->
  <altitude>0.0</altitude>
  <altitudeMode>clampToGround</altitudeMode>
  <LatLonBox>
    <north>180.0</north>
    <south>-180.0</south>
    <east>180.0</east>
    <west>-180.0</west>
    <rotation>0.0</rotation>
  </LatLonBox>
</GroundOverlay>
```

LatLonBox

A <GroundOverlay> includes a <LatLonBox> element that specifies the boundaries of the image in terms of its latitude and longitude.

The syntax for <LatLonBox> is as follows (see also Figure 5-8):

<north>
> Specifies the latitude of the north edge of the overlay image in decimal degrees from 0 to +/−90.

<south>
> Specifies the latitude of the south edge of the overlay image in decimal degrees from 0 to +/−90.

<east>
> Specifies the longitude of the east edge of the image in decimal degrees from 0 to +/−180.

<west>
> Specifies the longitude of the west edge of the image in decimal degrees from 0 to +/−180.

<rotation>
> Specifies a rotation of the overlay image around its center, in degrees. Values can be +/−180 degrees. The default is 0 (top of image points north). Rotations are specified in a counterclockwise direction.

The following example specifies a <LatLonBox> for a <GroundOverlay> element with no image.

GroundOverlayNoImage.kml

```
<?xml version="1.0" encoding="UTF-8"?>
<kml xmlns="http://www.opengis.net/kml/2.2">
  <GroundOverlay>
    <LatLonBox>
      <north>48.25</north>
      <south>48.24</south>
      <east>-90.86</east>
      <west>-90.87</west>
    </LatLonBox>
  </GroundOverlay>
</kml>
```

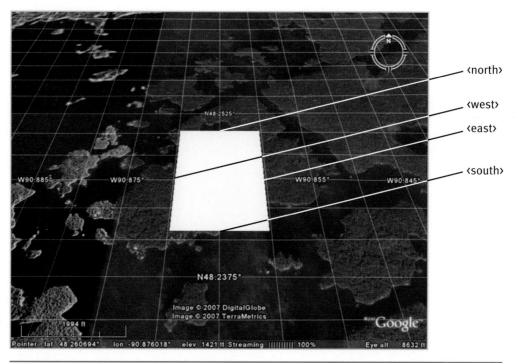

Figure 5-8 Ground overlay with no icon specified.

Figure 5-8 shows this overlay in Google Earth with longitude and latitude grid lines turned on.

> **Note**
>
> With KML, the edges of the overlay are stretched to fit the edges of the <LatLonBox>. Sophisticated GIS (geographical information system) software provides finer control over how an image is stretched over the terrain. One way to achieve more control over how the image is draped onto the Earth is to subdivide the image into a number of smaller rectangles and specify individual ground overlays with a <LatLonBox> for each.

Altitude and Altitude Mode

You can also specify an <altitude> and <altitudeMode> for a ground overlay. As described in Chapter 3, the value specified for <altitude> is always interpreted in terms of the altitude mode specified. In <GroundOverlay>, the only valid altitude modes are clampToGround (the default) or absolute.

Here is an example of adding a <GroundOverlay> (without an image) at an altitude of
500 meters above sea level:

```
<?xml version="1.0" encoding="UTF-8"?>
<kml xmlns="http://www.opengis.net/kml/2.2">
  <GroundOverlay>
    <altitude>500</altitude>
    <altitudeMode>absolute</altitudeMode>
    <LatLonBox>
      <north>48.25</north>
      <south>48.24</south>
      <east>-90.86</east>
      <west>-90.87</west>
    </LatLonBox>
  </GroundOverlay>
</kml>
```

Example of a GroundOverlay

The following example shows two ground overlays that are drawn on top of each other
according to their specified <drawOrder> element (see Figure 5-9). The top element
was processed using the SnagIt application to make white areas of the floorplan fully
transparent. Many photo-processing applications can perform this task, such as Photo-
Shop or GIMP (GNU Image Manipulation Program). Be sure to save the image as a
PNG or GIF image to preserve the transparency. The bottom image, a magnetometric
view of the site, is visible through the transparent parts of the top image.

GroundAndImage.kml

```
<?xml version="1.0" encoding="UTF-8"?>
<kml xmlns="http://www.opengis.net/kml/2.2">
  <Document>
    <name>Kom Firin with Sample Overlays</name>
    <open>1</open>
```

```
<description>A visit to an excavation at Kom Firin, a Ramesside site
            in the Nile Delta. Photos taken October 6, 2007.
</description>
<GroundOverlay>
  <name>Temple Floor Plan</name>
  <description>Floor plan showing a central courtyard with two rows
            of three columns each. Openings indicate probable
            location of gateways, which are thought to be about
            two meters wide.
  </description>
  <drawOrder>1</drawOrder>
  <Icon>
    <href>komfirin1.gif
    </href>
  </Icon>
  <LatLonBox>
    <north>30.865689</north>
    <south>30.86382</south>
    <east>30.491607</east>
    <west>30.48943</west>
    <rotation>-121.340933</rotation>
  </LatLonBox>
</GroundOverlay>
<GroundOverlay>
  <name>Magnetometric view of Kom Firin temple</name>
  <description>Magnetometry survey of the temple, surrounding
            fortified enclosure, and northern gate. Image
            courtesy of the British Museum.</description>
  <Icon>
    <href>3komfirin_3.jpg</href>
  </Icon>
  <LatLonBox>
    <north>30.866014</north>
    <south>30.862289</south>
    <east>30.492794</east>
    <west>30.488453</west>
    <rotation>-16.823374</rotation>
  </LatLonBox>
</GroundOverlay>
</Document>
</kml>
```

Figure 5-9 Two ground overlays showing different information about the dig at Kom Firin. The top image shows the temple floor plan, with transparent spaces that allow the underlying magneto-metric image to show through. (Images courtesy of the British Museum.)

Screen Overlay

A screen overlay is an image that is fixed to a specified location on the screen. Regardless of where the user navigates in the Earth browser, the screen overlay remains in the same position. As with ground overlays, the <href> child of <Icon> specifies the image for the overlay. If no image is specified, a rectangle is drawn with the specified size, color, and transparency.

The <ScreenOverlay> element allows you to specify the following:

- Size of the image
- Position of the image overlay on the screen
- Rotation of the image around a defined rotation point (if desired)

To position a screen overlay, you specify two locations—one on the screen and one on the image. The image is then "attached" to the screen by mapping these two points onto each other.

The Google Earth user interface does not provide a mechanism for creating screen overlays. You can create them with KML, as described here, or with a third-party application designed for this purpose.

Syntax for <ScreenOverlay>

The syntax for the <ScreenOverlay> element is as follows (see the section Syntax for <Overlay> earlier in this chapter, and Appendix A for the elements inherited from Feature and Overlay):

```
<ScreenOverlay id="ID">
  <!-- elements inherited from Feature -->
  .
  .
  .
  <!-- elements inherited from Overlay -->
  .
  .
  .
  <!-- elements specific to ScreenOverlay -->
  <overlayXY  x="1.0" y="1.0" xunits="fraction" yunits="fraction"/>
  <screenXY   x="1.0" y="1.0" xunits="fraction" yunits="fraction"/>
  <rotationXY x="1.0" y="1.0" xunits="fraction" yunits"fraction"/>
  <size       x="1.0" y="1.0" xunits="fraction" yunits="fraction"/>
  <rotation>0.0</rotation>
</ScreenOverlay>
```

Specifying X/Y Units for Image Overlays and Icons

The first four child elements of <ScreenOverlay> use x and y units that are identical to those used for the <hotSpot> child of <IconStyle>, described in Chapter 4. Here is a more detailed description of the three types of units: fraction, pixels, and insetPixels.

- "fraction" specifies a portion of the total image or screen, measured from the bottom-left corner (see Figure 5-10, top).
- "pixels" specifies the number of pixels in the x (horizontal) and y (vertical) directions, measured from the bottom-left corner (see Figure 5-10, middle).

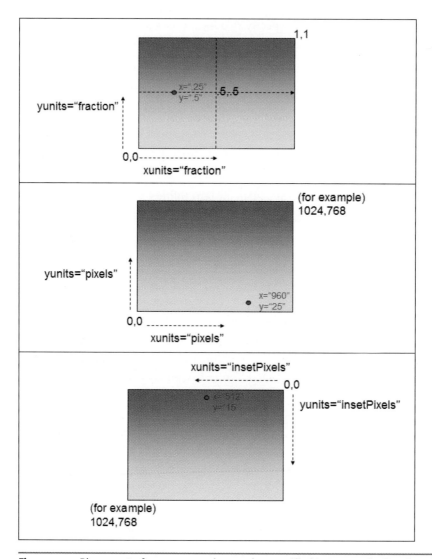

Figure 5-10 Placement of a screen overlay can be specified in terms of a *fraction* of the screen, *pixels* (measured from the lower-left corner), or *insetPixels* (measured from the upper-right corner). You can specify the "x" direction in one unit type and the "y" direction in a different unit type.

- `"insetPixels"` specifies the number of pixels in the *x* (horizontal) and *y* (vertical) directions, measured from the top-right corner (see Figure 5-10, top).

You can mix and match these units—*x* does not have to use the same units as its corresponding *y*, nor do screen units need to be the same as the units used to specify locations for the image.

Child Elements for <ScreenOverlay>

Here is a description of the <ScreenOverlay> child elements:

<overlayXY>

Specifies a point on (or outside of) the overlay image that is mapped to the screen coordinate specified in <screenXY>. This element has attributes for specifying the *x* and *y* values and the type of units used for each. The `xunits` and `yunits` attributes can be one of the following: `fraction`, `pixels`, or `insetPixels` (see the previous section Specifying X/Y Units for Image Overlays and Icons).

<screenXY>

Specifies a point on the screen that is mapped to the <overlayXY> coordinate. See <overlayXY> for a description of the attributes, which are the same for this element.

<rotationXY>

Specifies a point relative to the screen about which the screen overlay is rotated. For example, specify (.5, .5) for the values of *x* and *y* to indicate rotation about the center of the screen. The default rotation is around the upper-right corner (1,1). The amount of rotation is specified in <rotation>. See <overlayXY> for a description of the attributes, which are the same for this element.

<size>

Specifies the size of the image for the screen overlay. See <overlayXY> for a description of the attributes, which are the same for this element. Values are as follows:

−1 specifies to use the image as is, without resizing.

0 specifies to maintain the aspect ratio.

n sets the value of the dimension.

<rotation>

Indicates the angle of rotation of the screen overlay. The value is an angle in degrees counterclockwise from North (0). Values can be +/−180 (see Figure 5-11).

Example of a Simple Screen Overlay

The *ScreenOverlay.kml* example shows adding a screen overlay at the top-left corner of the screen.

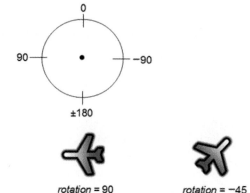

Figure 5-11 Rotations for a screen overlay are specified in degrees from 0 to +/– 180. Use the "rotationXY" attribute to specify rotations that are not around the center of the screen.

ScreenOverlay.kml

```
<?xml version="1.0" encoding="UTF-8"?>
<kml xmlns="http://www.opengis.net/kml/2.2">
  <ScreenOverlay>
    <Icon>
      <href>Images/0502BritishMuseumLogo.tif
      </href>
    </Icon>
    <overlayXY x="0" y="1" xunits="fraction" yunits="fraction"/>
    <screenXY x="0" y="1" xunits="fraction" yunits="fraction"/>
  </ScreenOverlay>
</kml>
```

Example of a Screen Overlay with <ListStyle>

The *ScreenOverlayWithListStyle.kml* example builds on the previous example by adding an inline <ListStyle> element that specifies a custom icon for the list view. It uses the <name> element to add the credits to the list view in a prominent manner.

ScreenOverlayWithListStyle.kml

```
<?xml version="1.0" encoding="UTF-8"?>
<kml xmlns="http://www.opengis.net/kml/2.2">
  <ScreenOverlay>
    <name>Used by permission of the British Museum</name>
    <Style>
```

```
        <ListStyle>
          <ItemIcon>
            <href>http://maps.google.com/mapfiles/kml/shapes/
                  homegardenbusiness.png</href>
          </ItemIcon>
        </ListStyle>
      </Style>
      <Icon>
        <href>Images/0502BritishMuseumLogo.tif
        </href>
      </Icon>
      <overlayXY x="0" y="1" xunits="fraction" yunits="fraction"/>
      <screenXY x="0" y="1" xunits="fraction" yunits="fraction"/>
    </ScreenOverlay>
</kml>
```

PhotoOverlay

Photo overlays are photographs that are directly embedded in the Earth's landscape. They can be 2D rectangles, adding scenic "billboards" to the Google Earth landscape. Photo overlays can also be projected onto cylinders or spheres to create virtual panoramas that the user can "fly into," explore, and inspect in detail. The photo overlay is placed at a specified location and oriented toward the viewpoint. If you include the <Point> child element, the photo overlay has an icon.

Gigapixel Photos

The <PhotoOverlay> feature can accommodate very large images containing many megapixels of data. Such images require you, as KML author, to provide a set of down-sampled versions of the image so that the Earth browser can efficiently load only the portion of the image that fits into the current view, and at the appropriate level of detail. See Advanced: Image Pyramids for Gigapixel Images later in this chapter, which describes the details of creating an *image pyramid*.

Syntax for <PhotoOverlay>

The syntax for the <PhotoOverlay> element is as follows (see the section Syntax for <Overlay> earlier in this chapter, and Appendix A for the elements inherited from Feature and Overlay):

```
<PhotoOverlay>
  <!-- elements inherited from Feature -->
  .
  .
  .

  <!-- elements inherited from Overlay -->
  .
  .
  .

  <!-- elements specific to PhotoOverlay -->
  <rotation>0.0</rotation>
  <ViewVolume>
    <leftFov>0.0</leftFov>
    <rightFov>0.0</rightFov>
    <bottomFov>0.0</bottomFov>
    <topFov>0.0</topFov>
    <near>0.0</near>
  </ViewVolume>
  <ImagePyramid>
    <tileSize>256</tileSize>
    <maxWidth>0</maxWidth>
    <maxHeight>0</maxHeight>
    <gridOrigin>lowerLeft</gridOrigin>
  </ImagePyramid>
  <Point>
    <coordinates>...</coordinates>
  </Point>
  <shape>rectangle</shape>
</PhotoOverlay>
```

The following sections are organized conceptually, building from simple to more complex. Refer to the Syntax section above for the ordering of these child elements within <PhotoOverlay> and Appendix A, which provides a complete reference for all elements.

Basics: Shape and Point

The image of a photo overlay is projected onto a <shape>, which can be rectangle (the default), cylinder (for partial or full cylindrical panoramas), or sphere (for spherical panoramas). The basic image can be created by a panoramic camera, or can be a series of individual photos that are "stitched" together using photo-processing software.

A <PhotoOverlay> has a <Point> child that is used in the same way that a <Placemark> uses a <Point>. The <Point> child adds an icon to the photo overlay and places the overlay at the specified location. This icon can be styled by the <IconStyle> and <ListStyle> elements.

Field of View

As you have learned, you can specify a viewpoint for any Feature using either the <LookAt> or <Camera> element. The <PhotoOverlay> element includes a <ViewVolume> element, which defines the *field of view*. Specifying the field of view is analogous to specifying the lens opening in a physical camera. A small field of view, like that of a telephoto lens, focuses on a small part of the scene. A large field of view, like that of a wide-angle lens, focuses on a large part of the scene.

The field of view for a photo overlay is defined by four planes, each of which is specified by an angle relative to the view vector. These four planes define the top, bottom, left, and right sides of the field of view, which has the shape of a truncated pyramid, as shown in Figure 5-12.

Figure 5-13 shows the <rightFov> and <leftFov> angles (*Top View*) and the <topFov> and <bottomFov> angles (*Side View*) of this pyramid. The <near> element specifies the measurement in meters along the viewing direction from the camera viewpoint to the photo overlay shape.

A typical camera has symmetrical values on either side of the view vector. Values for a typical camera are as follows:

```
<ViewVolume>
  <near>1000</near>
  <leftFov>-60</leftFov>
  <rightFov>60</rightFov>
  <bottomFov>-60</bottomFov>
  <topFov>60</topFov>
</ViewVolume>
```

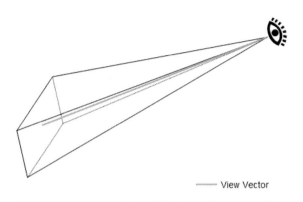

——— View Vector

Figure 5-12 The field of view is defined by four planes that are specified relative to the view vector.

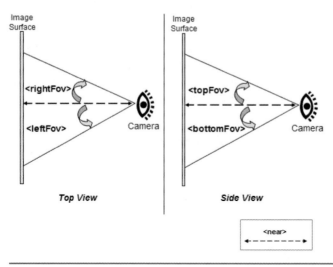

Figure 5-13 Four planes determine the field of view, which defines the portion of the photo overlay that is visible.

Field of View for a Rectangle

For a rectangle, <topFov> must be less than 90 degrees, and <bottomFov> must be greater than −90 degrees. If either of these limits is exceeded, the field of view plane will not intersect the image at all. The values for <bottomFov> and <leftFov> are usually negative.

Field of View for a Cylinder

For a cylindrical image, the axis of the cylinder matches the *up* vector (*y* axis) for the view. The radius of the cylinder is equal to <near>. For a cylinder, the ranges for the field of view are as follows:

```
-90 < bottomFov < topFov < 90
-180 < leftFov < rightFov < 180
```

Field of View for a Sphere

A spherical image is centered at the origin of the camera (the eye point). The radius of the sphere is equal to <near>. The ranges for the field of view elements are the same for a sphere as for a cylinder (see previous section).

Adjusting the View with the Rotation Element

If your photo has been rotated and deviates slightly from a desired horizontal view, you can specify a <rotation> to adjust how the photo is placed inside the field of view.

Advanced: Image Pyramids for Gigapixel Images

This section describes how to preprocess very large images so that they can be loaded efficiently by an Earth browser. Fortunately, you can now use third-party tools to create image pyramids for large images quickly and easily. The Google Earth PhotoOverlay Creator by Digital Urban and the software available for download from GigaPan at www.gigapan.org are examples of free software tools that will make this task a snap.

The main reason for creating an image pyramid is to maximize performance for viewing large photo images. As a rule of thumb, you do not need to create an image pyramid if your image is less than 2K by 2K pixels. Most modern graphics cards can handle images of up to 4K by 4K pixels. If your image is larger, you should probably create an image pyramid for your photo overlay so that it performs well on most computers.

How Image Pyramids Work

An image pyramid is a hierarchical set of images, each of which is an increasingly lower-resolution version of the original image. Each image in the pyramid is subdivided into tiles, so that only the portions in view need to be loaded. Google Earth calculates the current viewpoint and loads the tiles that are appropriate to the user's distance from the image. As the viewpoint moves closer to the photo overlay, Google Earth loads higher-resolution tiles. Since all the pixels in the original image can't be viewed on the screen at once, this preprocessing allows Google Earth to achieve maximum performance because it loads only the portions of the image that are in view, and only the pixel details that can be discerned by the user at the current viewpoint.

If your image is very large, you should create an image pyramid for it and modify the <href> in the <Icon> element to include specifications for the tiles in the pyramid. The following sections describe how to create the image pyramid by hand and how to specify the <href> for a gigapixel image. In fact, you will probably use a software utility to accomplish this task.

Syntax for <ImagePyramid>

```
<ImagePyramid>
   <tileSize>256</tileSize>
   <maxWidth>0</maxWidth>
   <maxHeight>0</maxHeight>
   <gridOrigin>lowerLeft</gridOrigin>    <!-- lowerLeft or upperLeft -->
</ImagePyramid>
```

<tileSize>

> Size of the tiles, in pixels. Tiles must be square, and <tileSize> must be a power of 2. A tile size of 256 (the default) or 512 is recommended. The original image is divided into tiles of this size, at varying resolutions.

<maxWidth>

> Width in pixels of the original image.

<maxHeight>

> Height in pixels of the original image.

<gridOrigin>

> Specifies where to begin numbering the tiles in each layer of the pyramid. A value of `lowerLeft` (default) specifies that row 1, column 1 of each layer is in the bottom-left corner of the grid. A value of `upperLeft` indicates to begin numbering in the upper-left corner of the grid.

The pixel size of the original image is specified in the <maxWidth> and <maxHeight> elements. The width and height can be any size and do not need to be a power of 2. You can fill out the remaining pixels with blank pixels, as described in the upcoming section Adding Fill to the Image.

Creating the Image Pyramid

These instructions assume your image pixel measurement is a power of 2. If your image pixel measurement is not a power of 2, you'll first need to add fill, as described in Adding Fill to the Image. Then follow these steps to create an image pyramid:

1. Starting with the original, full-size image, divide it into tile-sized pieces—for example, into blocks of 256 * 256 pixels each.

2. Shrink the image by a factor of 2.

3. Divide this new image into tile-sized squares.

4. Repeat steps 2 and 3 until the resulting image fits inside the tile size (for example, 256 * 256 pixels).

Figure 5-14 shows a small image pyramid created in this fashion.

Adding Fill to the Image

If the last tile in a row is not square, you'll need to add transparent fill pixels to make the tile square. Place the image so that the (0,0) tile is at the origin. (For example, if the origin is at the lower left, place the image in the lower left of the tile grid.) The row and columns that might need fill would then be at the right and top of the image. For best filtering, replicate the last row (or column) at the edge of the image. Then add fill (for example, black) to the remaining pixels in the tiles of the row (or column).

Example

As an example, consider an image whose dimensions are 3600 * 2700 pixels (roughly 10 megapixels). Here are the steps to create an image pyramid for this image:

1. Using a tile size of 256 pixels, you can subdivide the original image into a grid of 16 * 16 pixels. (This image ends up as level 4 in the final pyramid.)

2. Fill in the pixels to "square up" the partially filled tiles (as described in Adding Fill to the Image) in the last column (to the right) and the last row (at the top, assuming <gridOrigin> is lowerLeft).

3. Scale down the image by a factor of 2.

4. Subdivide this image into 256-pixel tiles. The image at this level consists of a grid of 8 * 8 tiles (level 3).

5. Scale the level 3 image down by a factor of 2.

6. Subdivide into tiles. The image at this level consists of a grid of 4 * 4 tiles (level 2).

7. Scale the level 2 image down by a factor of 2.

8. Subdivide into tiles. The image at this level consists of a grid of 2 * 2 tiles (level 1).

9. Scale the level 1 image down by a factor of 2.

10. The resulting image is 256 * 256 pixels, so this is the last level of the image pyramid (level 0).

The image pyramid for a 4096 * 4096 image has five levels, as shown in Table 5-2.

Level n thus has 2^n tiles in each direction.

Figure 5-14 shows Levels 0, 1, and 2 of a sample image pyramid.

Table 5-2 Sample Image Pyramid with Five Levels

Level	Number of Tiles	Size of Image (Pixels)
0	1	256 * 256
1	4 (2 * 2 grid)	512 * 512
2	16 (4 * 4 grid)	1024 * 1024
3	64 (8 * 8 grid)	2048 * 2048
4	256 (16 * 16 grid)	4096 * 4096

Level 0

Level 1

Level 2

Figure 5-14 An image pyramid consists of multiple versions of the same image. At each level, the image is subdivided into square tiles. Search the web for software tools that can create this image pyramid for you.

Numbering the Tiles

The tiles in each level are numbered so that Google Earth can fetch only the specific tiles that are appropriate for the current viewpoint. Each tile is identified by three values:

- *x value*   Row position in the grid
- *y value*   Column position in the grid
- *level*   Level in the image pyramid, with 0 being the highest level

By default, the origin (0,0) is at the lower left of the grid. If your image has an origin in the upper left, specify `upperLeft` for the <gridOrigin>.

Figure 5-15 illustrates numbering of the tiles at level 2 of the 10-megapixel image, with the origin in the lower left.

Specifying the URL of a Gigapixel Image

For gigapixel images, the <href> specification in the <Icon> element includes special entities to specify the *level*, *x*, and *y* values of the tiles Google Earth needs to fetch. For example, the URL for the image might be specified as follows:

```
http://server.company.com/bigphoto/$[level]/row_$[x]_column_[$y].jpg
```

Google Earth fills in the values for these entities when it makes the http request. For example, to request the tile in row 2, column 1, at level 3, Google Earth would fetch the following URL:

```
http://server.company.com/bigphoto/3/row_2_column_1.jpg
```

Level 2 (numbering the tiles)

Figure 5-15 In this example, the grid origin is at the lower left of the image, and tiles are numbered from lower left to upper right (*x, y*).

Transparency

If your image is fully opaque, use the JPEG format. If part of the image is opaque and part is transparent, you can mix PNG and JPEG tiles. Use the PNG format only for tiles that have transparency values. If you need to mix formats, omit the file extension from the <href> specification of the image file and include the file extension in the filename for each tile.

Example of a PhotoOverlay

The *PhotoOverlay.kml* example shows a cylindrical photo overlay and a view that is specified with the <Camera> element. Notice how the <description> includes a link to the Placemark that allows the user to fly into the panoramic photo overlay. Because this is a very large image, the creator of the KML file, Stefan Geens, created an image pyramid and includes parameters that describe it, so that Google Earth can request specific tiles to load rather than requesting the entire image.

PhotoOverlay.kml

```
<?xml version="1.0" encoding="UTF-8"?>
<kml xmlns="http://www.opengis.net/kml/2.2">
  <PhotoOverlay id="kom_firin_360">
    <name>Kom Firin 360</name>
    <description>
      <![CDATA[
        <p>Panorama view of the excavation of a
         Ramesside temple site by the British Museum team, visited
         October 6, 2007.</p><p><a href="#kom_firin_360">Fly into this
         panorama</a>.</p>
      ]]>
    </description>
    <Camera>
      <longitude>30.488247</longitude>
      <latitude>30.863415</latitude>
      <altitude>20</altitude>
      <heading>53.5</heading>
      <tilt>90</tilt>
      <roll>0</roll>
    </Camera>
    <Style>
      <IconStyle>
        <Icon>
          <href>http://maps.google.com/mapfiles/kml/shapes/camera.png
```

```
            </href>
          </Icon>
        </IconStyle>
      </Style>
      <Icon>
        <href>http://www.ogleearth.com/komfirin360/
            komfirin360_$[level]_$[x]_$[y].jpg</href>
      </Icon>
      <ViewVolume>
        <leftFov>-180</leftFov>
        <rightFov>180</rightFov>
        <bottomFov>-24.5</bottomFov>
        <topFov>12.7</topFov>
        <near>65</near>
      </ViewVolume>
      <ImagePyramid>
        <maxWidth>16390</maxWidth>
        <maxHeight>1757</maxHeight>
        <gridOrigin>upperLeft</gridOrigin>
      </ImagePyramid>
      <Point>
        <altitudeMode>relativeToGround</altitudeMode>
        <coordinates>30.488247,30.863415,13</coordinates>
      </Point>
      <shape>cylinder</shape>
    </PhotoOverlay>
</kml>
```

What's Next?

Chapter 6 introduces the network link, which is a powerful way to share and refresh your data over the network. Network links are also a useful way to organize large presentations into smaller files that can be loaded independently, both locally or across the network. Additional features of the <Link> element are discussed too, showing how you can refresh network links based on the user's view or changes in data, and how you can communicate certain information from the Earth browser back to the server.

Chapter 6

Network Links

After reading this chapter, you'll be able to do the following:

- Give several reasons why network links are useful.

- Create a network link that fetches a KML file from a web server.

- Create a network link that refreshes the fetched KML file every half-hour.

- Create a network link that refreshes the fetched KML file 5 seconds after the user moves to a new location in Google Earth.

- Explain the relationship between a web client and a web server.

Chapter Overview

A *network link* contains the URL of another KML file or KMZ archive. When Google Earth opens the source KML file, it also fetches and loads the KML file referenced in the <NetworkLink> element. This fetched KML file can be either *local* or *remote* (that is, residing on a web server). Linking to a file on a web server allows the Google Earth user to view data that is updated remotely or that requires special processing by a web server (Figure 6-1).

The fetched KML file can contain the following:

- A hierarchy of Feature elements
- One (optional) <NetworkLinkControl> element that controls the behavior of the source (fetching) KML file

This chapter begins by explaining what network links are and why they're useful. It describes the basics of client/server communication and gives a few pointers on setting up a web server to test KML network link functionality. You will also need to follow configuration instructions provided by the web server application of your choice to complete this setup.

After a network link has been loaded into Google Earth, it can be *refreshed* (that is, refetched and reloaded into Google Earth) based on changes in the user's view, on time-based parameters, or on changes to the <Link> element. This very important feature of network links is discussed next, along with an example of a view-based refresh to a network link.

Network links also allow Google Earth to *send client data to the server*, where user-created scripts can process the data before sending a response back to the client. The child elements of <NetworkLink> that provide this functionality are described:

- <viewFormat>
- <viewBoundScale>
- <httpQuery>

A *network link control* is a KML file that contains a <NetworkLinkControl> element and that resides on a web server. This chapter concludes by showing how network link controls specify or override fetching behavior of network links and also how network link controls can affect certain content elements within a network link.

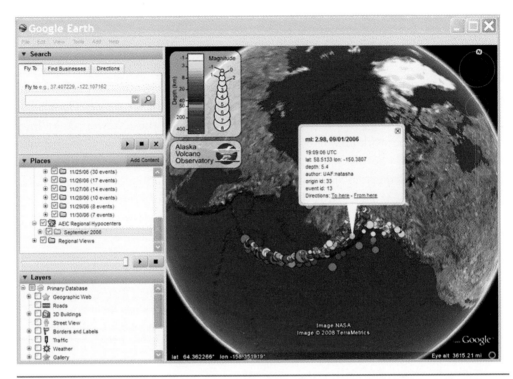

Figure 6-1 The Alaska Volcano Observatory monitors seismic data in the volcanic regions of Alaska and the Aleutian Islands. The data is transmitted using radio telemetry and telephone lines to laboratories at the University of Fairbanks and the USGS-Anchorage, where the data is analyzed and processed. The updated information is then published on the web server as a KML file so that remote Google Earth users can view it. (Courtesy of Alaska Volcano Observatory and the University of Alaska, Fairbanks; http://ge.images.alaska.edu.)

What Is a Network Link?

A KML network link references a KML file or KMZ archive on a local or remote network. This reference causes Google Earth to fetch the linked file, load it into memory, and display it in the 3D viewer of Google Earth. The fetched KML file can, in turn, contain a network link to another KML file, thus creating a hierarchy of network linked KML files.

The Network Link as a Grouping Mechanism

The <NetworkLink> element is derived from Feature, so it can have <name>, <visibility>, <open>, <description>, <Camera> or <LookAt>, or any of the other child elements of Feature, which have been discussed in earlier chapters. In addition, <NetworkLink> is a *grouping mechanism* and functions like a <Folder> in the list view of Google Earth. The Features in the fetched KML file appear as children of the <NetworkLink> in the list view. The network link, like a folder, has a checkbox and an icon in the list view (see Figure 6-2). The <listItemType> child of <ListStyle>, which was discussed in Chapter 4, Styles and Icons, can also be used to affect how the children of a network link appear in the list view. If a fetched KML file contains hundreds of Features, it's useful to create a <Style> for the network link and specify checkOffOnly or checkHideChildren so that the list view isn't cluttered with extraneous information.

> **Note**
>
> In Google Earth, even though the Features in the fetched KML file are inside a folder or document, this top-level container does not show up in the list view unless it has an ID assigned to it. See Chapter 7 for more information on IDs.

Network Links: Local and Remote

Despite the name, the target of a network link can be either local *or* remote. Network links are a useful way to split up very large files into smaller files that are more manageable. If you use relative file references, a cluster of files linked by <NetworkLink> elements can be hosted locally (on your computer system) or remotely, without modifying any file references used in the <href> element.

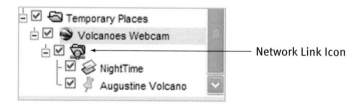

Figure 6-2 A network link has an icon in the list view and functions as a folder. The objects in the linked KML file appear as children of the network link in the list view of Google Earth.

Why Use Network Links?

Network links are useful in a number of different cases, especially the following:

- When data is distributed over a large area of the Earth's surface, the *view-based refresh* feature of <NetworkLink> enables Google Earth to perform a spatial search based on the current viewpoint and load only the data that is currently within the user's view.

- When data is changing frequently, the *interval refresh* feature of <NetworkLink> provides for timely refresh of the displayed data.

- For very large data sets, the *region* feature of <NetworkLink> allows you to control which parts of the data set are shown in a given view. (See Chapter 8, Dealing with Large Data Sets.)

- When you've already transmitted a large amount of data, you can use the *update* feature of <NetworkLinkControl> to make small changes to the data already fetched by the <NetworkLink>. (See Chapter 7, Dynamic KML.)

- For complex sets of KML files, you can partition the KML into multiple files that link to each other. This use applies to files hosted locally as well as files hosted remotely.

> **Note**
>
> For brevity, this chapter refers to the fetched file as simply a "KML file," but in all cases, the target of a network link can be a KMZ archive. Google Earth unpacks and loads the KMZ archive automatically, just as it does a simple KML file.

Client/Server Basics

The Google Earth application is actually a *web client* (located on your local computer system) that communicates over the Internet with any number of *web servers* (located somewhere on the web). As shown in Figure 6-3, Google Earth issues *requests* to these web servers, and the servers send back *responses* to these requests.

Typically, the web client communicates with a web server over HTTP (Hypertext Transfer Protocol). When the client issues a request, it actually sends an HTTP GET command to the server. This command includes the name of the requested file and other relevant information. The requested file on the web server can be a program or script that is written in a language such as HTML, Perl, JavaScript, PHP, MySQL, or XML. These programs all use CGI (Common Gateway Interface), which is a standard for writing applications that run on web servers.

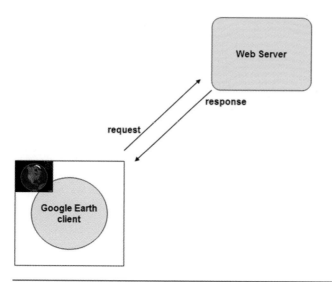

Figure 6-3 Google Earth is a web client that communicates with a web server.

In the case of a network link, Google Earth sends a request to the server for a KML file, as shown in Figure 6-4. The server returns a response that contains the KML file. Here, the KML "file" is actually a stream of bytes—not the filename, but its actual contents.

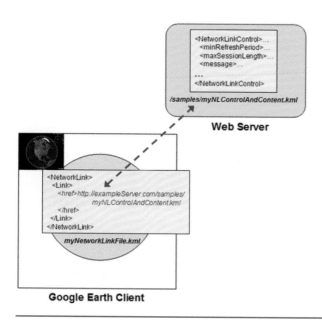

Figure 6-4 A network link contains the URL of a KML file that is fetched and loaded into Google Earth.

Setting Up a Server

Many different web server software packages are available, some more complex to configure and run than others. Apache, Microsoft Internet Information Services, iPlanet, WebSite, WebStar, and Lotus Domino are examples of popular web servers. The **lighttpd** (pronounced "lighty") web server (www.lighttpd.net), as its name suggests, is a lightweight web server that is relatively easy to install and configure.

Choose a server and install and configure it as specified. If you're mainly interested in testing KML examples, you will probably want a simple server such as lighttpd.

Configuring the Server for the KML/KMZ MIME Type

A MIME type tells the operating system what application to launch to display a particular file. MIME stands for Multipart Internet Mail Extensions. Although originally MIME types were used to describe e-mail formats, they are now used to identify many different types of content. For network links to work properly, the web server must be configured to recognize the KML and KMZ content-types. The exact syntax for the MIME type definition differs slightly for each web server application. The MIME type for KML files is

```
application/vnd.google-earth.kml+xml
```

The MIME type for KMZ files is

```
application/vnd.google-earth.kmz
```

For an Apache server, for example, you need to add these lines to the *httpd.conf* configuration file in order for KML/KMZ files to be recognized:

```
AddType application/vnd.google-earth.kml+xml .kml
AddType application/vnd.google-earth.kmz .kmz
```

For a lighttpd server (another web server that is easy to set up and use), you need to add these lines to the *lighttpd.conf* configuration file:

```
mimetype.assign = <
".kml" => "application/vnd.google-earth.kml+xml",
".kmz" => "application/vnd.google-earth.kmz"
```

Install and Configure the Server for Desired Language and Database Support

You will also need to install and configure your server with the languages required to run the scripts (if any) hosted on the server. The scripting example in this chapter requires PHP, and one of the Update examples in Chapter 7 requires Python. If the script queries a database, you will also need to follow the database software instructions for installation and configuration. (The example in this chapter queries a MySQL database.)

Strategies for Testing Network Links

If you use relative file references, you can test your network links locally and then move the entire file hierarchy to the web server when it is ready for production use—without modifying any file specifications inside the KML files. The file you send to the end user needs the *http://* specification to direct the Earth browser to the web server. Inside the KML files, though, the KML link specifications do not need the *http://* qualification (because all of the remaining file paths are relative paths, not absolute paths).

Absolute versus Relative File References

The source KML file (that is, the file containing the <NetworkLink> element) is considered the "root" file. The source file is the top of the file hierarchy. In the <href> element of the source file's <Link> element, external files are specified *relative to* this root.

For example, suppose you have a *doc.kml* file located in *C:\My Documents\Projects\ CityPlanning.* The *doc.kml* file contains a <NetworkLink> with a <Link> element that points to a KML file named *myHouses.kml.* The easiest solution is to place both files in the same directory (here, *CityPlanning;* see Figure 6-5). Then you simply refer to the linked file by its name:

```
<href>myHouses.kml</href>
```

As an alternative, you might have a subfolder within *CityPlanning* named *philadelphia.* If you place the *myHouses.kml* file in that directory as shown in Figure 6-6, the <href> in *doc.kml* would be

```
<href>philadelphia/myHouses.kml</href>
```

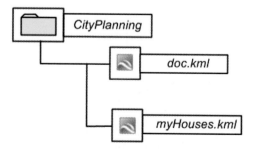

Figure 6-5 Placing the linked file in the same directory as the source KML file.

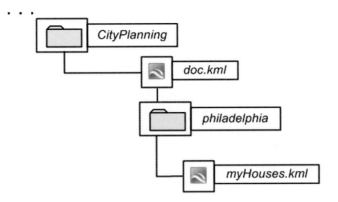

Figure 6-6 Placing the linked file in a subdirectory of the source KML file.

The equivalent absolute reference—that is, the complete file specification:

```
C:\My Documents\Projects\CityPlanning\Philadelphia\myHouses.kml
```

would also work as long as the files were hosted on your system. However, if you move the files to a new computer, the network link will break unless your original directory structure is replicated on the new computer system as well. As a result, it's best to use *relative references* for all link URLs.

Syntax for ‹NetworkLink›

The ‹NetworkLink› element contains all the elements of Feature, plus the elements shown below:

```
<NetworkLink id="ID">
  <!-- inherited from Feature element -->
  <name>...</name>
  <visibility>1</visibility>
  <open>0</open>
  <atom:author>...<atom:author>
  <atom:link />
  <address>...</address>
  <xal:AddressDetails>...</xal:AddressDetails>
  <phoneNumber>...</phoneNumber>
  <Snippet maxLines="2">...</Snippet>
  <description>...</description>
  <AbstractView>...</AbstractView>
```

```
<TimePrimitive>...</TimePrimitive>
<styleUrl>...</styleUrl>
<StyleSelector>...</StyleSelector>
<Region>...</Region>
<ExtendedData>...</ExtendedData>

<!-- specific to NetworkLink -->
<refreshVisibility>0</refreshVisibility>
<flyToView>0</flyToView>
<Link id="ID">
  <href>...</href>
  <refreshMode>onChange</refreshMode>
  <refreshInterval>4.0</refreshInterval>
  <viewRefreshMode>never</viewRefreshMode>
  <viewRefreshTime>4.0</viewRefreshTime>
  <viewBoundScale>1.0</viewBoundScale>
  <viewFormat>BBOX=
    [bboxWest],[bboxSouth],[bboxEast],[bboxNorth]</viewFormat>
  <httpQuery>...</httpQuery>
</Link>
</NetworkLink>
```

<refreshVisibility>

> Boolean value (0 or 1). A value of 0 (the default) leaves the visibility of a Feature within the control of the Google Earth user. A value of 1 indicates to reset the visibility of a Feature each time the <Link> is refreshed.

> When a KML file is refreshed (re-fetched), the fetched KML is fully reconstructed in Google Earth. The original instance of the file in Google Earth memory is destroyed, and a completely new version of the file is created. Thus, when a placemark balloon is open and the file is refreshed, the balloon closes because the file is being reloaded from scratch.

> Suppose a <NetworkLink> has <refreshVisibility> set to 1, and the fetched KML file contains a <Placemark> with its <visibility> set to 1. In this case, the placemark is visible when the network link first fetches the link. Next, suppose the user unchecks this placemark in the list view, making it invisible. When the network link is refreshed, the placemark is redrawn from scratch and is visible because its specified <visibility> in the KML file is 1 (TRUE).

<flyToView>

> Boolean value (0 or 1). A value of 0 (the default) indicates to ignore the AbstractView element (that is, <Camera> or <LookAt>). A value of 1 causes Google Earth to fly to the view of the <Camera> or <LookAt> in the <NetworkLinkControl> in the fetched KML file (if it exists). If the

<NetworkLinkControl> does not contain an AbstractView element, Google Earth flies to the <Camera> or <LookAt> element specified in the Feature child of the <kml> element in the fetched file (recall that the <kml> element has at most one Feature child). If the <kml> element does not have a <Camera> or <LookAt> specified, Google Earth uses the default view.

A value of 1 for this element means, for example, that Google Earth would fly to the <LookAt> view of the parent <Document> in the fetched file. It would not fly to the <LookAt> of the placemarks contained within the <Document>, even if the <LookAt> is specified at that lower level in the hierarchy. (This policy provides you, the KML author, with some control over the initial viewpoint for a KML file, but also provides an efficient means for Google Earth to locate the appropriate AbstractView quickly.)

Note that <flyToView> should be used with care, since it takes control of the view in Google Earth away from the user. In most cases, it feels more natural for the user to be in control of the view.

<Link>
<href>

In a <NetworkLink>, the target of the <href> within <Link> can be a KML file or KMZ archive, or it can be a program or script that returns a *.kml* or *.kmz* file (the actual bytes of the file, not simply the filename). For example, a server might be connected to a large database. When the server receives the network link request from Google Earth, it might in turn run a script that requests and processes data from the database, and then create and return a *.kml* file that results from this processing.

If the target of the <href> is a script or program, the file specification *must* include the *http://* specification. A script or program specified in a <NetworkLink> cannot be run locally.

<refreshMode>

Specifies a refresh mode based on time or on changes in the <Link> parameters. Values are

onChange (default)
    Refresh when the image is loaded and whenever the <Link> parameters change.

onInterval
    Refresh every *n* seconds, as specified in <refreshInterval>.

onExpire

Refresh the image when the expiration time is reached. This refresh mode uses the time specified in the <expires> element of <NetworkLinkControl>, described later in this chapter. If no <expires> element is specified, the HTTP header is examined to see if its header fields contain expiration parameters. (See Appendix A.)

<refreshInterval>

Specifies to refresh the image every *n* seconds.

<viewRefreshMode>

Specifies a view-based refresh mode. Values are

never (default)

Ignore changes in the view. Also ignore <viewFormat> parameters, if any.

onStop

Refresh the image *n* seconds after movement stops, where *n* is specified in <viewRefreshTime>.

onRequest

Refresh the image only when the user explicitly requests it. (For example, in Google Earth, the user right-clicks and selects Refresh in the Context menu.)

onRegion

Refresh the image when the Region becomes active. See Chapter 8, Dealing with Large Data Sets.

<viewRefreshTime>

Specifies the number of seconds to wait after the view changes before refreshing the image (used with **<viewRefreshMode>**onStop**</viewRefreshMode>**).

Note

The <Icon> element and the <Link> elements have the same set of child elements. <Icon> is used in the Overlay elements. <Link> is used in <NetworkLink> and <Model>.

The section Sending Additional Data to the Server with <httpQuery> later in this chapter completes the discussion of the remaining child elements of <Link> (and <Icon>).

Simple Network Link Example

This simple example of a network link references a file named *AugustineWebcam.kml*, which contains a screen overlay that links to a web camera focused on the Augustine Volcano (see Figure 6-7). This network link example assumes that both the source file and the web file are in the *same directory,* and therefore it uses relative references. If the files were not in the same directory, the file references would need to be adjusted.

Simple Network Link: Source File

```
<?xml version="1.0" encoding="UTF-8"?>
<kml xmlns="http://www.opengis.net/kml/2.2">
  <Document>
    <name>Volcanoes Webcam</name>
    <NetworkLink>
      <Link>
        <href>http://localhost:3000/AugustineWebcam.kml</href>
      </Link>
    </NetworkLink>
  </Document>
</kml>
```

Simple Network Link: Fetched File (AugustineWebcam.kml)

```
<?xml version="1.0" encoding="UTF-8"?>
<kml xmlns="http://www.opengis.net/kml/2.2">
  <Document>
    <name>Augustine Webcam</name>
    <LookAt>
      <longitude>-133.768512</longitude>
      <latitude>56.447578</latitude>
      <altitude>0</altitude>
      <heading>-10.595248</heading>
      <tilt>0</tilt>
      <range>7382344.561341</range>
      <altitudeMode>relativeToGround</altitudeMode>
    </LookAt>
    <ScreenOverlay>
      <name>Webcam Image</name>
      <Icon>    <!-- link to the web camera -->
        <href>http://www.avo.alaska.edu/webcam/augustine.jpg</href>
```

A <viewRefreshMode> with a value of `onStop` combined with a specified <viewRefreshTime> is useful from a performance standpoint because the server refreshes the network link only when the user has stopped roaming the globe and has actually paused to view a particular area. In addition, this mode enhances the user's experience because files aren't loading and interrupting the user's travels when he is still in transit.

See also the *Pizza.kml* sample for another example of refreshing a network link based on the user's view.

Advanced Example: Puff Volcanic Ash Tracking Model

This advanced example combines many KML features in a real-world application created by the Alaska Volcano Observatory (AVO). In conjunction with regional agencies, AVO monitors volcanoes across the North Pacific, including Kamchatka, the Aleutian Islands, the Alaska Mainland, and the northwestern United States. AVO is a joint program of the United States Geological Survey (USGS), the Geophysical Institute of the University of Alaska Fairbanks (UAFGI), and the State of Alaska Division of Geological and Geophysical Surveys (ADGGS).

The example uses network links to retrieve data from the observatory that is processed and updated every six hours. University of Alaska Fairbanks volcanologists Peter Webley and John Bailey have further developed the computer program, affectionately named "Puff," that takes current wind conditions and data about the ash particles produced by the current volcanic eruptions from each site, and then processes this data according to a complex mathematical model, and finally, outputs the information as a 3D model of the ash cloud in Google Earth (see Figure 6-8).

The program records ash particles and wind conditions at regular intervals and outputs an hourly snapshot of the ash plume at each location. Each snapshot has a time stamp, which acts as a signal to Google Earth to "play" the files in consecutive order, as if it were flipping through an animation sequence. (This is merely a preview of how to use the TimeSpan element—see Chapter 7 for the full story.) To view the full example, visit the Alaska Volcano Observatory website (http://puff.images.alaska.edu).

The Puff example includes one *.kml* file with network links that fetch updated data from the AVO server. Here is an excerpt from the beginning of this file, which shows

```
      <Link>
        <href>
          http://puff.images.alaska.edu/watch/Shiveluch/latest/avn-gfs/
          200801121100_kmz.kmz
        </href>
      </Link>
    </NetworkLink>
  .
  .
  .

    </Folder>
  </Document>
</kml>
```

The *.kmz* file referenced in the <Link> in the *PuffModel.kml* file contains two files: the *doc.kml* file (the main KML file) and *ash.tif*, which is the patterned dot image used to simulate the ash cloud. The ash cloud geometry is actually made up of thousands of Placemarks, each with its own icon that simulates a tiny portion of the ash cloud particles.

doc.kml (from 200801121100_kmz.kmz)

```
<?xml version="1.0" encoding="UTF-8"?>
<kml xmlns="http://www.opengis.net/kml/2.2">
  <Document>
    <name>Ash_Particles_for 200801121000</name>
    <Style id="PuffBalloon">
      <BalloonStyle>
        <text>
          <![CDATA[$[description]]]>
        </text>
      </BalloonStyle>
    </Style>
    <Style id="check-hide-children">
      <ListStyle>
        <listItemType>checkHideChildren</listItemType>
      </ListStyle>
    </Style>
    <styleUrl>#check-hide-children</styleUrl>
    <Placemark>
      <styleUrl>#PuffBalloon</styleUrl>
      <description>
        .
        .
        .
```

```
      </description>
      <Style>
        <IconStyle>
          <Icon>
            <href>ash.tif</href>
          </Icon>
        </IconStyle>
      </Style>
      <Point>
        <altitudeMode>absolute</altitudeMode>
        <coordinates>160.701477,56.811301,2565.582002</coordinates>
      </Point>
    </Placemark>
    . <!-- thousands of similar Placemark elements follow-->
    .
    .
  </Document>
</kml>
```

You can view the complete example online, or visit the AVO website for current, near real-time 3D ash cloud predictions.

Sending Information from Client-Side to Server-Side

This section describes the remaining features of the <Link> element. The elements discussed in this section are used when the <href> inside the <Link> element points to a remote file that is retrieved via HTTP. They are not used for local files.

For review and reference purposes, the syntax of <Link> is repeated here (elements introduced in this section are in boldface type):

```
<Link id="ID">
  <href>...</href>
  <refreshMode>onChange</refreshMode>
  <refreshInterval>4.0</refreshInterval>
  <viewRefreshMode>never</viewRefreshMode>
  <viewRefreshTime>4.0</viewRefreshTime>
  <viewBoundScale>1.0</viewBoundScale>
  <viewFormat>BBox=
     [bboxWest],[bboxSouth],[bboxEast],[bboxNorth]</viewFormat>
  <httpQuery>...</httpQuery>
</Link>
```

Sending Information about the Current View

The <viewFormat> and <viewBoundScale> elements are used by the Google Earth client to send information to the server about the user's current viewpoint. This information enables your CGI script on the server side to format a response efficiently and according to the current user state.

Format of the Query String

When a file is fetched, the URL that is sent to the server is composed of three pieces of information:

- The *href* (hypertext reference) that specifies the file to load
- An arbitrary format string that is created from (a) bounding box parameters for the current view or (b) parameters that you specify in the <viewFormat> element that describe the current viewpoint
- A second format string that is specified in the <httpQuery> element

If the file specified in <href> is a local file, the <viewFormat> and <httpQuery> elements are not used. See the section Example of View-Based Refresh later in this chapter for an example of a <NetworkLink> that sends a query string to a script located at the server.

Bounding Box Information (and More)

By default, the Google Earth client appends the following four parameters to the URL of the <href> in the network link:

```
BBOX=[bboxWest],[bboxSouth],[bboxEast],[bboxNorth]
```

These values represent the West, South, East, and North limits of an imaginary box that encloses the *current viewing area*. This box is called a *bounding box*, and this information matches the commonly used Web Map Service (WMS) bounding box specification.

If you specify an empty <viewFormat> element, no bounding box information is sent to the server.

You can also specify a custom set of viewing parameters to add to the query string. If you supply a format string, it is used *instead of* the bounding box information. If you also want the bounding box information included, you need to add those parameters along with the custom parameters.

Use the <viewBoundScale> element to scale the bounding box parameters before sending them to the server. A value less than 1 specifies to use less than the full view (screen). A value greater than 1 specifies to fetch an area that extends beyond the edges of the current view.

Additional Parameters for <ViewFormat>

You can use any of the following parameters in your format string. Include the parameter name (and square brackets) as values in the <viewFormat> element of <Link>. When the Google Earth client issues its request to the server for the link, Google Earth will substitute the appropriate current value at the time it creates the request.

[lookatLon], [lookatLat]
: Longitude and latitude of the point that <LookAt> is viewing

[lookatRange], [lookatTilt],[lookatHeading]
: Values used by the <LookAt> element (see <LookAt> in Appendix A)

[lookatTerrainLon], [lookatTerrainLat], [lookatTerrainAlt]
: Point on the terrain in degrees/meters that <LookAt> is viewing

[cameraLon], [cameraLat], [cameraAlt]
: Degrees/meters of the eye point for the <Camera>

[horizFov], [vertFov]
: Horizontal, vertical field of view for the <Camera>

[horizPixels], [vertPixels]
: Size in pixels of the 3D viewer in Google Earth

[terrainEnabled]
: Indicates whether the 3D viewer in Google Earth is currently showing terrain

Sending Additional Data to the Server with <httpQuery>

The <httpQuery> element is used to send additional information to the server about the Google Earth client issuing the request. Include the parameter(s) as shown here, and Google Earth substitutes the appropriate value at the time it creates the request.

[clientVersion]
: Version of the Earth browser sending the request

[kmlVersion]
: KML version supported by the Earth browser sending the request

[clientName]
>   Name of the Earth browser sending the request

[language]
>   Language currently used by the Earth browser

For example, to tell the network link control's server the horizontal and vertical dimensions of the 3D viewer in Google Earth, the current state of the Terrain checkbox, the client application name, the client application version, and the current language enabled in the client, you would include the following elements in the <Link> element of the fetching <NetworkLink>:

```
<Link>
  <href>http://localhost:3000/AugustineWebcamRevised.kml</href>
  <viewFormat>[horizPixels],[vertPixels],[terrainEnabled]
  </viewFormat>
   <httpQuery>[clientVersion],[clientName],[language]</httpQuery>
</Link>
```

Example of View-Based Refresh

This example, created by Mano Marks, generates KML placemarks on the fly, based on the user's current view. A script written in PHP queries a MySQL database that contains listings of pizzerias across the United States. Placemarks are created for all pizzerias within a 400-mile radius of the center of the user's view. The *Pizzas.kml* file is located on the client side (Google Earth), and the *genxml.php* script is located at the server along with the database.

The *Pizzas.kml* example contains the <NetworkLink> with the <viewRefreshMode> of onStop. When the user stops panning in Google Earth for 4 seconds, Google Earth sends the current bounding box information to the server along with the URL specified in the <NetworkLink>. The <Link> in <NetworkLink> also specifies a value for the <httpQuery> element (radius=400). This string is appended to the query string sent to the server, as described in the previous section, Format of the Query String. For example, if the user pauses over Chicago, Google Earth would send a string like this to the server:

```
http://localhost:8081/genkml.php?+BBOX=[-87.964613],[41.659033],
[-87.281816],[42.095123];?radius=400
```

Pizzas.kml

```xml
<?xml version="1.0" encoding="UTF-8"?>
<kml xmlns="http://www.opengis.net/kml/2.2">
  <NetworkLink>
    <name>View-Based Refresh Example</name>
    <open>1</open>
    <Link>
      <href>http://manomarks.net/genxml.php?</href>
      <viewRefreshMode>onStop</viewRefreshMode>
      <httpQuery>radius=400</httpQuery>
    </Link>
  </NetworkLink>
</kml>
```

The *genxml.php* file is the PHP script that queries the pizzeria database on the server and returns all entries that are within 400 miles of the center of the bounding box for the current view.

genxml.php

```php
<?php
 $username = 'manomark';
 $password = 'Lbgtq1969';
 $database = 'manomark_manotest';
 $server = 'db123a.pair.com';
error_reporting(0);
function parseLocation(){
$radius = $_GET['radius'];
if (!$radius) $radius = 200;
$bbox = $_GET['BBOX'];
$bbox = split(",",$bbox);
$west = $bbox[0];
$south = $bbox[1];
$east = $bbox[2];
$north = $bbox[3];
$center_lat = (($north - $south)/2) + $south;
$center_lng = (($east - $west)/2) + $east;
$location = array("center_lat"=>$center_lat,
"center_lng"=>$center_lng,"radius"=>$radius);
return $location;
}
$location = parseLocation();
```

```php
$center_lat = $location['center_lat'];
$center_lng = $location['center_lng'];
$radius = $location['radius'];
// Start XML file, create parent node
$dom = new DOMDocument("1.0");
$node = $dom->createElement("kml");
$kmlnode = $dom->appendChild($node);
$foldernode = $dom->createElement("Folder");
$parnode = $kmlnode->appendChild($foldernode);
$opennode = $dom->createElement("open","1");
$parnode->appendChild($opennode);
// Opens a connection to a mySQL server
$connection=mysql_connect($server, $username, $password);
if (!$connection) {
die("Not connected : " . mysql_error());
}
// Set the active mySQL database
$db_selected = mysql_select_db($database, $connection);
if (!$db_selected) {
die ("Can\'t use db : " . mysql_error());
}
// Search the rows in the markers table
$query = "SELECT address, name, lat, lng, ( 3959 * acos( cos("
."radians(".$center_lat.") ) * cos( radians( lat ) ) * cos( radians( lng )"
."- radians(" . $center_lng . ") ) + sin( radians(".$center_lat.") ) *"
."sin( radians( lat ) ) ) AS distance FROM markers HAVING distance < "
.$radius. " ORDER BY distance LIMIT 0 , 20";
$result = mysql_query($query);
if (!$result) {
die("Invalid query: " . mysql_error());
}
//header("Content-type: application/vnd.google-earth.kml+xml");
// Iterate through the rows, adding XML nodes for each
while ($row = @mysql_fetch_assoc($result)){
$node = $dom->createElement("Placemark");
$placenode = $parnode->appendChild($node);
$namenode = $dom->createElement("name",htmlentities ($row['name']));
$placenode->appendChild($namenode);
$descriptioncdata = $dom->createCDATASection("<b>Address:</b> " .
$row['address'] ."<br/><b>Distance:</b> " . $row['distance']);
$descriptionnode=$dom->createElement("description");
$descriptionnode->appendChild($descriptioncdata);
```

```
$placenode->appendChild($descriptionnode);
$coor = $row['lng'] . "," . $row['lat'];
$pointnode = $dom->createElement("Point");
$placenode->appendChild($pointnode);
$coornode = $dom->createElement("coordinates", $coor);
$pointnode->appendChild($coornode);
}
echo $dom->saveXML();
?>
```

Figure 6-9 shows an example of the pizzeria placemarks that are displayed when the user pauses near Chicago.

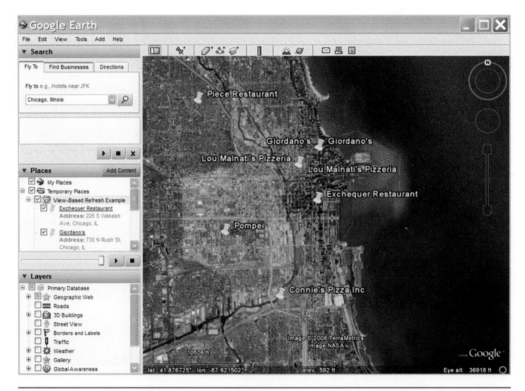

Figure 6-9 This example creates KML on the fly by querying a database of pizzerias based on the user's current viewpoint; see *Pizzas.kml*. (Example created by Mano Marks.)

Network Link Controls

A <NetworkLinkControl> element is contained in the *fetched* KML file (the remote KML file on the server).

A <NetworkLinkControl> performs three general functions:

- It specifies or overrides the fetching behavior of a network link.
- It operates on the content within the fetching network link.
- It operates on content that was previously fetched by a network link and is currently in memory in Google Earth. (See Chapter 7 for how to use a network link control to *update* content that was previously loaded into Google Earth.)

When a KML file is loaded via a network link, it follows the path shown in Figure 6-10:

1. The *.kml* file is fetched from the server. If the fetched file contains a <NetworkLinkControl> element, the fetching process is subject to the controls specified in that <NetworkLinkControl> element.

2. If the file is fetched over the nework, it is sent via HTTP and loaded into the local system's cache (temporary storage).

3. The user's computer then reads the file, parses it, and loads it into RAM (memory) in a form known as an *object model.* This in-memory representation of the KML is ready to be drawn in the computer's frame buffer (graphics hardware).

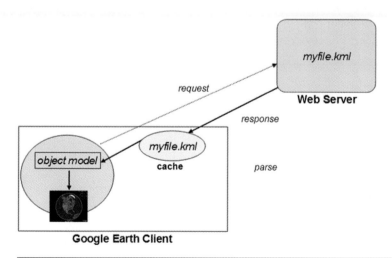

Figure 6-10 A file fetched by a network link is subject to conditions specified in the <NetworkLinkControl> element (if present).

4. The computer draws the graphics in Google Earth, and the user views the fetched file.

Syntax for <NetworkLinkControl>

The <NetworkLinkControl> element is a direct child of <kml>. A <kml> element can contain 0 or 1 <NetworkLinkControl> element.

The syntax for the <NetworkLinkControl> element is as follows:

```
<NetworkLinkControl>
  <minRefreshPeriod>0.0</minRefreshPeriod>
  <maxSessionLength>-1.0</maxSessionLength>
  <cookie>...</cookie>
  <message>...</message>
  <linkName>...</linkName>
  <linkDescription>...</linkDescription>
  <linkSnippet maxLines="2">...</linkSnippet>
  <expires>...</expires>
  <Update>...</Update>                  <!-- See Chapter 7-->
  <AbstractView>...</AbstractView>      <!-- LookAt or Camera -->
</NetworkLinkControl>
```

<minRefreshPeriod>

(default=0.0) Specifies the minimum allowed time between fetches of the file. The value is specified in seconds (it's a `double` value, which means the value can include a decimal value). This element allows the server to throttle fetches of a file and to tailor refresh rates to an acceptable load. The value specified in this element overrides the refresh values specified in the <Link> child of the <NetworkLink> in the source *.kml* file.

<maxSessionLength>

Specifies the maximum number of seconds for which the client <NetworkLink> can remain connected to the server. The default value of −1 indicates to leave the connection open.

<cookie>

The server specifies this <cookie> string, which the client appends to the URL query the next time the network link is refreshed. You can use this data in a server script to provide more intelligent handling on the server side, including version querying and conditional file delivery. The exact sequence is as follows:

1. The server generates the <NetworkLinkControl> and sets the value of <cookie> to a string, for example "count=0".

2. The client <NetworkLink> remembers this cookie.

3. When the client requests a refresh of the <NetworkLink>, it appends `"count=0"` to its *http://* request.

4. The server parses the request URL and looks for the cookie.

5. At this point, the server returns to step 1, and in this case would probably increment the count by 1: `"count=1"`.

The cookie is not required to be of the form *name=value*, but this form is commonly understood by most server-side CGI (Common Gateway Interface) modules. Note that the KML cookie is not the same thing as a web page (HTTP) cookie.

<message>

The server specifies this <message> string, which appears as a pop-up dialog on the user's screen when the network link is first loaded into Google Earth, or when it is changed in the network link control (on the server side). Note that it does not appear every time the file is refreshed, since this could be annoying to the user.

<linkName>

The server specifies this <linkName>, which is used as the name of the network link in the list view of Google Earth. It overrides the <name>, if any, specified for the <NetworkLink> in the file that resides on the client side.

<linkDescription>

The server specifies this <linkDescription>, which is used as the description of the network link in the list view of Google Earth. It overrides the <description>, if any, specified for the <NetworkLink> in the file that resides on the client side.

<linkSnippet maxLines="2">

The server specifies this <linkSnippet>, which is used as the snippet of the network link in the list view of Google Earth. It overrides the <Snippet>, if any, that is specified for the <NetworkLink> in the file that resides on the client side. The `maxLines` attribute specifies the maximum number of lines to display and overrides the value of `maxlines` if specified in the <Snippet> of the <NetworkLink> on the client side.

<expires>

Specifies a date and time at which the link should be refreshed. This value takes effect only if the <refreshMode> in <Link> has a value of `onExpire`. (See the section Refresh Based on Time or Change earlier in this chapter.)

<Update>
    <targetHref>
    <Change>
    <Create>
    <Delete>

> This element allows you to specify any number of Change, Create, and Delete elements for a KML file that has previously been loaded with a <NetworkLink>. See Chapter 7 for information on how to specify updates.

AbstractView

> Specifies a <Camera> or <LookAt> element that is the viewpoint for the network link.

Example of Server Overrides

This simple example shows how the server can override the <name> and <description> of a network link. It also shows how to specify a <message> that appears on the user's screen when the KML file is first loaded. See Figure 6-11 for the results of fetching this network link—does it show the name and description as specified in the network link file or in the network link control file?

Experiment by modifying different fields in the <NetworkLink> and in the <NetworkLinkControl> to see how the network link control overrides the values specified in the original network link. Then try substituting a different message in the net-

Figure 6-11 This example shows how the network link control can override values specified in the fetching network link file (see *BasicNetworkLink.kml* and *AugustineWebcamRevised.kml*).

work link control. If you've set up a web server, move the *AugustineWebcamRevised.kml* file to the server, change the <href> in the network link, and try fetching *AugustineWebcamRevised.kml* over the network.

BasicNetworkLink.kml

```
<?xml version="1.0" encoding="UTF-8"?>
<kml xmlns="http://www.opengis.net/kml/2.2">
  <Document>
    <name>Volcanoes Webcam</name>
    <NetworkLink>
      <name>Original Name on Client Side</name>
      <description>
        <![CDATA[
      This image is very dark in the winter!
      ]]>
      </description>
      <Link>
        <href>http://localhost:3000/AugustineWebcamRevised.kml</href>
      </Link>
    </NetworkLink>
  </Document>
</kml>
```

AugustineWebcamRevised.kml

```
<?xml version="1.0" encoding="UTF-8"?>
<kml xmlns="http://www.opengis.net/kml/2.2">
  <NetworkLinkControl>
    <message>
      <![CDATA[
    This image is updated every 6 hours.
    ]]>
    </message>
    <linkName>Network Link Control Example</linkName>
    <linkDescription>
      <![CDATA[
    Can you see anything?
    ]]>
    </linkDescription>
  </NetworkLinkControl>
  <Document>
    <name>Augustine Webcam</name>
    <LookAt>
```

Chapter Overview

This chapter explores several techniques for creating KML objects that move or change in some way. The first technique involves using the *Update* element within a *network link control* to *change*, *delete*, or *add* elements to a file previously loaded by a network link. This chapter builds on the topics introduced in Chapter 6, which covers the basic functioning of network links and network link controls.

The second technique used to create dynamic KML is the time primitives: *TimeStamp* and *TimeSpan*. A time primitive is included as the child of any Feature element (<Placemark>, Overlay, Container, or <NetworkLink>) and is used to limit the display of that Feature to a given instant in time or period of time. When a KML file contains Features with time primitives, the Earth browser automatically displays a time slider that corresponds to the range of times included in the KML file.

An important new concept introduced in this chapter is the use of *identifiers* for elements that will be updated by a network link control. After the Key Concepts section, the chapter is divided into two main sections, one describing use of the Update element in detail, and one describing KML's time primitives.

Key Concepts

Most of the key concepts required by this chapter are introduced in Chapter 6, Network Links. This section provides additional details on specifying and using identifiers in KML.

Identifiers

Any KML element that is derived from <*Object*> can have an identifier (id) assigned to it. Identifiers are used to uniquely specify a *Style*, for example, so that it can be referenced by multiple Features (see Chapter 4, Styles and Icons). Another common use for identifiers is to uniquely specify the element that is to be modified by an *Update* operation, described later in this chapter. The third use for identifiers in KML is in *fragment URIs*, described later in this Key Concepts section. Chapter 8, Dealing with Large Data Sets, discusses a fourth use for identifiers: identifying a <Schema> that declares custom data types.

An identifier is defined inside the opening tag for an element. For example, as shown in Chapter 4, this is how you would assign an ID to a <BalloonStyle> element:

```
<Style id="grayBlueScheme">
  <BalloonStyle >
    <bgColor>ffffabb2</bgColor>
    <textColor>ff8d8d8d</textColor>
    <displayMode>default</displayMode>
  </BalloonStyle
</Style>
```

Placemark elements in this file can use this style by referencing its ID with a # sign:

```
<Placemark>
  <name>Customized Placemark</name>
  <description>This balloon has a blue gray background</description>
  <styleUrl>#grayBlueScheme</styleUrl>
  <Point>
    <coordinates>-80.210836,34.679252,0</coordinates>
  </Point>
</Placemark>
```

Identifiers are most useful (and less intimidating) if they are descriptive strings that provide a clue about their associated element. Technically, a KML identifier is an XML NCName and must start with a letter, . (period), - (dash), or _ (underscore). An id cannot start with an integer, but it can contain integers. It cannot contain white space. Identifiers support the Unicode character set (which includes, for example, ideographs).

Fragment URIs

In KML, the <href> and <styleUrl> elements can contain values of type anyURI. A URI (Uniform Resource Identifier) is the precise term for what is commonly referred to as a URL (Uniform Resource Locator). The URI specifies a resource (such as a KML file, HTML file, image, or movie) on the web and is actually composed of a number of pieces:

SCHEME	HOST	PATH	FRAGMENT	QUERY STRING
http://	myServer.com	/greece/cities	#athens	?a=24&c=35
file:/		myDirectory/Jan/		

You're already familiar with the *scheme*, *host*, and *path* components. The *fragment* component is used in a KML feature anchor (Chapter 2) to identify a particular object in a KML file by referring to its ID (preceded by a # sign). When the user clicks an <href> link that includes a fragment URI, by default the Earth browser flies to the Feature whose ID matches the fragment. If the Feature has a <LookAt> or <Camera> element, the Feature is viewed from the specified viewpoint.

For example, including this URI in a balloon description creates a hyperlink that, when clicked, opens the specified KML file and flies to the placemark with the ID "myHomeTown."

```
<description>
  <![CDATA[
    <a href="http://myServer.com/biographies.kml#myHomeTown">
      Where It All Started</a>
  ]]>
</description>
```

Within a given KML file, you can just use the fragment URI by itself (for example, #historicMarker) to refer to objects defined within the same file.

For information on the query string, see Chapter 6, Network Links.

Updating KML

The KML update feature is useful when you have already transmitted a large amount of data using a network link and subsequently want to change a relatively small amount of data in the previously fetched file. An alternative to using the <Update> element is to refresh the previously fetched file using a refresh based on time or change, as described in Chapter 6, Network Links. With time-based and view-based refreshes, the entire KML file (including all referenced models, textures, and images) is deleted from memory, refetched, and reloaded into memory. In contrast, with <Update>, only the specified elements are changed. The tradeoff, then, is that while an update requires a bit more framework to set up, greater efficiency can result for very large data sets.

There are three types of updates:

- Create
- Change
- Delete

A given <NetworkLinkControl> can specify any number of each of these types, and the updates will be performed in the order they are listed in the <NetworkLinkControl>. The target KML file of the update operation must have been previously loaded by a <NetworkLink>, and, for security purposes, the file specified in the network link control's <targetHref> must reside on the same server as the network link control.

General Outline of the Update Mechanism

Before focusing on the specific syntax for the <Update> element, it is helpful to gain a general "feel" for how the update mechanism is set up. A certain amount of indirection is involved, since one network link on the client side requests the original KML from the server, and a second network link on the client side requests the update KML from the server. Figures 7-1 and 7-2 show this scenario.

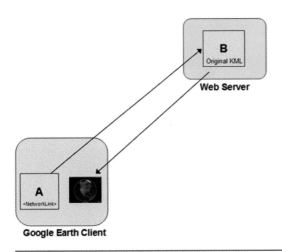

Figure 7-1 Conceptually, four KML files are used to perform an update. In step 1, network link A fetches KML file B.

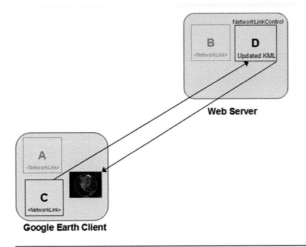

Figure 7-2 In step 2, network link C fetches KML update file D.

For security, the two KML files fetched via network links—that is, the original fetched file (B) and the file with the updates (D)—must reside on the same server. This requirement protects the integrity of the data by limiting access to the target data.

Syntax for <Update> Child of <NetworkLinkControl>

The syntax for the <Update> child of <NetworkLinkControl> is as follows:

```
<NetworkLinkControl>
  .
  .
  .
  <Update>
    <targetHref>...</targetHref>
    <Change>...</Change>
    <Create>...</Create>
    <Delete>...</Delete>
  </Update>
  .
  .
  .
</NetworkLinkControl>
```

<Update>

The <Update> element can have any number of <Change>, <Create>, and <Delete> child elements, which are executed in the order they appear.

<targetHref>

Specifies the KML to update. This file must be on the same server as the file that contains the Update KML file.

<Change>

Modifies the values in a KML element that has already been loaded with a <NetworkLink>. The child of the <Change> element can be any Object element. This Object element must have an id defined for it in the original KML file. Within the Change element, the child to be modified must include a targetId attribute that references the original element's id. In the modified element, only the values listed in <Change> are replaced; all other values remained untouched. When <Change> is applied to a set of coordinates, the new coordinates replace the current coordinates.

<Create>

Adds an element to KML that has already been loaded with a <NetworkLink>. The child of the <Create> element is *always* a Container element (that is, either a <Document> or a <Folder>). This Container element must have an id defined for it in the original KML file. Within the Create element, the child to be created must include a targetId attribute that references the original element's id. After the update occurs, this new element becomes part of the original file. To perform subsequent updates on this element, use the URI of the original KML file (file B in Figure 7-1).

<Delete>

Removes an element from a file that has already been loaded with a <NetworkLink>. The child of the <Delete> element is *always* a Feature element (<NetworkLink>, <Placemark>, <GroundOverlay>, <PhotoOverlay>, <ScreenOverlay>, <Document>, <Folder>). This object must have an id defined for it in the original KML file. Within the Delete element, the child to be deleted must include a targetId attribute that references the original element's id.

For any Update operation, you specify two targets:

- targetHref

  Specifies the file to update. (In these simple examples, this is file B shown in Figure 7-1.) This file must be on the same server as the file that contains the update KML file. (Note that although the targetHref specifies a filename, the update actually occurs in the KML *content* for this file, which has already been loaded into Google Earth memory. The file on disk remains unchanged.)

- targetId

  Specifies the original id of the object to be updated. The targetId is used within the <Change>, <Create>, and <Delete> elements to tie the new KML data with the data that was previously loaded. (In our simple examples, the <Update> is part of file D, shown in Figure 7-2.)

Creating an Element Using <Update>

This example shows how to add a placemark to KML that has been previously loaded into Google Earth with a network link.

Example of Update Create

The following simple example of using <Update> to create an object contains four files that correspond to the four files shown in Figures 7-1 and 7-2. (The first letter of each filename indicates which file it corresponds to.)

This file, located on the client side, contains the network link that loads the original KML into the Earth browser.

aMyPlacemark.kml (Network Link load)

```
<?xml version="1.0" encoding="UTF-8"?>
<kml xmlns="http://www.opengis.net/kml/2.2">
  <NetworkLink>
    <name>Creating Placemarks Example</name>
    <description>Check the box to see the placemark</description>
    <visibility>0</visibility>
    <Link>
      <href>http://localhost:3000/bOnePlacemark.kml</href>
    </Link>
  </NetworkLink>
</kml>
```

This file, located on the server side, contains the original KML to be loaded into the Earth browser.

bOnePlacemark.kml (Original KML)

```
<?xml version="1.0" encoding="UTF-8"?>
<kml xmlns="http://www.opengis.net/kml/2.2">
  <Folder id="targetFolder">
    <name>All My Children</name>
    <Placemark>
      <name>My First Placemark</name>
      <visibility>1</visibility>
      <Snippet>original snippet</Snippet>
      <description>original description</description>
      <Point>
        <coordinates>130.166977,-14.403440</coordinates>
      </Point>
    </Placemark>
  </Folder>
</kml>
```

This file, located on the client side, contains the network link that loads the updated KML into the Earth browser.

cCreateMore.kml (Network Link update)

```
<?xml version="1.0" encoding="UTF-8"?>
<kml xmlns="http://www.opengis.net/kml/2.2">
  <NetworkLink>
    <name>Add New Placemark</name>
    <description>Check the box to see the placemark</description>
    <visibility>0</visibility>
    <Link>
      <href>http://localhost:3000/dUpdatePlacemarkData.kml</href>
    </Link>
  </NetworkLink>
</kml>
```

This file, located on the server side, contains the new placemark to be added to `"targetFolder"` in the original KML file (*bOnePlacemark.kml*). The <targetHref> in <Update> must match exactly the <href> in the <Link> element of the fetching NetworkLink (in file *aMyPlacemark.kml*). Include the full file specification, beginning with *http://*.

dUpdatePlacemarkData.kml (Update KML)

```
<?xml version="1.0" encoding="UTF-8"?>
<kml xmlns="http://www.opengis.net/kml/2.2">
  <NetworkLinkControl>
    <Update>
      <targetHref>http://localhost:3000/bOnePlacemark.kml</targetHref>
      <Create>
        <Folder targetId="targetFolder">
          <Placemark>
            <name>Newly Created Placemark</name>
            <visibility>1</visibility>
            <Snippet>Sydney Australia</Snippet>
            <description>
              new description and new location
            </description>
            <Point>
              <coordinates>151.209522,-33.861718</coordinates>
            </Point>
          </Placemark>
```

```
      </Folder>
    </Create>
  </Update>
 </NetworkLinkControl>
</kml>
```

Changing an Element Using <Update>

This example shows how to change the coordinates, name, description, and snippet for a placemark that has been previously loaded into Google Earth with a network link.

Example of Update Change

These four files correspond to the files shown in Figure 7-2.

This file, located on the client side, contains the network link that loads the original KML into the Earth browser.

aPlacemark.kml (Network Link load)

```
<?xml version="1.0" encoding="UTF-8"?>
<kml xmlns="http://www.opengis.net/kml/2.2">
  <NetworkLink>
    <name>My Placemark Test</name>
    <description>Check the box to see the placemark</description>
    <visibility>0</visibility>
    <Link>
      <href>http://localhost:3000/bOriginalPlacemark.kml</href>
    </Link>
  </NetworkLink>
</kml>
```

This file, located on the server side, contains the original KML to be loaded into the Earth browser.

bOriginalPlacemark.kml (Original KML)

```
<?xml version="1.0" encoding="UTF-8"?>
<kml xmlns="http://www.opengis.net/kml/2.2">
  <Placemark id="targetPlacemark">
    <name>Original Placemark Name</name>
    <visibility>1</visibility>
    <Snippet>original snippet</Snippet>
    <description>original description</description>
```

```
    <Point>
      <coordinates>-122.000,37.000</coordinates>
    </Point>
  </Placemark>
</kml>
```

This file, located on the client side, contains the network link that loads the updated KML into the Earth browser.

cChangeMe.kml (Network Link update)

```
<?xml version="1.0" encoding="UTF-8"?>
<kml xmlns="http://www.opengis.net/kml/2.2">
  <NetworkLink>
    <name>Change My Placemark</name>
    <description>Check the box to see the placemark</description>
    <visibility>0</visibility>
    <Link>
      <href>http://localhost:3000/dUpdatePlacemark.kml</href>
    </Link>
  </NetworkLink>
</kml>
```

This file, located on the server side, contains the new name, description, snippet, and coordinates for the placemark ("targetPlacemark") that was previously loaded into the Earth browser (*bOriginalPlacemark.kml*).

dUpdatePlacemark.kml (Update KML)

```
<?xml version="1.0" encoding="UTF-8"?>
<kml xmlns="http://www.opengis.net/kml/2.2">
  <NetworkLinkControl>
    <Update>
      <targetHref>http://localhost:3000/bOriginalPlacemark.kml
      </targetHref>
        <Change>
          <Placemark targetId="targetPlacemark">
            <name>New Placemark</name>
            <visibility>1</visibility>
            <Snippet>Moving across the ocean</Snippet>
            <description>
              <![CDATA[
              new description, new location
              ]]>
```

```
        </description>
        <Point>
          <coordinates>140.837,-3.26921</coordinates>
        </Point>
      </Placemark>
    </Change>
  </Update>
 </NetworkLinkControl>
</kml>
```

Deleting an Element Using <Update>

This example shows how to delete a placemark from a file that has been previously loaded into Google Earth with a network link.

Example of Update Delete

These four files correspond to the files shown in Figure 7-2.

This file, located on the client side, contains the network link that loads the original KML into the Earth browser.

aPlacemark.kml (Network Link load)

```
<?xml version="1.0" encoding="UTF-8"?>
<kml xmlns="http://www.opengis.net/kml/2.2">
  <NetworkLink>
    <name>Deleting Placemarks Example</name>
    <description>Check the box to see the placemark</description>
    <visibility>0</visibility>
    <Link>
      <href>http://localhost:3000/bOriginalPlacemarks.kml</href>
    </Link>
  </NetworkLink>
</kml>
```

This file, located on the server side, contains the original KML to be loaded into the Earth browser.

bOriginalPlacemarks.kml (Original KML)

```
<?xml version="1.0" encoding="UTF-8"?>
<kml xmlns="http://www.opengis.net/kml/2.2">
  <Folder>
```

```
      <Placemark id="eastMarker">
        <name>Eastern Placemark</name>
        <visibility>1</visibility>
        <Point>
          <coordinates>-67.99,-54.2312</coordinates>
        </Point>
      </Placemark>
      <Placemark id="westMarker">
        <name>Western Placemark</name>
        <visibility>1</visibility>
        <Point>
          <coordinates>-73.0128,-54.3714</coordinates>
        </Point>
      </Placemark>
    </Folder>
</kml>
```

This file, located on the client side, contains the network link that loads the updated KML into the Earth browser.

cDeleteOne.kml (Network Link update)

```
<?xml version="1.0" encoding="UTF-8"?>
<kml xmlns="http://www.opengis.net/kml/2.2">
  <NetworkLink>
    <name>Delete a Placemark</name>
    <visibility>0</visibility>
    <Link>
      <href>http://localhost:3000/dRemoveOnePlacemark.kml</href>
    </Link>
  </NetworkLink>
</kml>
```

This file, located on the server side, specifies the placemark ("eastMarker") to delete from the file that was previously loaded into the Earth browser (*bOriginalPlacemarks.kml*).

dRemoveOnePlacemark.kml (Update KML)

```
<?xml version="1.0" encoding="UTF-8"?>
<kml xmlns="http://www.opengis.net/kml/2.2">
  <NetworkLinkControl>
    <Update>
      <targetHref>http://localhost:3000/bOriginalPlacemarks.kml
```

```
      </targetHref>
      <Delete>
        <Placemark targetId="eastMarker"></Placemark>
      </Delete>
    </Update>
  </NetworkLinkControl>
</kml>
```

Advanced Update Example with Script

This example, written by Bent Hagemark, uses a Python script to generate the original fetched KML file and the updates to it. (It thus replaces files B and D in Figure 7-2 with one file, the Python script, *continents.py*.) The script uses the <cookie> element of <NetworkLinkControl> to store a count value that is used to index into a table of coordinates stored in the continents variable. Here are the two files, *continents.kml* (which fetches the file from the server) and *continents.py* (which resides on the server, constructs the KML when requested, and returns it to the client). A description of the sequence of events as the client requests the file and refreshes it follows the sample code listings.

continents.kml

```
<NetworkLink>
  <name>Continents tour</name>
  <description>Enable the check to start the tour</description>
  <visibility>0</visibility>
  <flyToView>1</flyToView>
  <Link>
    <href>http://localhost:3000/cgi-bin/continents.py</href>
    <refreshMode>onInterval</refreshMode>
    <refreshInterval>6</refreshInterval>
  </Link>
</NetworkLink>
```

continents.py

```python
#!/usr/bin/python

# This script is CGI script which generates KML.
# If no cookie is found an initial KML file is generated.
# If the CGI variable "count=num" is found an Update KML is generated.
```

```
import cgi
import socket

# The hostname _must_ match the <href> in the fetching NetworkLink/Link.
hostname = localhost:3000
href = 'http://%s/cgi-bin/continents.py' % hostname
minrefreshperiod = 7  # seconds

# This list has LookAt data (name, lon, lat, range) for each continent.
continents = []
continents.append(('nowhere', 0, 0, 0))  # offset 0 is unused
continents.append(('Australia', 134.6, -20.47, 3500000))
continents.append(('Antarctica', 138.3, -86.37, 4700000))
continents.append(('Europe', 18.37, 49.18, 3400000))
continents.append(('Africa', 13.15, -1.01, 5600000))
continents.append(('South America', -67.09, -22.48, 5600000))
continents.append(('Asia', 102, 33.7, 4700000))
continents.append(('North America', -100.7, 31.7, 4200000))

# The <cookie> content appears in the CGI params list.
fs = cgi.FieldStorage()
if fs.has_key('count'):
  # We found count=val in the CGI params.  Break out the value.
  # The original KML sets count=1.  Increment here to find 1st entry.
  count = int(fs['count'].value) + 1
  # This indexes the continents list.  After entry 7 cycle back to 1.
  if count > 7:
    count = 1
else:
  # No cookie found.  Set the count to trigger sending the original KML.
  count = 0


def Original():
  k = []
  k.append('<kml>')
  k.append('<NetworkLinkControl>')
  k.append('<minRefreshPeriod>%d</minRefreshPeriod>' % minrefreshperiod)
  k.append('<cookie>count=0</cookie>')
  k.append('</NetworkLinkControl>')
  k.append('<Placemark>')
  k.append('<name>Moving point</name>')
  k.append('<Point id=\"pt0\">')
  k.append('<coordinates>0,0</coordinates>')
```

```
  k.append('</Point>')
  k.append('</Placemark>')
  k.append('</kml>')
  return '\n'.join(k)


# This is always called with 1 <= count <= 7
def Update(count, targethref):
  global continents
  name = continents[count][0]
  longitude = continents[count][1]
  latitude = continents[count][2]
  range = continents[count][3]
  k = []
  k.append('<kml>')
  k.append('<NetworkLinkControl>')
  k.append('<minRefreshPeriod>%d</minRefreshPeriod>' % minrefreshperiod)
  k.append('<message>Arriving %s</message>' % name)
  k.append('<cookie>count=%d</cookie>' % count)
  k.append('<Update>')
  k.append('<targetHref>%s</targetHref>' % targethref)
  k.append('<Change>')
  k.append('<Point targetId=\"pt0\">')
  k.append('<coordinates>%f,%f</coordinates>' % (longitude, latitude))
  k.append('</Point>')
  k.append('</Change>')
  k.append('</Update>')
  k.append('<LookAt>')
  k.append('<longitude>%f</longitude>' % longitude)
  k.append('<latitude>%f</latitude>' % latitude)
  k.append('<range>%d</range>' % range)
  k.append('</LookAt>')
  k.append('</NetworkLinkControl>')
  k.append('</kml>')
  return '\n'.join(k)


print 'Content-type: text/plain'
print

if count == 0:
  print Original()
else:
  print Update(count, href)
```

The order of events for this example is as follows:

1. The *continents.kml* file is loaded for the first time.

2. The network link in *continents.kml* fetches the script contained in its <href> element.

3. This fetch causes the script to run for the first time. No <cookie> element is present in the URI that was sent to the server.

4. The script runs and sends the following KML to the client in response to its first fetch (note that the KML includes a <cookie> element with a count of 0):

```
<kml>
  <NetworkLinkControl>
    <minRefreshPeriod>7</minRefreshPeriod>
    <cookie>count=0</cookie>
  </NetworkLinkControl>
  <Placemark>
    <name>Moving point</name>
    <Point id="pt0">
    <coordinates>0,0</coordinates>
    </Point>
  </Placemark>
</kml>
```

5. When the user refreshes *continents.kml* for the first time, the network link again fetches the <href>, but this time it dutifully returns the cookie that was sent by the server:

```
http://localhost:3000/cgi-bin/continents.py?count=0
```

6. The script sees the cookie with count=0, increments the count to 1, and uses that value to index into the table, which has Australia as its first entry. This is the KML that is sent to Google Earth:

```
<kml>
  <NetworkLinkControl>
    <minRefreshPeriod>7</minRefreshPeriod>
    <message>Arriving Australia</message>
    <cookie>count=1</cookie>
    <Update>
      <targetHref>http://localhost:3000/cgi-bin/continents.py
      </targetHref>
      <Change>
        <Point targetId="pt0">
          <coordinates>134.600000,-20.470000</coordinates>
        </Point>
      </Change>
```

```
    </Update>
    <LookAt>
      <longitude>134.600000</longitude>
      <latitude>-20.470000</latitude>
      <range>3500000</range>
    </LookAt>
  </NetworkLinkControl>
</kml>
```

7. At the next refresh, the `count=1`, so the script increments the `count` to 2, and uses that value to index into the table, which has Antarctica as its second entry. This is the KML that is sent to Google Earth:

```
<kml>
  <NetworkLinkControl>
    <minRefreshPeriod>7</minRefreshPeriod>
    <message>Arriving Antarctica</message>
    <cookie>count=2</cookie>
    <Update>
      <targetHref>http://localhost:3000/cgi-bin/continents.py
      </targetHref>
      <Change>
        <Point targetId="pt0">
          <coordinates>138.300000,-86.370000</coordinates>
        </Point>
      </Change>
    </Update>
    <LookAt>
      <longitude>138.300000</longitude>
      <latitude>-86.370000</latitude>
      <range>4700000</range>
    </LookAt>
  </NetworkLinkControl>
</kml>
```

8. For subsequent fetches, the general process is the same: The client returns the server's cookie. The server increments the `count` by 1 and then creates the KML by indexing into the `continents` table using that value. After the `count` reaches 7, it cycles back to a value of 1.

> **Note**
>
> This example requires that the user close the balloon for each new location; otherwise, the user will experience balloon build-up. Note too that the network link control specifies the refresh rate of 7 seconds in the <minRefreshPeriod> element. It is a good safeguard to specify the refresh rate in the network link

control. It would be possible for the fetching network links on the client side to specify aggressive refresh rates that could overwhelm your server. Recall that a refresh rate specified in <NetworkLinkControl> overrides the values specified on the client side.

Time and Animation in KML

This section describes how to use the KML time elements to limit the display of a Feature to a single point in time (TimeStamp) or period of time (TimeSpan). The time elements offer a relatively easy way to provide sophisticated animations in an Earth browser. When a KML file contains time elements, the Earth browser automatically creates a time slider that corresponds to the beginning and ending times in the file. The user can then "play" the file using the time slider play button or by moving the slider itself.

Because there are many ways to use the time elements, the examples in this chapter should be used as a starting point. Common uses include the following:

- Importing data from a GPS tracking device and using a <TimeStamp> element for each time and location. Typically, the time stamp would be associated with a placemark to show the location (see the Animated Placemark example later in this chapter).

- Associating KML Features with time stamps to create graphical representations of trends or movements. As an example, view Declan Butler's KML file illustrating the spread of avian flu, shown in Figure 7-3.

- Animating ground overlays by specifying a series of time spans for a set of images. An example of this use is the visualization shown in Figure 7-4, created by Valery Hronusov using data provided by Ron Blakey. This animation shows how the Earth's continents evolved over a period of 600 million years to their current configuration.

- Animating a model by specifying a different time span for successive positions of the model. James Stafford's stunning animation of the London Eye giant Ferris wheel illustrates this technique (see Figure 7-5).

Specifying the Time

In both the <TimeStamp> and <TimeSpan> elements, the time is specified in a `dateTime` format defined according to the XML Schema standard (www.w3.org/TR/xmlschema-2/#isoformats). The value is expressed in the following form:

yyyy-mm-ddThh:mm:sszzzzzz

where

yyyy

Is a four-digit value that specifies the year (for example, 1950).

mm

Is a two-digit value that specifies the month between 01 and 12 (for example, 02 for February.

dd

Is a two-digit value that specifies the day of the month between 01 and 31, depending on the month (for example, 28).

T

Is the separator between the date and the time.

Figure 7-3 Placemarks with time stamps create a powerful animation to show how avian flu has spread across the globe in recent years. (KML visualization created by Declan Butler, www.declanbutler.info.)

hh

Is a two-digit value for hour (between 00 and 24). If the value of the hour element is 24, then the values of the minutes element and the seconds element must be 00 and 00.

mm

Is a two-digit value for minutes (between 00 and 59).

ss

Is a two-digit value for seconds (usually between 00 and 59, although the XML specification allows a value of 60 for "leap seconds").

zzzzzz

Is either **Z** for a time specification that uses UTC *or* the time offset in relation to UTC (**+hh:mm** or **-hh:mm**). For more information on UTC (Coordinated Universal Time), see the following section.

The dateTime value can be expressed as a date only (**yyyy-mm-dd**).

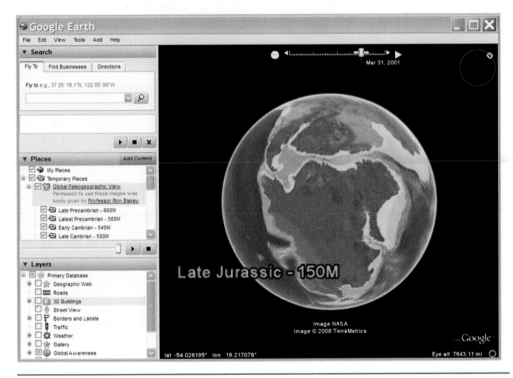

Figure 7-4 This animation uses a series of ground overlays, each associated with a time span, to show how the Earth's continents have evolved over a span of 600 million years. (KML visualization created by Valery Hronusov using data provided by Ron Blakey, Northern Arizona University, http://earth.google.com/gallery/index.html.)

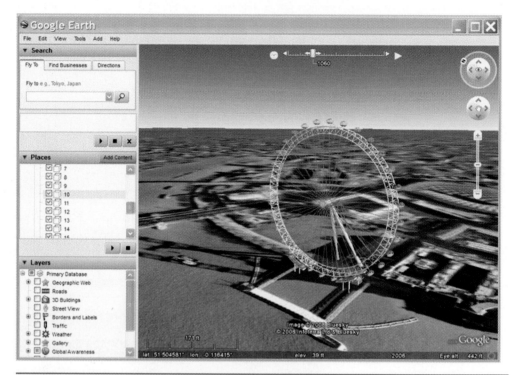

Figure 7-5 James Stafford created this animation of the London Eye using a series of Placemarks, each with a different rotation of the model for the giant Ferris wheel. The ‹TimeSpan› elements specify the relative amount of time to display the model in each position (www.barnabu.co.uk). (Actual playback speed is controlled by the user.)

UTC (Coordinated Universal Time)

UTC is a worldwide standard for expressing time. This standard replaced Greenwich Mean Time (GMT) as the international standard for time in 1972. UTC is also referred to as "Zulu time," which is why the XML time specification used by KML includes a "z" if the time is specified in UTC. Local time zones can be specified as offsets of UTC (+ or − UTC, which is measured from the Prime Meridian).

If you want to specify local time with an offset from UTC, you can look up the UTC offset on the web. One source of information can be found at

`http://www.timeanddate.com/worldclock/city.html`

For example, offsets for some major cities are as follows:

- New York City, United States: UTC −5 hours (or −4 hours during daylight savings time)
- Sydney, Australia: UTC +10 hours (or +11 during daylight savings time)
- Beijing, China: UTC −8 hours (no daylight savings time changes)

Examples of Specifying Time

Here are some examples of specifying times using the XML format:

Year
> Here is the specification for the year 1990:
>
> ```
> <when>1990</when>
> ```

Year and Month
> Here is the specification for May 1990:
>
> ```
> <when>1990-05</when>
> ```

Year, Month, and Day
> Here is the specification for May 17, 1990:
>
> ```
> <when>1990-05-17</when>
> ```

Date and Time (UTC)
> In this example, T is the separator between the calendar and the hourly notation of time, and Z indicates UTC. Seconds are required.
>
> ```
> <when>1990-05-17T07:30:25Z</when>
> ```

Date and Time (with conversion to UTC)
> This example gives a local time in New York City (10:30:15), followed by the conversion to UTC (−5 hours):
>
> ```
> <when>1990-05-17T10:30:15-05:00</when>
> ```

Syntax for <TimeStamp>

The <TimeStamp> element represents a single moment in time. It can be the child of any Feature element. The syntax for this element is as follows:

```
<TimeStamp id="ID">
   <when>...</when>
</TimeStamp>
```

\<when\>

> Specifies a `dateTime` element, as described in the section Specifying the Time earlier in this chapter.

Syntax for \<TimeSpan\>

The \<TimeSpan\> element represents a period of time. It can be the child of any Feature element. The syntax for this element is as follows:

```
<TimeSpan id="ID">
  <begin>...</begin>
  <end>...</end>
</TimeSpan>
```

\<begin\>

> Specifies the `dateTime` that marks the beginning of the time to display this Feature. If the \<begin\> time is unspecified, the beginning of the time period is unbounded.

\<end\>

> Specifies the `dateTime` that marks the end of the time to display this Feature. If the \<end\> time is unspecified, the end of the time period is unbounded.

Time Stamps and GPS Data

A time stamp is typically associated with a point placemark. Displaying the placemark icon briefly at each position along a path has the effect of animating the placemark. This technique is especially useful in creating KML displays of data imported from a GPS tracking device. Because the device samples data at a regular interval, the placemark animates at the same rate along its path.

Time stamps are usually used for lightweight data sets that are shown in multiple locations (for example, placemarks with simple icons that seem to move along a path). In such cases, multiple Features are often in view at the same time as they are shown in slightly different locations at different times. The time slider in the Google Earth user interface includes a time window that selects a "slice" of the time slider and moves from beginning to end of the time period.

The following two examples use the \<TimeStamp\> element to animate a placemark. The first example uses data collected from a GPS device. The second uses a large dataset collected by scientists studying the outbreak of avian flu.

Example of Time Stamp with GPS Data

This example animates a custom icon (a hiker's profile) along a path of point placemarks whose coordinates were captured with a GPS device. The time stamps are tightly sampled, so the placemark icon moves quickly along the path when the user plays the KML file (see Figure 7-6).

First, check out the following code excerpt for its use of the <TimeStamp> element, which specifies dates and times in Zulu format. Then examine its use of the <Style> element—it's a good review of what you learned in Chapter 4, Styles and Icons. The first placemark includes a custom icon, a paddle marked "A," to indicate the start of the hike. The last placemark includes a custom icon, a paddle marked "B," to indicate the end of the hike. The <Document> also defines a <ListStyle> with a <listItemType> of checkHideChildren. After the <Document> *defines* the style, it *references* it so that the list style applies to all of the document's children. As a result, the numerous placemarks are hidden in the list view of Google Earth.

Figure 7-6 An animated point placemark moves along a path according to the time stamps in each placemark. The ‹Document› for this file contains a ‹ListStyle› element with a ‹listItemType› of checkHideChildren that prevents the hundreds of placemarks from cluttering the list view.

Here is an excerpt from the code for this example:

TimeStampGPSExample.kml

```xml
<?xml version="1.0" encoding="UTF-8"?>
<kml xmlns="http://www.opengis.net/kml/2.2">
  <Document>
    <name>Points with TimeStamps</name>
    <!-- defines the styles used by the placemarks and list view -->
    <Style id="paddle-a">
      <IconStyle>
        <Icon>
          <href>http://maps.google.com/mapfiles/kml/paddle/A.png</href>
        </Icon>
        <hotSpot x="32" y="1" xunits="pixels" yunits="pixels"/>
      </IconStyle>
    </Style>
    <Style id="paddle-b">
      <IconStyle>
        <Icon>
          <href>http://maps.google.com/mapfiles/kml/paddle/B.png</href>
        </Icon>
        <hotSpot x="32" y="1" xunits="pixels" yunits="pixels"/>
      </IconStyle>
    </Style>
    <Style id="hiker-icon">
      <IconStyle>
        <Icon>
          <href>http://maps.google.com/mapfiles/ms/icons/hiker.png</href>
        </Icon>
        <hotSpot x="0" y=".5" xunits="fraction" yunits="fraction"/>
      </IconStyle>
    </Style>
    <Style id="check-hide-children">
      <ListStyle>
        <listItemType>checkHideChildren</listItemType>
      </ListStyle>
    </Style>
    <styleUrl>#check-hide-children</styleUrl>
    <Placemark>     <!-- first placemark, has Paddle A icon -->
      <TimeStamp>
        <when>2007-01-14T21:05:02Z</when>
      </TimeStamp>
```

```
    <styleUrl>#paddle-a</styleUrl>
    <Point>
      <coordinates>-122.536226,37.86047,0</coordinates>
    </Point>
  </Placemark>
  <Placemark>
    <TimeStamp>
      <when>2007-01-14T21:05:20Z</when>
    </TimeStamp>
    <styleUrl>#hiker-icon</styleUrl>
    <Point>
      <coordinates>-122.536422,37.860303,0</coordinates>
    </Point>
  </Placemark>
  <Placemark>
    <TimeStamp>
      <when>2007-01-14T21:05:43Z</when>
    </TimeStamp>
    <styleUrl>#hiker-icon</styleUrl>
    <Point>
      <coordinates>-122.536688,37.860072,0</coordinates>
    </Point>
  </Placemark>
  <Placemark>
    <TimeStamp>
      <when>2007-01-14T21:06:04Z</when>
    </TimeStamp>
    <styleUrl>#hiker-icon</styleUrl>
    <Point>
      <coordinates>-122.536923,37.859855,0</coordinates>
    </Point>
  </Placemark>
  <Placemark>
    <TimeStamp>
      <when>2007-01-14T21:06:24Z</when>
    </TimeStamp>
    <styleUrl>#hiker-icon</styleUrl>
    <Point>
      <coordinates>-122.537116,37.85961000000001,0</coordinates>
    </Point>
  </Placemark>
  <Placemark>
    <TimeStamp>
      <when>2007-01-14T21:06:46Z</when>
```

```
        </TimeStamp>
        <styleUrl>#hiker-icon</styleUrl>
        <Point>
          <coordinates>-122.537298,37.859336,0</coordinates>
        </Point>
      </Placemark>
      <Placemark>
        <TimeStamp>
          <when>2007-01-14T21:07:07Z</when>
        </TimeStamp>
        <styleUrl>#hiker-icon</styleUrl>
        <Point>
          <coordinates>-122.537469,37.85907,0</coordinates>
        </Point>
      </Placemark>
      .
      .
      .

      <Placemark>    <!-- last placemark, has Paddle B icon -->
        <TimeStamp>
          <when>2007-01-14T22:36:20Z</when>
        </TimeStamp>
        <styleUrl>#paddle-b</styleUrl>
        <Point>
          <coordinates>-122.536248,37.860445,0</coordinates>
        </Point>
      </Placemark>
    </Document>
</kml>
```

Example of Time Stamp with Animated Placemark Data

This example is a brief excerpt of the data presented in Declan Butler's visualization of the outbreak of avian flu shown in Figure 7-3. It uses the same technique as the previous example, with a <TimeStamp> element for each <Placemark>. Instead of showing movement along a path, this KML shows how time stamps can be used to compare relative times and locations for discrete events.

The placemarks are all from Turkey and use Style_13, the style defined in the original KML for Turkey. (In the original KML, a separate style is defined for each country.) This brief example provides a good review of styles, style maps, and shared styles.

Google Earth creates a time slider that ranges from September 30, 2005, to February 20, 2007, because this is the span of time covered by this set of placemarks.

For simplicity, most of the balloon data has been omitted from this example. If you're interested in how the balloon descriptions are formatted, click the placemarks for the cities of Batman or Diyarbakir in this shortened version of the original.

AvianFluExcerpt.kml

```xml
<?xml version="1.0" encoding="UTF-8"?>
<kml xmlns="http://www.opengis.net/kml/2.2">
  <Document>
    <StyleMap id="Style_13">
      <Pair>
        <key>normal</key>
        <styleUrl>#Style_13n</styleUrl>
      </Pair>
      <Pair>
        <key>highlight</key>
        <styleUrl>#Style_13h</styleUrl>
      </Pair>
    </StyleMap>
    <Style id="Style_13n">
      <IconStyle>
        <scale>0.78125</scale>
        <Icon>
          <href>Style_13n.png</href>
        </Icon>
      </IconStyle>
      <LabelStyle>
        <scale>0</scale>
      </LabelStyle>
      <PolyStyle>
        <color>ff000000</color>
        <fill>1</fill>
        <outline>0</outline>
      </PolyStyle>
      <BalloonStyle>
        <color>ffdcf5f5</color>
        <textColor>ff000000</textColor>
        <text>$[description]</text>
      </BalloonStyle>
    </Style>
    <Style id="Style_13h">
```

```
        <IconStyle>
          <scale>0.78125</scale>
          <Icon>
            <href>Style_13h.png</href>
          </Icon>
        </IconStyle>
        <LabelStyle>
          <color>ff00ffff</color>
          <scale>1</scale>
        </LabelStyle>
        <PolyStyle>
          <color>ff000000</color>
          <fill>1</fill>
          <outline>0</outline>
        </PolyStyle>
        <BalloonStyle>
          <color>ffdcf5f5</color>
          <textColor>ff000000</textColor>
          <text>$[description]</text>
        </BalloonStyle>
      </Style>
  <Folder>
        <name>Data</name>
        <visibility>1</visibility>
        <Placemark id="pm288">
          <name>Adana</name>
          <description>Turkey</description>
          <TimeStamp>
            <when>2006-01-15</when>
          </TimeStamp>
          <styleUrl>#Style_13</styleUrl>
          <Point id="g288">
            <altitudeMode>clampToGround</altitudeMode>
            <coordinates>35.49832811,37.027542491,0</coordinates>
          </Point>
        </Placemark>
        <Placemark id="pm289">
          <name>Adiyaman</name>
          <description>Turkey</description>
          <TimeStamp>
            <when>2006-01-07</when>
          </TimeStamp>
          <styleUrl>#Style_13</styleUrl>
          <Point id="g289">
```

```
        <altitudeMode>clampToGround</altitudeMode>
        <coordinates>38.25,37.75,0</coordinates>
      </Point>
  </Placemark>
  <Placemark id="pm290">
    <name>Adiyaman</name>
    <description>Turkey</description>
    <TimeStamp>
      <when>2006-01-13</when>
    </TimeStamp>
    <styleUrl>#Style_13</styleUrl>
    <Point id="g290">
        <altitudeMode>clampToGround</altitudeMode>
        <coordinates>38.287163037,37.745354829,0</coordinates>
    </Point>
  </Placemark>
  <Placemark id="pm293">
    <name>Agri</name>
    <description>Turkey</description>
    <TimeStamp>
      <when>2005-12-31</when>
    </TimeStamp>
    <styleUrl>#Style_13</styleUrl>
    <Point id="g293">
        <altitudeMode>clampToGround</altitudeMode>
        <coordinates>44.135769502,39.62933027,0</coordinates>
    </Point>
  </Placemark>
  <Placemark id="pm294">
    <name>Agri</name>
    <description>Turkey</description>
    <TimeStamp>
      <when>2005-11-25</when>
    </TimeStamp>
    <styleUrl>#Style_13</styleUrl>
    <Point id="g294">
        <altitudeMode>clampToGround</altitudeMode>
        <coordinates>42.592256972,39.834565669,0</coordinates>
    </Point>
  </Placemark>
  <Placemark id="pm295">
    <name>Agri</name>
    <description>Turkey</description>
    <TimeStamp>
```

```
        <when>2005-11-29</when>
      </TimeStamp>
      <styleUrl>#Style_13</styleUrl>
      <Point id="g295">
        <altitudeMode>clampToGround</altitudeMode>
        <coordinates>43.088015653,39.505741873,0</coordinates>
      </Point>
    </Placemark>
    <Placemark id="pm337">
      <name>Aksaray</name>
      <description>Turkey</description>
      <TimeStamp>
        <when>2006-01-07</when>
      </TimeStamp>
      <styleUrl>#Style_13</styleUrl>
      <Point id="g337">
        <altitudeMode>clampToGround</altitudeMode>
        <coordinates>33.8545596715,38.4068859713,0</coordinates>
      </Point>
    </Placemark>
      .
      .
      .
  </Folder>
  </Document>
</kml>
```

Time Spans and Ground Overlays

Use the <TimeSpan> element to display a series of polygons or image overlays that transition instantly from one to the next. Time spans are used in cases where only one Feature is in view at a given time and the Features occupy the same location. This technique is typically used to show the changes in polygons and in images such as ground overlays—for example, to show the retreating path of glaciers, the spread of volcanic ash, and the extent of logging efforts over the years.

Be sure the <TimeSpan> elements in your KML file are contiguous and do not overlap. For data sets with time spans, the Google Earth user interface time slider includes a pointer that moves smoothly along the time slider from the beginning to the end of the time period. The transition from one Feature to the next is an instant change.

The following example uses the <TimeSpan> element to animate a series of ground overlays.

Example of Time Span with Ground Overlay

This example animates a series of ground overlays based on data collected by Ron Blakcy. Valery Hronusov has used some creative license in specifying the `dateTimes` used in the <TimeSpan> elements, since the KML `dateTime` format is limited to four digits for the year specification, and this visualization covers a span of 600 million years.

The online example shows three of the 26 geologic eras contained in the original visualization by Valery Hronusov. A separate <Folder> contains the name and data for each era. The <TimeSpan> defined within each <Folder> applies to all Features within that <Folder>. Each <Folder> contains two Features:

- A <GroundOverlay> with the image showing the continent formation for that era.
- A <Placemark> with a <name> that is used as the label for the ground overlay. This is a kind of "trick," since the Placemark's point has an altitude of 1,000,000 meters and a <scale> value of 8 for the <LabelStyle>. Since the sole use of this <Placemark> is to provide a label for the <GroundOverlay>, the <Placemark> has a null <Icon> value.

Note too that each <Folder> has a <ListStyle> element that specifies a background color for its entry in the list view. These entries form an attractive gradation from dark orange for the earliest eras to yellow for the present era. The <ListStyle> has a <listItemType> child with a value of `checkHideChildren`, since it would be distracting (and possibly confusing) to view separate entries for the <Placemark> and <GroundOverlay>.

PaleoGlobeExcerpt.kml

```
<kml xmlns="http://www.opengis.net/kml/2.2">
  <Document>
    <name>Global Paleogeographic</name>
    <description><![CDATA[Permission to use these images was kindly
        given by
        <a href="http://jan.ucc.nau.edu/~rcb7/">Professor Ron Blakey
        </a>]]>
    </description>
    <Folder>
      <name>Latest Precambrian - 560M</name>
      <open>1</open>
      <TimeSpan>
        <begin>2000-02-09</begin>
        <end>2000-02-29T23:00:00Z</end>
      </TimeSpan>
```

```
<Style>
  <ListStyle>
    <listItemType>checkHideChildren</listItemType>
    <bgColor>ff0039ff</bgColor>
  </ListStyle>
</Style>
<Placemark>
  <name>Latest Precambrian - 560M</name>
  <Style>
    <IconStyle>
      <scale>0</scale>
      <Icon>
      </Icon>
    </IconStyle>
    <LabelStyle>
      <color>ff0039ff</color>
      <scale>8</scale>
    </LabelStyle>
  </Style>
  <Point>
    <extrude>1</extrude>
    <altitudeMode>relativeToGround</altitudeMode>
    <coordinates>0,89.99,1000000</coordinates>
  </Point>
</Placemark>
<Placemark>
  <name>Latest Precambrian - 560M</name>
  <Style>
    <IconStyle>
      <scale>0</scale>
      <Icon>
      </Icon>
    </IconStyle>
    <LabelStyle>
      <color>ff0039ff</color>
      <scale>8</scale>
    </LabelStyle>
  </Style>
  <Point>
    <extrude>1</extrude>
    <altitudeMode>relativeToGround</altitudeMode>
    <coordinates>0,-89.99,1000000</coordinates>
  </Point>
</Placemark>
```

```
<GroundOverlay>
  <name>Latest Precambrian - 560M</name>
  <drawOrder>4</drawOrder>
  <Icon>
    <href>files/560Marect.jpg</href>
  </Icon>
  <LatLonBox>
    <north>90</north>
    <south>-90</south>
    <east>180</east>
    <west>-180</west>
  </LatLonBox>
</GroundOverlay>
    </Folder>
    .
    .
    .
  </Document>
</kml>
```

What's Next?

Congratulations! You've now studied the basic components of KML. The final chapter in this guide deals with two advanced subjects that are useful for KML files that contain large data sets. *Regions* allow you to specify additional conditions under which data is shown (based on where the user is looking and how far away the user is from the objects being viewed). The *extended data* mechanism is used for custom, typed data and allows you to add new data types to KML and preserve them when the file is saved and reloaded.

Chapter 8

Dealing with Large Data Sets

After reading this chapter, you'll be able to do the following:

- List three uses for Regions.

- Create a set of Placemarks that include Regions to make them active.

- Create (or locate) a Model that can be shown in three levels of detail and use Regions to display the different versions of the Model.

- Use Regions to display a set of GroundOverlays.

- Explain what a super-overlay is used for. List the two KML elements that are used in a super-overlay.

- Outline a simple data set that could use the extended data feature to preserve its fields and types.

Chapter Overview

This chapter deals with two concepts that can be considered among the more advanced features of KML: *regions* and *extended data*. Readers with some programming background will probably be comfortable implementing everything described here. If you're relatively new to programming, the discussion of fields and types in the extended data section may be less familiar to you, but the basic patterns should be clear. The most difficult topic covered here is super-overlays, and that is because the text describes all the details behind this implementation. In fact, almost everyone will use a software utility to create the super-overlay, so the details presented in this chapter are mainly of interest to implementors who need to get "under the hood" to understand the details of this feature.

The first half of this chapter deals with the <Region> element, which can be included in any KML Feature. Regions can be used in a number of ways:

- To reduce clutter when multiple Features are packed closely together in one spot (see Figure 8-1)

Figure 8-1 Too much data for one view! The Swiss transit system includes over 15,000 stations with over 18,000 connections between them. Subdividing this data into separate files using region-based network links creates multiple small files that are fetched over the network and at a level of detail that the user can handle at one time. (See Figure 8-11 for the Super-Overlay solution to this problem by Bent Hagemark.)

- To add clarity by separating different types of data into layers that are swapped in or out depending on what is in the current view

- To fade Features in and out of view

- To increase performance by splitting up very high-resolution images into more manageable chunks that are loaded only when they are in view

- To increase performance by loading Models with different levels of detail that correspond to the amount of screen space currently being used to show the Model

The second half of this chapter deals with the <ExtendedData> element, which offers three different ways to add custom data to KML. Casual users can probably skip this section. It is generally of interest to users who have large databases, where the names and types of each data field are fed into KML files and need to be preserved when the file is written out. These data sets are specialized for widely different applications—real estate, volcanology, immunology, astronomy, geology—and thus it's important to provide a flexible mechanism for extending KML in a simple way.

Key Concepts

This section explains key concepts related to regions. Basically, a region defines a geographical area. Features that specify a <Region> element are visible only when two conditions are met:

- The area defined by the <Region> is currently in view.

- The area defined by the <Region>, when projected onto the screen, falls within the specified LOD range (see Level of Detail [LOD] Range later in this chapter).

When these two conditions are met, the region is said to be active. When a region is active, its related Features are drawn on the screen (assuming <visibility> is set to 1).

Since regions allow you to control how Features pop in and out of sight in relation to the current view, they can be very useful in helping you control and sort out large data sets into presentations that are both more attractive and more easily comprehended. As the chapter examples show, though, regions can also be used with simple data (even a single ground overlay) for interesting effects.

Super-overlays, which are ground overlays that use region-based network links, are explained later in a separate section. The key concepts explained here apply also to super-overlays. Figure 8-2 shows a sample super-overlay.

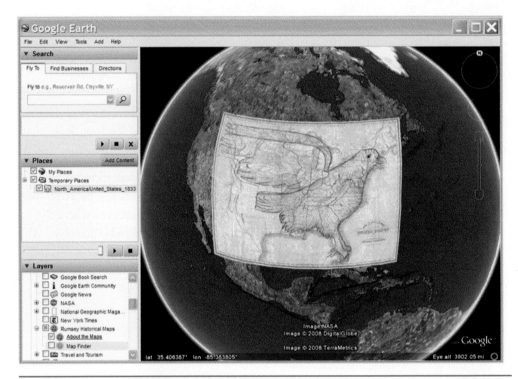

Figure 8-2 This 1833 engraving shows an eagle superimposed on a map of the United States. Google Earth includes a layer of maps from the David Rumsey Map Collection that have been converted into a set of super-overlays for efficient rendering at all resolutions. (Image courtesy of David Rumsey Map Collection, www.davidrumsey.com.)

Bounding Box for Regions

A Region defines a geographical area in its <LatLonAltBox> element. This area can be either a flat box bounded by *North/South/East/West* coordinates or a 3D box bounded by *North/South/East/West/minimumAltitude/maximumAltitude* coordinates (see Figure 8-3).

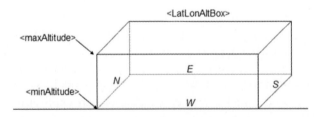

Figure 8-3 A bounding box defines a geographic area of interest for a Region.

A 2D box located at a specified altitude would also require <minAltitude> and <maxAltitude> elements. The <minAltitude> and <maxAltitude> elements are affected by one additional element, the <altitudeMode> element, which was introduced in Chapter 3. This area is commonly referred to as a *bounding box*, since it defines the boundaries for a 3D box.

> **Note**
>
> Typically, the Feature that includes the Region is located somewhere within the area defined by the <LatLonAltBox>, but it's important to note that this is not a requirement. The <LatLonAltBox> and the location of the Feature may have no relation to each other.

Level of Detail (LOD) Range

LOD is an abbreviation for *level of detail*. <Lod> describes the size of the projected region on the screen that is required in order for the region to be considered active.

The LOD range is defined by <minLodPixels> at the lower (smaller) end, and <maxLodPixels> at the higher (larger) end. This range is a size in pixels that relates to the size of the region when projected onto screen space.

The value of <minLodPixels> element is a measurement, in screen pixels, that represents the minimum limit of the visibility range for a given region. The Earth browser calculates the size of the region when projected onto screen space. Then it computes the square root of the region's area. (If, for example, the region is square and located at the Equator, the viewpoint is directly above the region, and the region is not tilted, this measurement is equal to the *width of the projected Region*.) If this measurement falls within the limits defined by <minLodPixels> and <maxLodPixels> (and if the <LatLonAltBox> is in view), the region is active. If this limit is not reached, the region is not active, and the associated geometry is not drawn.

You must specify a value for <minLodPixels>. The <maxLodPixels> element has a default value of −1, which indicates active to infinite size.

Open the *ScreenRulers.kml* example in an Earth browser and examine the crosshairs shown in this file. The crosshairs are screen overlays presented with radio buttons that allow you to select a size of 64, 128, 256, or 512 pixels for the *x* and *y* rulers. These rulers will help you visualize the different projection sizes in relation to your screen and will aid you in setting the values for <minLodPixels> and <maxLodPixels>. The *WineRegions.kml* example later in this chapter is a good example of setting values for these elements.

```xml
<?xml version="1.0" encoding="UTF-8"?>
<kml xmlns="http://www.opengis.net/kml/2.1">
<!--
    Radio-folders of screen overlays measuring a certain number of
    screen pixels in vertical and horizontal dimensions. (Note how
    icon-less overlays draw polygons.)
-->
<Document>
  <name>Rulers</name>
  <open>1</open>
  <Style id="rf">
    <ListStyle>
      <listItemType>radioFolder</listItemType>
    </ListStyle>
  </Style>
  <Folder>
    <name>Horizontal</name>
    <open>1</open>
    <styleUrl>#rf</styleUrl>
    <Placemark>
      <name>off</name>
    </Placemark>
    <ScreenOverlay>
      <name>64 px</name>
      <color>aaaaffaa</color>
      <Icon>
        <href/>
      </Icon>
      <overlayXY x="0.5" y="0.5" xunits="fraction" yunits="fraction"/>
      <screenXY x="0.5" y="0.5" xunits="fraction" yunits="fraction"/>
      <rotationXY x="0" y="0" xunits="fraction" yunits="fraction"/>
      <size x="64" y="8" xunits="pixels" yunits="pixels"/>
    </ScreenOverlay>
    <ScreenOverlay>
      <name>128 px</name>
      <color>aaaaffaa</color>
      <Icon>
        <href/>
      </Icon>
      <overlayXY x="0.5" y="0.5" xunits="fraction" yunits="fraction"/>
      <screenXY x="0.5" y="0.5" xunits="fraction" yunits="fraction"/>
      <rotationXY x="0" y="0" xunits="fraction" yunits="fraction"/>
      <size x="128" y="8" xunits="pixels" yunits="pixels"/>
```

```
      </ScreenOverlay>
      <ScreenOverlay>
        <name>256 px</name>
        <color>aaaaffaa</color>
        <Icon>
          <href/>
        </Icon>
        <overlayXY x="0.5" y="0.5" xunits="fraction" yunits="fraction"/>
        <screenXY x="0.5" y="0.5" xunits="fraction" yunits="fraction"/>
        <rotationXY x="0" y="0" xunits="fraction" yunits="fraction"/>
        <size x="256" y="8" xunits="pixels" yunits="pixels"/>
      </ScreenOverlay>
      <ScreenOverlay>
        <name>512 px</name>
        <color>aaaaffaa</color>
        <Icon>
          <href/>
        </Icon>
        <overlayXY x="0.5" y="0.5" xunits="fraction" yunits="fraction"/>
        <screenXY x="0.5" y="0.5" xunits="fraction" yunits="fraction"/>
        <rotationXY x="0" y="0" xunits="fraction" yunits="fraction"/>
        <size x="512" y="8" xunits="pixels" yunits="pixels"/>
      </ScreenOverlay>
    </Folder>
    <Folder>
      <name>Vertical</name>
      <open>1</open>
      <styleUrl>#rf</styleUrl>
      <Placemark>
        <name>off</name>
      </Placemark>
      <ScreenOverlay>
        <name>64 px</name>
        <color>aaaaffaa</color>
        <Icon>
          <href/>
        </Icon>
        <overlayXY x="0.5" y="0.5" xunits="fraction" yunits="fraction"/>
        <screenXY x="0.5" y="0.5" xunits="fraction" yunits="fraction"/>
        <rotationXY x="0" y="0" xunits="fraction" yunits="fraction"/>
        <size x="8" y="64" xunits="pixels" yunits="pixels"/>
      </ScreenOverlay>
      <ScreenOverlay>
        <name>128 px</name>
        <color>aaaaffaa</color>
```

```
      <Icon>
        <href/>
      </Icon>
      <overlayXY x="0.5" y="0.5" xunits="fraction" yunits="fraction"/>
      <screenXY x="0.5" y="0.5" xunits="fraction" yunits="fraction"/>
      <rotationXY x="0" y="0" xunits="fraction" yunits="fraction"/>
      <size x="8" y="128" xunits="pixels" yunits="pixels"/>
    </ScreenOverlay>
    <ScreenOverlay>
      <name>256 px</name>
      <color>aaaaffaa</color>
      <Icon>
        <href/>
      </Icon>
      <overlayXY x="0.5" y="0.5" xunits="fraction" yunits="fraction"/>
      <screenXY x="0.5" y="0.5" xunits="fraction" yunits="fraction"/>
      <rotationXY x="0" y="0" xunits="fraction" yunits="fraction"/>
      <size x="8" y="256" xunits="pixels" yunits="pixels"/>
    </ScreenOverlay>
    <ScreenOverlay>
      <name>512 px</name>
      <color>aaaaffaa</color>
      <Icon>
        <href/>
      </Icon>
      <overlayXY x="0.5" y="0.5" xunits="fraction" yunits="fraction"/>
      <screenXY x="0.5" y="0.5" xunits="fraction" yunits="fraction"/>
      <rotationXY x="0" y="0" xunits="fraction" yunits="fraction"/>
      <size x="8" y="512" xunits="pixels" yunits="pixels"/>
    </ScreenOverlay>
  </Folder>
</Document>
</kml>
```

Fade Range

The <Lod> element also specifies the number of pixels to be used for fading from transparent to opaque and fading from opaque to transparent. The <minFadeExtent> is the distance over which the geometry fades between fully opaque and fully transparent. This ramp value, expressed in screen pixels, is applied at the minimum end of the LOD (visibility) limits.

Similarly, the <maxFadeExtent> is the distance over which the geometry fades between fully opaque and fully transparent at the maximum end of the LOD (visibility) limits. See the following section, Detailed Description of the <Lod> Element, for details on how this ramp value is calculated.

Detailed Description of the <Lod> Element

Figure 8-4 shows a visual representation of the <Lod> child elements.

The following pseudo-code explains how the Earth browser uses the <Lod> elements to calculate the visibility and fade ranges for a Region's objects:

```
if (P < minLodPixels)
   opacity=0                                      //#1 in Figure 8-4
else if(P < minLodPixels + minFadeExtent)
   opacity=(P - minLodPixels)/minFadeExtent   //#2 in Figure 8-4
else if (P < maxLodPixels - maxFadeExtent)
   opacity=1                                      //#3 in Figure 8-4
else if (P < maxLodPixels)
   opacity=(maxLodPixels-P)/maxFadeExtent    //#4 in Figure 8-4
else
   opacity=0                                      //#5 in Figure 8-4
```

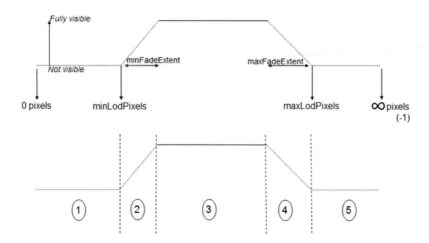

Figure 8-4 The Level of Detail (LOD) range defines minimum and maximum bounds for the size of the Region when projected onto the screen. If the projected Region is outside this Range, its affected Features are not visible.

How Regions Relate to View Refresh Mode

The <Link> and <Icon> elements include a <viewRefreshMode> element that can have a value of onRegion. The value of onRegion indicates to refresh the file or network link whenever the associated Region becomes active. This is a very efficient mechanism because the KML file is fetched only when the Region is in view and meets the visibility range specifications. This view-based refresh of onRegion also underlies the functioning of a super-overlay, described later in this chapter.

Cascading Regions

In a hierarchy of Features, multiple Features can specify Regions. In a Container or NetworkLink hierarchy, Regions defined within a parent element apply also to all child elements unless the child defines its own Region locally. The *WineRegions.kml* example later in this chapter provides an example of setting Region values both locally and within a parent Container element.

In KML, Regions, Time elements, and the <atom> elements (Chapter 3) all have this cascading effect. For example, a TimeSpan element specified in a <Document> applies to all Features lower in the file hierarchy unless overridden by a local TimeSpan defined locally inside another Feature later in the file. Features within a file fetched by a network link are similarly controlled by the values for Regions, Time elements, and the <atom> elements when specified in their parent fetching file. (Note that this behavior is different from shared styles, which do not cascade through the hierarchy. Each Feature must explicitly reference the shared style in a <styleUrl> element.)

Super-Overlays

A super-overlay is a collection of ground overlays that are fetched by Region-based NetworkLinks. A Region-based NetworkLink is simply a NetworkLink that contains a <viewRefreshMode> of onRegion in its <Link> element. These overlays are arranged in a special type of hierarchy that facilitates efficient processing by an Earth browser. As mentioned earlier, this chapter contains all the details about constructing this hierarchy. You will probably use a software utility, such as the Regionator utility, to construct the image tile hierarchy.

Regions

This section provides simple examples of using Regions to affect how your data is shown in an Earth browser.

Syntax for <Region>

The syntax for <Region> is as follows:

```
<Region id="ID">
  <LatLonAltBox id="ID">
    <north>180.0</north>
    <south>-180.0</south>
    <east>180.0</east>
    <west>-180.0</west>
    <minAltitude>0.0</minAltitude>
    <maxAltitude>0.0</maxAltitude>
    <altitudeMode>clampToGround</altitudeMode>
  </LatLonAltBox>
  <Lod id="ID">
    <minLodPixels>0.0</minLodPixels>
    <maxLodPixels>-1.0</maxLodPixels>
    <minFadeExtent>0.0</minFadeExtent>
    <maxFadeExtent>0.0</maxFadeExtent>
  </Lod>
</Region>
```

<LatLonAltBox>

Specifies a bounding box that describes an area of interest defined by geographic coordinates and altitudes.

<north>

Specifies the latitude of the north edge of the bounding box, in decimal degrees from to +/−90.

<south>

Specifies the latitude of the south edge of the bounding box, in decimal degrees from to +/−90.

<east>

Specifies the longitude of the east edge of the bounding box, in decimal degrees from to +/−180.

<west>
   Specifies the longitude of the west edge of the bounding box, in decimal degrees from to +/−180.

<minAltitude>
   Minimum altitude of the Region bounding box, specified in meters (and interpreted according to the <altitudeMode> specification).

<maxAltitude>
   Maximum altitude of the Region bounding box, specified in meters (and interpreted according to the <altitudeMode> specification).

<altitudeMode>
   Can be either `clampToGround` (ignores the altitude specifications), `relativeToGround` (adds the altitude specification to the current ground elevation), or `absolute` (relative to sea level).

<Lod>
<minLodPixels>
   Measurement in screen pixels that represents the minimum limit of the visibility range for a given Region. Google Earth calculates the size of the Region when projected onto screen space. Then it computes the square root of the Region's area. If this measurement falls within the limits defined by <minLodPixels> and <maxLodPixels> (and if the <LatLonAltBox> is in view), the Region is "active." If this limit is not reached, the associated geometry is considered too far from the user's viewpoint to be drawn.

<maxLodPixels>
   Measurement in screen pixels that represents the maximum limit of the visibility range for a given Region. A value of −1, the default, indicates "active to infinite size."

<minFadeExtent>
   Distance over which the geometry fades between fully opaque and fully transparent. This ramp value, expressed in screen pixels, is applied at the minimum end of the LOD (visibility) limits.

<maxFadeExtent>
   Distance over which the geometry fades between fully transparent and fully opaque. This ramp value, expressed in screen pixels, is applied at the maximum end of the LOD (visibility) limits.

Example of GroundOverlay with Region

The *HistoricOverlay.kml* example constructs a Region for a 2D overlay at ground level. The black-and-white image used for the ground overlay contains historical data showing a portion of Mountain View, California, in 1991. As the user zooms in on the area, the overlay becomes visible. Figure 8-5 shows what the overlay looks like when it is first visible. The example file also includes a white LineString to make the overlay stand out better.

In this example, <minLodPixels> is 128, which means that the GroundOverlay comes into view when it occupies 128 square pixels on the screen. (The example uses the default value of −1 for <maxLodPixels>, which means that it will remain visible as the user zooms in at this angle.) The image used for this overlay is 256 square pixels.

HistoricOverlay.kmz

```
<?xml version="1.0" encoding="UTF-8"?>
<kml xmlns="http://www.opengis.net/kml/2.2">
  <Document>
    <name>Flat Region</name>
    <open>1</open>
    <Region>
      <LatLonAltBox>
        <north>37.430419921875</north>
        <south>37.41943359375</south>
        <east>-122.080078125</east>
        <west>-122.091064453125</west>
        <minAltitude>0</minAltitude>
        <maxAltitude>0</maxAltitude>
      </LatLonAltBox>
      <Lod>
        <minLodPixels>128</minLodPixels>
        <maxLodPixels>-1</maxLodPixels>
      </Lod>
    </Region>
    <GroundOverlay>
      <name>Mountain View DOQQ</name>
      <Icon>
        <href>historicOverlay.kmz/files/image.JPEG</href>
      </Icon>
      <LatLonBox>
        <north>37.430419921875</north>
        <south>37.41943359375</south>
        <east>-122.080078125</east>
        <west>-122.091064453125</west>
```

```
      </LatLonBox>
    </GroundOverlay>
    <Placemark>
      <name>overlay border</name>
      <LineString>
        <tessellate>1</tessellate>
        <coordinates>
          -122.091064,37.43042,0
          -122.080078,37.43042,0
          -122.080078,37.419434,0
          -122.091064,37.419434,0
          -122.091064,37.43042,0
        </coordinates>
      </LineString>
    </Placemark>
  </Document>
</kml>
```

Figure 8-5 The black-and-white ground overlay is not visible until its area on the screen is equal to <minLodPixels>. This image shows the ground overlay coming into view at its minimum size (128 pixels).

The <LatLonAltBox> for this data does not need to include the <minAltitude> and <maxAltitude> elements because the data is flat and is at ground level. The bounding box for the data in the Region's <LatLonAltBox> is identical to the boundaries of the ground overlay's <LatLonBox>.

Also, within the KML file, notice that the Region is a sibling of the image (or geometry) whose visibility it affects.

Try loading this file into an Earth browser and experiment with different viewpoints. Watch when the Region comes into view and out of view, depending on how much of the screen area it requires. Note that if you tilt the view far enough or if you zoom out quite a bit, the overlay disappears because it takes up too little screen space to meet the <minLodPixels> requirement.

Region for a 3D Model

The *UnitedNationsModel.kml* example shows how to construct a Region that contains 3D objects at ground level. The <LatLonAltBox> for this Region contains a <maxAltitude> of 300 meters since that is the height of the building. You'll probably recognize these buildings as the United Nations complex in New York City (see Figure 8-6).

It's important to notice that the boundaries of the Region's <LatLonAltBox> do not necessarily match up exactly with the longitude and latitude boundaries of the Model. The coordinates for the Model are relative to its own local origin, which may be offset from the actual position of the Model on the Earth.

UnitedNationsModel.kmz

```
<?xml version='1.0' encoding='UTF-8'?>
<kml xmlns="http://www.opengis.net/kml/2.2">
  <Document>
    <name>3D Region on Ground</name>
    <Placemark>
      <name>United Nations Headquarters</name>
      <visibility>0</visibility>
      <Region>
        <Lod>
          <minLodPixels>128</minLodPixels>
        </Lod>
        <LatLonAltBox>
          <north>40.750683130314</north>
          <south>40.748162385230</south>
          <east>-73.966608428427</east>
          <west>-73.969476624071</west>
```

```
              <minAltitude>0</minAltitude>
              <maxAltitude>300</maxAltitude>
              <altitudeMode>absolute</altitudeMode>
            </LatLonAltBox>
        </Region>
        <Model>
            <altitudeMode>absolute</altitudeMode>
            <Location>
              <longitude>-73.967763927199</longitude>
              <latitude>40.749458312255</latitude>
              <altitude>0.406173708576</altitude>
            </Location>
            <Link>
              <href>models/un.dae</href>
            </Link>
        </Model>
      </Placemark>
    </Document>
</kml>
```

Figure 8-6 Regions are an efficient mechanism for displaying complex models. The objects are displayed only when the Region is active.

Region for a 2D Overlay at Altitude

The *CloudRegionAtAltitude.kml* example shows how you would display a 2D overlay above the Earth's surface at a specified altitude. This technique is useful for data showing weather fronts and air traffic patterns. Here, the example shows a small cloud cover at an altitude of 100,000 meters above sea level.

CloudRegionAltitude.kmz

```xml
<?xml version="1.0" encoding="UTF-8"?>
<kml xmlns="http://www.opengis.net/kml/2.2">
  <Document>
    <name>Flat Region at Altitude</name>
    <GroundOverlay>
      <name>Cloud overlay</name>
      <Region>
        <LatLonAltBox>
          <north>33.75</north>
          <south>22.5</south>
          <east>-45</east>
          <west>-56.25</west>
          <minAltitude>100000</minAltitude>
          <maxAltitude>100000</maxAltitude>
          <altitudeMode>absolute</altitudeMode>
        </LatLonAltBox>
        <Lod>
          <minLodPixels>128</minLodPixels>
        </Lod>
      </Region>
      <Icon>
        <href>files/image.PNG</href>
      </Icon>
      <altitude>100000</altitude>
      <altitudeMode>absolute</altitudeMode>
      <LatLonBox>
        <north>33.75</north>
        <south>22.5</south>
        <east>-45</east>
        <west>-56.25</west>
      </LatLonBox>
    </GroundOverlay>
  </Document>
</kml>
```

The Region's <LatLonAltBox> specifies a value of 100,000 meters for both the <minAltitude> and <maxAltitude> elements. (The value is the same for both elements, since the Overlay is 2D and has no thickness.) The <altitudeMode> is `absolute`, which means that this value is relative to sea level.

Notice that the <altitude> value of the GroundOverlay is also 100,000 (that is, it matches the altitude value of the Region's bounding box), and the <altitudeMode> of the GroundOverlay matches the value specified for the Region's <altitudeMode>.

Case Study: Simplifying a Data Set

This example uses a small set of Placemarks taken from an extensive data set on "Wine Regions of the World," compiled by Antonio Rocha Graca into a comprehensive KML file (http://bbs.keyhole.com/ubb/showthreaded.php?Number=303649). The original file defines 10 general geographic wine districts and 187 Placemarks for officially designated appellations. For purposes of example, this case study uses only 39 Placemarks and three general geographic wine districts.

KML Regions allow you to gradually reveal more information based on what is in the current view. Without Regions, all the data is in view all the time. This example shows you how to subdivide your data into *layers* that correspond to different types of information appropriate to different views. Here is how the *WineRegions.kmz* example behaves:

1. When the user first pans to France, from very far away, no Placemarks are visible.

2. As the view moves closer, Placemarks for five major appellations come into view.

3. As the view moves even closer, the pink labels for three Regions appear.

4. Finally, at the closest range, the Placemarks within each Region appear.

Figure 8-7 shows a partially zoomed-in view of this area of France, with one label still visible and a number of wine appellations displayed (the most detailed level).

Step 1: Creating a Few Major Placemarks

The first part of this example defines a KML Region that encompasses the country of France. This Region affects the display of the five Placemarks that are included in its folder. These Placemarks come into view when the Region takes up 256 pixels on the screen (on a 1024 x 768-pixel screen, this would be about one-fourth of the screen). Here is the code for this Region, which has the largest LatLonAltBox of the Regions used in this example:

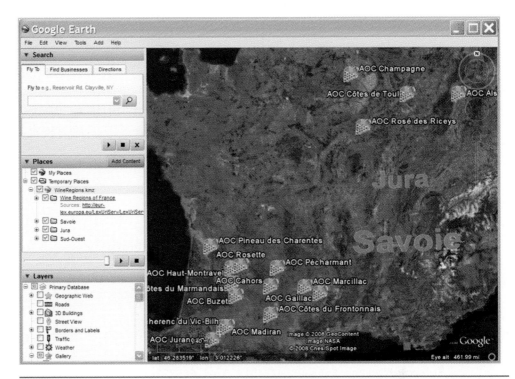

Figure 8-7 As the view zooms in on different areas of France, first the regional label and then the Placemarks for the official wine appellations come into view. KML Regions are a useful way to present data selectively based on its relationship to the current view. (Example is an excerpt from a complete study by Antonio Rocha Graca: http://bbs.keyhole.com/ubb/ showthreaded.php?Number=303649.)

WineRegions.kmz

```
      .
      .
      .

<Folder>
  <Region>
    <LatLonAltBox>
      <north>49.69366283018918</north>
      <south>42.8733871401169</south>
      <east>7.925664021372573</east>
      <west>-1.901208894918117</west>
    </LatLonAltBox>
    <Lod>
      <minLodPixels>256</minLodPixels>
```

```
      <maxLodPixels>-1</maxLodPixels>
    </Lod>
  </Region>
  <Placemark>
    <name>AOC Alsace</name>
    <styleUrl>#grapes</styleUrl>
    <Point>
      <coordinates>7.65924575839081,48.66041665081331,0</coordinates>
    </Point>
  </Placemark>
  <Placemark>
    <name>AOC Champagne</name>
    <styleUrl>#grapes</styleUrl>
    <Point>
      <coordinates>4.003005551108324,49.15478304226884,0
      </coordinates>
    </Point>
  </Placemark>
  <Placemark>
    <name>AOC Côtes de Toul</name>
    <styleUrl>#grapes</styleUrl>
    <Point>
      <coordinates>5.881205628481412,48.68672206064913,0
      </coordinates>
    </Point>
  </Placemark>
  <Placemark>
    <name>AOC Pineau des Charentes</name>
    <styleUrl>#grapes</styleUrl>
    <Point>
      <coordinates>-0.5221844434881291,45.32287528374275,0
      </coordinates>
    </Point>
  </Placemark>
  <Placemark>
    <name>AOC Rosé des Riceys</name>
    <styleUrl>#grapes</styleUrl>
    <Point>
      <coordinates>4.370713480581088,47.98064677028222,0
      </coordinates>
     </Point>
  </Placemark>
</Folder>
```

Step 2: Dividing Placemarks into a Set of Regions

Our example uses Placemarks from three geographic areas in France: Jura, Sud-Ouest, and Savoie. To use Regions, place each set of Placemarks in a Folder with the name of the geographic area. Then define a Region that bounds the Placemarks geographically and specifies a minimum pixel area (256 pixels) required to view them, as shown in this code excerpt:

```
     .
     .
     .
<Folder>
   <name>Savoie</name>
   <Region>
     <LatLonAltBox>
        <north>46.96365480582551</north>
        <south>44.65021261041166</south>
        <east>7.786675059794294</east>
        <west>4.240731679647905</west>
     </LatLonAltBox>
     <Lod>
        <minLodPixels>256</minLodPixels>
        <maxLodPixels>-1</maxLodPixels>
     </Lod>
   </Region>
   <Placemark>
     <name>AOC Bugey</name>
     <styleUrl>#grapes</styleUrl>
     <Point>
        <coordinates>5.709459459670144,45.76446876257237,0
        </coordinates>
     </Point>
   </Placemark>
```

```
<Placemark>
  <name>AOC Crépy</name>
  <styleUrl>#grapes</styleUrl>
  <Point>
    <coordinates>6.319411169117089,46.29540977670803,0
    </coordinates>
  </Point>
</Placemark>
<Placemark>
  <name>AOC Roussette du Bugey</name>
  <styleUrl>#grapes</styleUrl>
  <Point>
    <coordinates>5.277542722916067,46.16285192426042,0
    </coordinates>
  </Point>
</Placemark>
   .
   .
   .
```

All Placemarks in this Folder are affected by the Region defined in the same Folder.

Step 3: Adding Another Layer: Labels for the Regions

To help the user categorize the data and to reduce the number of Placemarks on the screen at any one time, you can create extra layers that filter the data in some way. In this example, when the view is farther away (and therefore the Region takes up less screen space), a Ground Overlay containing pink labels appears for each geographic area instead of the actual Placemarks. The labels for Jura, Sud-Ouest, and Savoie are *.png* images with pink letters and a transparent background. The <LatLonAltBox> for each GroundOverlay label matches the <LatLonAltBox> for the Placemarks' Region, but the GroundOverlay's LOD range is different, since the label pops in and out of view before the actual Placemarks. Specifically, the LOD range for Savoie is specified as 125 pixels for the minimum range and 256 for its maximum range. When the GroundOverlay label reaches its maximum size (256), it is no longer active and is replaced by the Placemarks, which have a minimum LOD of 256 pixels.

```
   .
   .
   .

<GroundOverlay>
  <Region>
    <LatLonAltBox>
      <north>46.96365480582551</north>
```

```
      <south>44.65021261041166</south>
      <east>7.786675059794294</east>
      <west>4.240731679647905</west>
    </LatLonAltBox>
    <Lod>
      <minLodPixels>125</minLodPixels>
      <maxLodPixels>256</maxLodPixels>
    </Lod>
    </Region>
  <Icon>
    <href>labelImages/savoie.png</href>
  </Icon>
  <LatLonBox>
    <north>45.95148218410907</north>
    <south>44.90439800077383</south>
    <east>7.799963830912753</east>
    <west>3.589059539181228</west>
  </LatLonBox>
</GroundOverlay>
    .
    .
    .
```

When working with GroundOverlays and Regions, be sure to take the native resolution of your image into consideration. If you specify a value for <maxLodPixels> that is greater than the resolution of the image, the image will be stretched. In some cases, this may not be the effect you desire, because the resulting image may be jagged or blurred.

Step 4: Adding a Fade Effect to the Labels

The following code causes the labels to fade in and out gradually. Edit the *doc.kml* file in the *WineRegions.kmz* archive (change the suffix to *.zip*, and then unzip it) to remove the comments around these lines and see the effect of these <Lod> child elements:

```
<minFadeExtent>200</minFadeExtent>
<maxFadeExtent>200</maxFadeExtent>
```

Super-Overlays

This section describes how to create a super-overlay—a hierarchy of regions and network links that can be used to efficiently serve a large set of imagery. Super-overlays allow you to take advantage of network links and their ability to determine (1) whether a given region is within view and (2) whether its projected size is appropriate to the view area. If both conditions are met, the region is "active," and the network link loads the data associated with the region. If the region is inactive, no data is loaded.

Simple Example of a Region-Based NetworkLink

Here is a simple example that shows a single region-based network link to illustrate a few basic principles of this technique. The <viewRefreshMode> in the parent (fetching) file, *UkraineRegion.kml*, has a value of onRegion, which specifies to load the network link data only when its region is active. The larger region (Ukraine) has a <LatLonAltBox> defined for it. When the Ukraine Region becomes active, a linestring that matches the boundaries of the region's <LatLonAltBox> is displayed. The smaller region (*RomaniaRegion.kml*) is fetched only when its sibling region in the "Romania NetworkLink" becomes active. When its region is active, *RomaniaRegion.kml* displays a linestring that matches its (smaller) <LatLonAltBox>.

Notice that the *RomaniaRegion.kml* file also defines a region for the Romania linestring. In our example, this region could be omitted because it matches the region of its parent file (*UkraineRegion.kml*). The region could, however, be replaced by a local region that would override the region of the parent file. Also, if the *RomaniaRegion.kml* file is loaded independently, it's useful to have the region defined locally.

UkraineRegion.kml

```
<?xml version="1.0" encoding="UTF-8"?>
<kml xmlns="http://www.opengis.net/kml/2.2">
<Document>
  <name>Nested Regions</name>
  <Region>
    <LatLonAltBox>
      <north>56.25</north>
      <south>45</south>
      <east>33.75</east>
      <west>22.5</west>
    </LatLonAltBox>
    <Lod>
      <minLodPixels>128</minLodPixels>
      <maxLodPixels>1024</maxLodPixels>
    </Lod>
  </Region>
  <Placemark>
    <name>ukraineRegion</name>
```

```
    <LineString>
      <tessellate>1</tessellate>
      <coordinates>
        22.5,45,0
        33.75,45,0
        33.75,56.25,0
        22.5,56.25,0
        22.5,45,0
      </coordinates>
    </LineString>
  </Placemark>
  <NetworkLink>
    <name>Romania NetworkLink</name>
    <Region>
      <LatLonAltBox>
        <north>50.625</north>
        <south>45</south>
        <east>28.125</east>
        <west>22.5</west>
      </LatLonAltBox>
      <Lod>
        <minLodPixels>128</minLodPixels>
        <maxLodPixels>1024</maxLodPixels>
      </Lod>
    </Region>
    <Link>
      <href>RomaniaRegion.kml</href>
      <viewRefreshMode>onRegion</viewRefreshMode>
    </Link>
  </NetworkLink>
</Document>
</kml>
```

RomaniaRegion.kml

```
<?xml version="1.0" encoding="UTF-8"?>
<kml xmlns="http://www.opengis.net/kml/2.2">
<Document>
  <name>Romania Document</name>
    <Region>
      <LatLonAltBox>
        <north>50.625</north>
        <south>45</south>
        <east>28.125</east>
```

```
      <west>22.5</west>
    </LatLonAltBox>
    <Lod>
      <minLodPixels>128</minLodPixels>
      <maxLodPixels>1024</maxLodPixels>
    </Lod>
  </Region>
<Placemark>
  <name>RomaniaRegion</name>
  <LineString>
    <tessellate>1</tessellate>
    <coordinates>
      22.5,45,0
      28.125,45,0
      28.125,50.625,0
      22.5,50.625,0
      22.5,45,0
    </coordinates>
  </LineString>
</Placemark>
</Document>
</kml>
```

Example of a Super-Overlay

To see how a super-overlay image hierarchy is used, load the *Mountain View Archives* example file into Google Earth. This very large collection of ground overlays shows the city of Mountain View in 1991 (see Figure 8-8). Experiment by zooming in and out of the overlay and watch how details in the imagery change.

 Mountain View Archives Super-Overlay example: Go to http://kml-samples.googlecode.com/svn/ trunk/kml_handbook and then select the file mvdoqq.kml.

Preparing Your Data for a Super-Overlay

In the sample super-overlay, the original Mountain View image, with dimensions of 7008 × 6720 pixels, is subdivided into hundreds of small ground overlays. These overlays, or *tiles*, are arranged in a five-level hierarchy. For purposes of example, the discussion here uses a simple three-level hierarchy and a set of 21 overlays, but the principles involved are the same. Note that this is just one approach to creating a hierarchy of region-based network links and that there are other ways to implement this mechanism.

Figure 8-8 Example of using region-based network links to efficiently load a very large data set. This file presents historical imagery for the city of Mountain View (a 1991 DOQQ). The oblique view shown here loads only five small tiles to represent this image. (White linestrings have been added to highlight the tile boundaries.)

To create a super-overlay, you need to do the following:

1. Prepare the imagery by subdividing it into manageable chunks (a tile size of 256 × 256 pixels is recommended).
2. Create the KML files that set up the regions, links, network links, and, in this case, the files containing the ground overlays.

> **Note**
>
> This section provides the details about how to set up a region-based network link hierarchy. If you are interested in creating super-overlays, be sure to check out the software tools that create such hierarchies programmatically. For example, see the Regionator and related tools at http://code.google.com/p/regionator/.

Step 1: Prepare the Imagery

Pick a standard size for your tiles, which are the subdivided images (of varying resolutions) that Google Earth will load as their associated regions become active. For purposes of example, we'll use 256 × 256 pixels for our tiles, which is small enough to be manageable.

1. Start with the original, full-resolution image. Subdivide it into four tiles, and then subdivide each of those tiles into four tiles.

2. Continue subdividing until you have tiles of the target size (in our example, 256 × 256 pixels).

   Let's assume our original image is 1024 × 1024 pixels. Figure 8-9 shows the hierarchy that results when it is subdivided. (If your image size is not a multiple of 2, use tile sizes that are a multiple of 2 in all but the last row and column.)

3. Next, resample each tile in the hierarchy to the standard size you've chosen (for example, 256 × 256 pixels).

These resampled tiles will have less detail, but will be associated with regions that are active at smaller screen areas, so the loss in detail will be imperceptible to the user.

Figure 8-10 shows three levels of detail in the hierarchy for this sample piece of imagery. When the user looks at the region from the greatest distance, Google Earth displays the thumbnail view. This view is stretched over its entire <LatLonAltBox> (but since the projected size is small—256 square pixels—there is no actual loss of visual information). As the user zooms in on the scene, the region is divided into four regions.

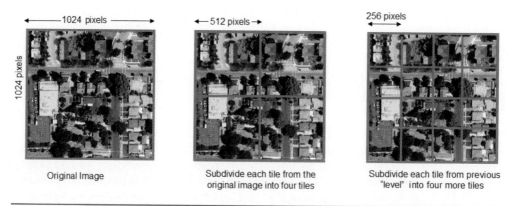

Figure 8-9 To create a super-overlay hierarchy, subdivide the original image into four smaller units until you reach a tile size of 256 × 256 pixels.

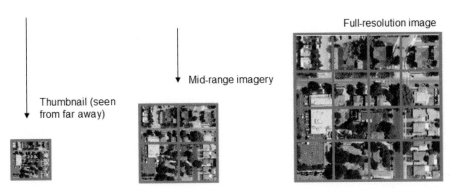

Figure 8-10 After you have divided the original image into levels with tiles of decreasing size, resample all tiles to the standard size you've chosen (for example, 256-by-256 pixels).

Each of these four "tiles" has the same size as the thumbnail image but provides more detailed imagery.

If the user continues to zoom in on the area, portions of the full-resolution imagery come into view, depending on the specified screen pixel range for the region's <LatLonAltBox>. Areas in the distance retain the less detailed imagery that was loaded first because their regions have not become active. In Google Earth, after you've loaded the *Mountain View Archives* example, enable Boxes and check out Placemarks A and B, which use linestrings around the regions to show multiple levels of the hierarchy at one time.

Notice that the sample uses the same values for <minLodPixels> and <maxLodPixels> for all regions (at all levels of the hierarchy). It's the <LatLonAltBox> that determines which level of the hierarchy should be loaded, and which tile(s) within the region.

Step 2: Prepare the KML Files

For each image, prepare a KML file that associates the <GroundOverlay> with a <Region> and a <NetworkLink>. Each KML file in this set has the following elements:

- A <Region> (with <LatLonAltBox>, <minLodPixels>, and <maxLodPixels> so that the Earth browser can determine whether the region is active at any given time)
- A set of network links to the child files (the tiles in the next level of the hierarchy)
- The <GroundOverlay> for this <Region>

This sample shows the top-level KML file for the Mountain View DOQQ example. For <maxLodPixels>, it specifies −1, which has the special meaning "active to infinite size." Without this specification, the entire hierarchy might never be triggered (for example, if you were flying along close to the Earth's surface and never crossed the region's <minLodPixels> limit).

```
<?xml version="1.0" encoding="UTF-8"?>
<kml xmlns="http://www.opengis.net/kml/2.2">
  <NetworkLink>
    <name>SuperOverlay: MV DOQQ</name>
    <Region>
      <LatLonAltBox>
        <north>37.44140625</north>
        <south>37.265625</south>
        <east>-121.9921875</east>
        <west>-122.16796875</west>
      </LatLonAltBox>
      <Lod>
        <minLodPixels>128</minLodPixels>
        <maxLodPixels>-1</maxLodPixels>
      </Lod>
    </Region>
    <Link>
      <href>http://mw1.google.com/mw-earth-vectordb/kml-samples/
        mv-070501/1.kml</href>
      <viewRefreshMode>onRegion</viewRefreshMode>
    </Link>
  </NetworkLink>
</kml>
```

The following file shows a region in the *Mountain View Archives* example (*179.kml*). This file contains five <href> tags: Four refer to the four KML files in the next level of the image hierarchy, and one refers to the image file used for the <GroundOverlay> for this tile.

```
<?xml version="1.0" encoding="UTF-8"?>
<kml xmlns="http://www.opengis.net/kml/2.2">
  <Document>
    <Region>
      <Lod>
        <minLodPixels>128</minLodPixels><maxLodPixels>-1</maxLodPixels>
      </Lod>
      <LatLonAltBox>
        <north>37.430419921875</north><south>37.41943359375</south>
        <east>-122.091064453125</east><west>-122.10205078125</west>
      </LatLonAltBox>
```

```
    </Region>
<NetworkLink>
  <name>001120</name>
  <Region>
    <Lod>
      <minLodPixels>128</minLodPixels><maxLodPixels>-1</maxLodPixels>
    </Lod>
    <LatLonAltBox>
      <north>37.430419921875</north><south>37.4249267578125</south>
      <east>-122.0965576171875</east><west>-122.10205078125</west>
    </LatLonAltBox>
  </Region>
  <Link>
    <href>180.kml</href>
    <viewRefreshMode>onRegion</viewRefreshMode>
  </Link>
</NetworkLink>
<NetworkLink>
  <name>001121</name>
  <Region>
    <Lod>
      <minLodPixels>128</minLodPixels><maxLodPixels>-1</maxLodPixels>
    </Lod>
    <LatLonAltBox>
      <north>37.430419921875</north><south>37.4249267578125</south>
      <east>-122.091064453125</east><west>-122.0965576171875</west>
    </LatLonAltBox>
  </Region>
  <Link>
    <href>185.kml</href>
    <viewRefreshMode>onRegion</viewRefreshMode>
  </Link>
</NetworkLink>
<NetworkLink>
  <name>001122</name>
  <Region>
    <Lod>
      <minLodPixels>128</minLodPixels><maxLodPixels>-1</maxLodPixels>
    </Lod>
    <LatLonAltBox>
      <north>37.4249267578125</north><south>37.41943359375</south>
      <east>-122.0965576171875</east><west>-122.10205078125</west>
    </LatLonAltBox>
  </Region>
```

```
  <Link>
    <href>190.kml</href>
    <viewRefreshMode>onRegion</viewRefreshMode>
  </Link>
</NetworkLink>
<NetworkLink>
  <name>001123</name>
  <Region>
    <Lod>
      <minLodPixels>128</minLodPixels><maxLodPixels>-1</maxLodPixels>
    </Lod>
    <LatLonAltBox>
      <north>37.4249267578125</north><south>37.41943359375</south>
      <east>-122.091064453125</east><west>-122.0965576171875</west>
    </LatLonAltBox>
  </Region>
  <Link>
    <href>195.kml</href>
    <viewRefreshMode>onRegion</viewRefreshMode>
  </Link>
</NetworkLink>
<GroundOverlay>
  <drawOrder>5</drawOrder>
  <Icon>
    <href>179.JPEG</href>
  </Icon>
  <LatLonBox>
    <north>37.430419921875</north><south>37.41943359375</south>
    <east>-122.091064453125</east><west>-122.10205078125</west>
  </LatLonBox>
</GroundOverlay>
  </Document>
</kml>
```

Swiss Transit Example

Region-based network links are also a useful technique for the efficient display of large sets of placemarks. Figure 8-1 presented the problem—Figure 8-11 offers the solution. Bent Hagemark created the Swiss Transit example, which loads information on train stations and connections between them, greatly simplifying the amount of data fetched and displayed to the user at any given time by using KML Regions. Take a look at this example, which also illustrates the use of the <MultiGeometry> and <StyleMap> elements.

Figure 8-11 Using region-based network links, this KMZ file showing the Swiss Transit system displays detailed information only when the stations are close to the user's view. Stations of lesser importance pop out of sight as the viewpoint moves away from them. (Example by Bent Hagemark, http://kml-samples.googlecode.com/svn/trunk/kml_handbook/ch-sbb.kml.)

Swiss Transit example of a Region-based NetworkLink hierarchy: Go to http://kml-samples.googlecode.com/svn/trunk/kml_handbook and then select the file ch-sbb.kml.

Extended Data

KML offers three ways to add custom data to a KML Feature. Which approach you choose depends on the kind of data you're adding as well as how you plan to use the data in your KML presentation. Specifically, the <ExtendedData> element provides the following mechanisms:

- **Arbitrary XML data** (basic) allows you to *preserve user data* within a KML file. Google Earth passes this data along with the file and saves it, but does not use it.

- **<Data> element** (basic) allows you to add *untyped name/value pairs* to the user data associated with a given Feature (<NetworkLink>, <Placemark>, <GroundOverlay>, <PhotoOverlay>, <ScreenOverlay>, <Document>, or <Folder>). These name/value pairs are displayed in the balloon by default. This information can also be used for entity replacement in the <text> element of <BalloonStyle>. See the section Using the <BalloonStyle> Element as a Template later in this chapter.

- **<Schema> and <SchemaData> elements** (advanced) allow you to add *typed data* to the user data associated with a given Feature.

> **Note**
>
> These three mechanisms can be combined in the same file. If you're adding different types of data from different sources, it may be appropriate to use the typed data approach (Schema/SchemaData) for some of the custom data and to use untyped data (Data) for other custom data.

Which Approach Should You Use?

If you simply need to pass data along with a KML file and do not need the Earth browser to process the data, use the arbitrary XML data feature, which allows you to reference an XML namespace prefix and pass along the data in the current KML context. For more information, see the next section, Adding Arbitrary XML Data to a Feature.

In most cases the <Data> element offers the simplest and most powerful mechanism for adding untyped data to a KML Feature. This method is relatively easy to implement, and it offers the advantage of facilitating the use of a <BalloonStyle> template, which can be applied to all placemarks in a KML file. See Entity Replacement for Extended Data Elements later in this chapter for an example of this use.

The <Schema> and <SchemaData> elements allow you to add *typed user data*. These elements are offered primarily for users with GIS (Geographic Information System) data. If you have typed data that is used by an external computer application, you will probably need to use the <Schema> and <SchemaData> elements to add structured data types to a Feature. (Google Earth does not use this typed information, but your other application may require it.) Casual users will probably not need the more technical aspects offered by this mechanism. Like <Data>, <SchemaData> facilitates use of templates for BalloonStyle.

Adding Arbitrary XML Data to a Feature

The simplest way to add user data to a Feature is to add the data directly as a value of <ExtendedData>. Google Earth preserves this data but does not process it.

Custom data elements added in this way need to include a namespace prefix (xmlns:prefix="namespace"), as shown in the *SimpleUserData.kml* example. This prefix can be added to the <kml> element or to the <ExtendedData> element. The external namespace prefix must qualify each instance of user data. In the example shown here, the namespace prefix is defined as "camp."

SimpleUserData.kml

```
<?xml version="1.0" encoding="UTF-8"?>
<kml xmlns="http://www.opengis.net/kml/2.2">
  <Document>
    <name>Adding Arbitrary Data to KML</name>
    <Placemark>
      <name>CampsiteData</name>
      <!-- Imported schema requires use of namespace prefix -->
      <ExtendedData xmlns:camp="http://campsites.com">
        <camp:number>14</camp:number>
        <camp:parkingSpaces>2</camp:parkingSpaces>
        <camp:tentSites>4</camp:tentSites>
      </ExtendedData>
      <Point>
        <coordinates>-114.041,53.7199</coordinates>
      </Point>
    </Placemark>
  </Document>
</kml>
```

Adding Untyped Name/Value Pairs

The <Data> element is a simple yet powerful mechanism for adding untyped name/value pairs to a KML Feature.

Syntax for <Data>

The <Data> element is a child of <ExtendedData>. The syntax for the <Data> element is defined as follows:

```
<ExtendedData>
  <Data name="string">
    <displayName>...</displayName>
    <value>...</value>
  </Data>
    .
    .
    .
</ExtendedData>
```

\<Data name=" ">

> The name attribute is a unique identifier for this piece of data. This name is used
> to identify the name/value pair within the KML file. (The \<displayName> is used
> by the Earth browser for display purposes.)

\<displayName>

> Specifies a user-friendly name for this piece of data, used for display purposes in
> the balloon. This element can contain CDATA that includes spaces, URLs, and
> hyperlinks.

\<value>

> Specifies the value for this data (a string).

The *NameValuePairs.kml* example shows a placemark that contains custom data about
several holes in a golf course. Figure 8-12 shows how the name/value pairs are displayed
in the balloon using default formatting. Since no \<displayName> was specified, the
name attribute is used as the name.

NameValuePairs.kml

```
<?xml version="1.0" encoding="UTF-8"?>
<kml xmlns="http://www.opengis.net/kml/2.2">
  <Document>
    <name>My Golf Course Example</name>
    <Placemark>
      <name>Clubhouse</name>
      <ExtendedData>
        <Data name="holeNumber">
          <value>1</value>
        </Data>
        <Data name="holeYardage">
          <value>234</value>
        </Data>
        <Data name="holePar">
```

```xml
          <value>4</value>
        </Data>
      </ExtendedData>
      <Point>
        <coordinates>-111.956,33.5043</coordinates>
      </Point>
    </Placemark>
    <Placemark>
      <name>By the lake</name>
      <ExtendedData>
        <Data name="holeNumber">
          <value>5</value>
        </Data>
        <Data name="holeYardage">
          <value>523</value>
        </Data>
        <Data name="holePar">
          <value>5</value>
        </Data>
      </ExtendedData>
      <Point>
        <coordinates>-111.95,33.5024</coordinates>
      </Point>
    </Placemark>
  </Document>
</kml>
```

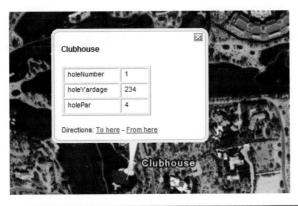

Figure 8-12 By default, the name/value pairs contained in a ‹Data› element are displayed in the balloon in tabular form.

Using the <BalloonStyle> Element as a Template

As you learned in Chapter 4, you can define a <Style> once and assign an `id` to it. After defining the <Style> in this manner, you can reference it multiple times within the KML file (or within other KML files) using the <styleUrl> element. A style defined in this way is referred to as a *shared style*. As you learned in Chapter 2, the <text> element within <BalloonStyle> supports *entity replacement*. Individual values can be substituted for each instance of the entity. Standard entities that can be replaced are as follows:

$[name]
> Replaced with the <name> of the <Placemark>

$[description]
> Replaced with the <description> of the <Placemark>

$[address]
> Replaced with the <address> of the <Placemark>

$[id]
> Replaced with the `id` of the <Placemark>

$[Snippet]
> Replaced with the <snippet> of the <Placemark>

$[geDirections]
> Replaced with the To/From driving directions of the <Placemark>

Entity Replacement for Extended Data Elements

Google Earth also supports entity replacement of certain extended data elements within the <text> element of <BalloonStyle>. The following entities can be referenced within the <text> element:

Variable	Replaced With	Example
$[nameAttributeOfDataElement]	Contents of <value> element	1, 234, 4
$[nameAttribute/displayName]	Contents of <displayName> element	Hole Number, Hole Yardage

The *BalloonStyleTemplate.kml* example creates a <BalloonStyle> template for the previous simple golf course example. For each placemark balloon, Google Earth substitutes the name of the placemark and then writes out information containing the hole number, par, and yardage for each individual hole (see Figure 8-13). Balloon style templates

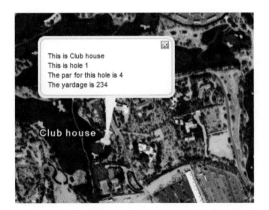

Figure 8-13 Balloon style templates are an efficient way to present custom data for a large set of placemarks. This example uses entity replacement to substitute unique data values for each balloon.

and entity replacement are a very useful and economic way of replicating complex styles for large numbers of placemarks. Be sure to experiment with this technique if you have large amounts of balloon data.

BalloonStyleTemplate.kml

```
<?xml version="1.0" encoding="UTF-8"?>
<kml xmlns="http://www.opengis.net/kml/2.2">
  <Document>
    <name>Data+BalloonStyle</name>
    <Style id="golf-balloon-style">
      <BalloonStyle>
        <text>
          <![CDATA[
          This is $[name]
          This is hole $[holeNumber]
          The par for this hole is $[holePar]
          The yardage is $[holeYardage]
          ]]>
        </text>
      </BalloonStyle>
    </Style>
    <!-- Shared style sample
      Two Placemarks use the same balloon template-->
    <Placemark>
```

```
    <name>Clubhouse</name>
    <styleUrl>#golf-balloon-style</styleUrl>
    <ExtendedData>
      <Data name="holeNumber">
        <value>1</value>
      </Data>
      <Data name="holeYardage">
        <value>234</value>
      </Data>
      <Data name="holePar">
        <value>4</value>
      </Data>
    </ExtendedData>
    <Point>
      <coordinates>-111.956,33.5043</coordinates>
    </Point>
  </Placemark>
  <Placemark>
    <name>By the lake</name>
    <styleUrl>#golf-balloon-style</styleUrl>
    <ExtendedData>
      <Data name="holeNumber">
        <value>5</value>
      </Data>
      <Data name="holeYardage">
        <value>523</value>
      </Data>
      <Data name="holePar">
        <value>5</value>
      </Data>
    </ExtendedData>
    <Point>
      <coordinates>-111.95,33.5024</coordinates>
    </Point>
  </Placemark>
 </Document>
</kml>
```

Adding Typed Data to a Feature

The <Schema> and <SchemaData> elements allow you to add typed data to a Feature.
Certain GIS and programming applications require this feature because they deal with
typed data.

To add a custom type to a KML Feature, you perform two basic tasks:

1. Create the <Schema> element, which declares your new type.
2. Create instances of the new type using the <SchemaData> element.

The <Schema> element is always a child of <Document>. The <ExtendedData> element is a child of the Feature that contains the custom data.

Syntax for <Schema>

A <Schema> element contains one or more <SimpleField> elements. In the <SimpleField>, the <Schema> declares the type and name of the custom field. It optionally specifies a <displayName> (the user-friendly form, with spaces and proper punctuation used for display in an Earth browser) for this custom field.

A <Document> can contain zero or more <Schema> elements. The syntax for the <Schema> element is defined as follows:

```
<Schema name="string" id="ID">
  <SimpleField type="string" name="string">
    <displayName>...</displayName>
  </SimpleField>
</Schema>
```

<Schema name= " " id= " ">
> The name attribute is optional and is used for entity replacement to qualify the namespace. The id attribute is required and must be unique within this KML document. The id attribute is referenced when instances of this type are created (using <SchemaData>).

<SimpleField type= " " name= " ">
> A <SimpleField> must have both a type and a name defined for it; otherwise, it is ignored. The type can be one of the following: bool, double, float, int, uint, short, ushort, or string.
>
> The name attribute is used for entity replacement in the <text> element of <BalloonStyle>.

<displayName>
> Specifies an optional name to be used by the Earth browser when it displays this field. Use the [CDATA] element to escape standard HTML markup.

Syntax for <SchemaData>

The <SchemaData> element is a child of <ExtendedData>. The syntax for the <SchemaData> element is defined as follows:

```
<ExtendedData>
  .
  .
  .
  <SchemaData schemaUrl="anyURI">
    <SimpleData name=""> ... </SimpleData>   <!-- string -->
  </SchemaData>
  <namespace_prefix:other>...</namespace_prefix:other>
</ExtendedData>
```

<SchemaData schemaUrl= " ">

This element is used in conjunction with <Schema> to add typed custom data to a KML Feature. The <Schema> element (identified by the schemaUrl attribute) declares the custom data type. The actual data objects ("instances" of the custom data) are defined using the <SchemaData> element.

The schemaUrl attribute references the id of the <Schema> that declares the type, just as a <styleUrl> references the id of a <Style> that has been previously declared.

The schemaUrl can be a full URL, a reference to a Schema ID defined in an external KML file, or a reference to a Schema ID defined in the same KML file. All of the following specifications are acceptable:

```
schemaUrl="http://host.com/PlacesIHaveLived.kml#my-schema-id"
schemaUrl="AnotherFile.kml#my-schema-id"
schemaUrl="#schema-id"    <!-- same file -->
```

If schemaUrl is an http address, the Earth browser fetches this file across the network. There can be only one instance of a given user-defined type per placemark.

<SimpleData name= " ">

Assigns a value to the custom data field identified by the name attribute. The type and name of this custom data field are declared in the <Schema> element.

Example of Typed Custom Data

The *TrailSchemaData.kml* example declares a user-defined type named ScenicVista. This type contains three fields: TrailHeadName, TrailLength, and ElevationGain. The TrailHeadName field contains values of type string. The

`TrailLength` field contains values of type `double`. The `ElevationGain` field contains values of type `int`. The placemark named `Easy trail` contains an instance of this user type. This instance has a value of "Pi in the sky" for its `TrailHeadName` field, a value of 3.14159 for its `TrailLength` field, and a value of 10 for its `ElevationGain` field.

TrailSchemaData.kml

```xml
<?xml version="1.0" encoding="UTF-8"?>
<kml xmlns="http://www.opengis.net/kml/2.2">
  <Document>
    <name>ExtendedData+SchemaData</name>
    <open>1</open>

    <!-- Declare the type "TrailHeadType" with 3 fields -->
    <Schema name="TrailHeadType" id="TrailHeadTypeId">
      <SimpleField type="string" name="TrailHeadName">
        <displayName><![CDATA[<b>Trail Head Name</b>]]></displayName>
      </SimpleField>
      <SimpleField type="double" name="TrailLength">
        <displayName><![CDATA[<i>Length in miles</i>]]></displayName>
      </SimpleField>
      <SimpleField type="int" name="ElevationGain">
        <displayName><![CDATA[<i>Change in altitude</i>]]></displayName>
      </SimpleField>
    </Schema>

      <TrailHeadType>
        <TrailHeadName>...</TrailHeadName>
        <TrailLength>...</TrailLength>
        <ElevationGain>...</ElevationGain>
      </TrailHeadType>
    -->

    <!--Instantiate some Placemarks extended with TrailHeadType fields-->
    <Placemark>
      <name>Easy trail</name>
      <ExtendedData>
        <SchemaData schemaUrl="#TrailHeadTypeId">
          <SimpleData name="TrailHeadName">Pi in the sky</SimpleData>
          <SimpleData name="TrailLength">3.14159</SimpleData>
          <SimpleData name="ElevationGain">10</SimpleData>
        </SchemaData>
```

```
      </ExtendedData>
      <Point>
        <coordinates>-122.000,37.002</coordinates>
      </Point>
    </Placemark>
    <Placemark>
      <name>Difficult trail</name>
      <ExtendedData>
        <SchemaData schemaUrl="#TrailHeadTypeId">
          <SimpleData name="TrailHeadName">Mount Everest</SimpleData>
          <SimpleData name="TrailLength">347.45</SimpleData>
          <SimpleData name="ElevationGain">10000</SimpleData>
        </SchemaData>
      </ExtendedData>
      <Point>
        <coordinates>-121.998,37.0078</coordinates>
      </Point>
    </Placemark>
  </Document>
</kml>
```

Figure 8-14 shows the balloon for one of these placemarks, which use default styling.

Figure 8-14 By default, custom typed data is displayed in the balloon in tabular form, with the name in the left column and the value in the right column.

Example Using Entity Replacement

The Schema/SchemaData mechanism also supports entity replacement in the <text> element of the <BalloonStyle> element. The <displayName> of <Schema> allows you to supply a user-friendly version for a custom data type. Changing the string once in the <Schema> has the effect of changing the <displayName> for all Features that contain that type.

In the <text> element of the <BalloonStyle> element, use the following syntax to qualify the <displayName>:

```
$[TYPENAME/TYPEFIELD/displayName]
```

where

TYPENAME
    is the name attribute of <Schema>

TYPEFIELD
    is the name attribute of <SimpleField>

displayName
    is the <displayName> element within <SimpleField>

The *SchemaDataAndBalloonStyle.kml* example adds a BalloonStyle template to the previous SchemaData example. As in the Golf Course example, the template is created using the <Style>, <BalloonStyle>, and <text> elements at the beginning of the Document. Each Placemark in the file references this style template (named ExtendedData+ SchemaData).

Figure 8-15 shows presenting the same data as the previous example (Figure 8-14), but with a customized <BalloonStyle> template.

SchemaDataAndBalloonStyle.kml

```
<?xml version="1.0" encoding="UTF-8"?>
<kml xmlns="http://www.opengis.net/kml/2.2">
  <Document>
    <name>ExtendedData+SchemaData</name>
    <open>1</open>
    <!-- Create a balloon template referring to the user-defined type -->
    <Style id="trailhead-balloon-template">
      <BalloonStyle>
        <text>
          <![CDATA[
```

Figure 8-15 A custom ‹BalloonStyle› template presents the data/value pairs in paragraph form for all placemarks with user-defined fields.

```
      <h2>My favorite trails!</h2>
      <br/><br/>
      The $[TrailHeadType/TrailHeadName/displayName] is
      <i>$[TrailHeadType/TrailHeadName]</i>.
      The trail is $[TrailHeadType/TrailLength] miles.<br/>
      The climb is $[TrailHeadType/ElevationGain] meters.<br/><br/>
      ]]>
      </text>
    </BalloonStyle>
  </Style>

  <!-- Declare the type "TrailHeadType" with 3 fields -->
  <Schema name="TrailHeadType" id="TrailHeadTypeId">
    <SimpleField type="string" name="TrailHeadName">
      <displayName><![CDATA[<b>Trail Head Name</b>]]></displayName>
    </SimpleField>
    <SimpleField type="double" name="TrailLength">
      <displayName><![CDATA[<i>The length in miles</i>]]></displayName>
    </SimpleField>
    <SimpleField type="int" name="ElevationGain">
      <displayName><![CDATA[<i>change in altitude</i>]]></displayName>
    </SimpleField>
  </Schema>

  <!--Instantiate some Placemarks extended with TrailHeadType fields-->
  <Placemark>
```

```
<name>Easy trail</name>
<styleUrl>#trailhead-balloon-template</styleUrl>
<ExtendedData>
  <SchemaData schemaUrl="#TrailHeadTypeId">
    <SimpleData name="TrailHeadName">Pi in the sky</SimpleData>
    <SimpleData name="TrailLength">3.14159</SimpleData>
    <SimpleData name="ElevationGain">10</SimpleData>
  </SchemaData>
</ExtendedData>
<Point>
  <coordinates>-122.000,37.002</coordinates>
</Point>
</Placemark>
<Placemark>
  <name>Difficult trail</name>
  <styleUrl>#trailhead-balloon-template</styleUrl>
  <ExtendedData>
    <SchemaData schemaUrl="#TrailHeadTypeId">
      <SimpleData name="TrailHeadName">Mount Everest</SimpleData>
      <SimpleData name="TrailLength">347.45</SimpleData>
      <SimpleData name="ElevationGain">10000</SimpleData>
    </SchemaData>
  </ExtendedData>
  <Point>
    <coordinates>-121.998,37.0078</coordinates>
  </Point>
</Placemark>
</Document>
</kml>
```

What's Next?

You're now at the end of the "teaching" part of this book. Appendix A, KML Reference, will be your constant companion as you create new KML and polish your old work. It's time to experiment, practice, and explore the power of KML. Be sure to make use of the rapidly growing KML community: Search the web for inspiring examples. Then create and share your own!

Appendix A

KML Reference

This section contains an alphabetical reference for all KML types and elements. Figure A-1 shows the class tree for KML elements that have derived elements. In this diagram, elements to the right on a particular branch in the tree are extensions of the elements to their left. For example, Placemark is a special kind of Feature. It contains all the elements that belong to Feature, and it adds some elements that are specific to the Placemark element. The syntax section for each KML element indicates where a given element *inherits* elements from an ancestor in the class tree.

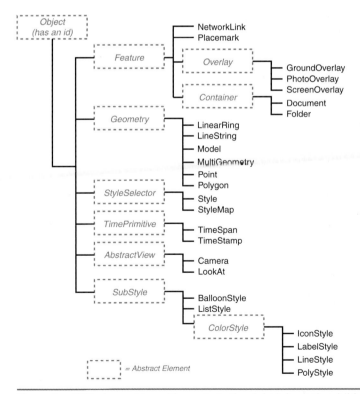

Figure A-1 KML element tree. Elements to the right inherit the children of their ancestors to the left.

Abstract Elements

The class tree diagram also indicates which elements are *abstract elements* (shown in dotted boxes). You cannot create an abstract element directly in a KML file. Abstract elements are an efficient way for the underlying Earth browser code to create complex elements that have a number of elements in common. Each abstract element is a *substitution group*. For example, any element derived from the <Geometry> abstract element can be substituted for any other element derived from <Geometry>. The derived elements have special uses, but their general usage is the same for siblings of the same ancestor in the tree.

Complex Versus Simple Elements

A *complex element* contains other elements. A *simple element* contains a string or numeric value and may contain attributes, but it does not contain other elements. In general, complex elements in KML begin with a capital letter, and simple elements begin with a lowercase letter. This reference section is an alphabetical reference of the complex elements in KML. A complex element is often referred to as the *parent* of its simple elements. Similarly, a simple element is referred to as the *child* of its complex element.

Basic Syntax Rules for KML

KML is an XML grammar and file format and follows general rules for XML. Specifically:

- Case is significant. Each element name must be spelled exactly as shown in this reference section, and with the same capitalization used here.
- Order is significant. The order of elements within a complex element must reflect the order shown in this reference.
- Child elements can belong only to the allowed parent elements, as listed in the syntax section for each complex element. (The Contains and Contained By sections for each element list additional allowed parent/child relationships.)

In Google Earth, you can enable error checking mode to warn you of misplaced elements or other KML errors.

Header

This reference describes KML Version 2.2. Each KML file must begin with the following lines:

```
<?xml version="1.0" encoding="UTF-8"?>
<kml xmlns="http://www.opengis.net/kml/2.2">
```

If the file contains celestial data rather than Earth data, also include `hint="target=sky"` as shown here:

```
<kml xmlns="http://www.opengis.net/kml/2.2" hint="target=sky">
```

Default Values

Every KML element has a default value. If you omit a KML element from a complex element, the default value is used for that element. There are no required elements in KML 2.2.

How to Use This Reference

This reference is a supplement to the first eight chapters of *The KML Handbook*, which teach you how to create and edit raw KML. It intentionally leaves out the details and nuances from its descriptions so that it will be a handy, compact, day-to-day syntax reference. You can copy the syntax sections directly into your KML code, substituting your own values for the default values listed there. This syntax section also lists the KML type for each element value. For enumerated values, all valid choices are also listed in the syntax section.

KML Schema File

The KML schema (*ogckml22.xsd*) is located at www.opengeospatial.org. KML is expected to expand, so check the website for *The KML Handbook* and the Open Geospatial Consortium for the most up-to-date information. Future versions of KML are required to be compatible with earlier versions.

Don't Forget to Test Different Earth Browsers

Some Earth browsers and mapping applications support a subset of the KML elements described here. This book documents the full KML 2.2 Specification, an Open Geospatial Consortium standard (documented on www.opengeospatial.org). Be sure to test your KML in the Earth browsers and applications that you expect to display it.

KML Types

KML uses common XML types such as `boolean`, `string`, `double`, `float`, and `int`. In addition, it defines a number of field element types. The following table lists some of the most commonly used types defined in KML and links to sample elements that use them:

Type	Value	Example Use
altitudeModeEnum	`clampToGround, relativeToGround, absolute`	See <LookAt> and <Region>
angle90	a value −90.0 and ≤ 90.0	See <latitude> in <Model>
angle180	a value −180 and ≤ 180	See <longitude> in <Model>
anglepos180	a value 0.0 and ≤ 180.0	See <tilt> in <LookAt>
angle360	a value −360.0 and ≤ 360.0	See <heading> in <Orientation>
color	hexBinary value: *aabbggrr*	See any element that extends ColorStyle
colorModeEnum	`normal, random`	See any element that extends ColorStyle
dateTime	*dateTime, date, gYearMonth, gYear*	See <TimeSpan> and <TimeStamp>
displayModeEnum	`default, hide`	See <BalloonStyle>
gridOriginEnum	`lowerLeft, upperLeft`	See <PhotoOverlay>
itemIconStateEnum	`open, closed, error, fetching0, fetching1, fetching2`	See <state> in <ItemIcon>
listItemTypeEnum	`radioFolder, check, checkHideChildren`	See <ListItemType> in <ListStyle>
refreshModeEnum	`onChange, onInterval, onExpire`	See <Link>
shapeEnum	`rectangle, cylinder, sphere`	See <PhotoOverlay>
styleStateEnum	`normal, highlight`	See <StyleMap>
unitsEnum	`fraction, pixels, insetPixels`	See <hotSpot> in <IconStyle>, <ScreenOverlay>
vec2	x=double xunits=*kml:unitsEnum* y=double yunits=*kml:unitsEnum*	See <hotSpot> in <IconStyle>, <ScreenOverlay>
viewRefreshEnum	`never, onRequest, onStop, onRegion`	See <Link>

AbstractView

```
<!-- AbstractView id="ID"  -->               <!-- Camera, LookAt -->
<-- /AbstractView -->
```

Description

This is an abstract element and cannot be used directly in a KML file. This element is the base element for the <Camera> and <LookAt> elements.

‹BalloonStyle›

```
<BalloonStyle id="ID">
  <bgColor>ffffffff</bgColor>              <!-- kml:color -->
  <textColor>ff000000</textColor>          <!-- kml:color -->
  <text>...</text>                         <!-- string -->
  <displayMode>default</displayMode>       <!-- kml:displayModeEnum -->
</BalloonStyle>
```

Description

Specifies how the description balloon for a Feature is drawn. The <bgColor>, if specified, is used as the background color of the balloon. See Chapter 2, Placemarks and Balloons.

Elements Specific to BalloonStyle

‹bgColor›

Background color of the balloon. Color and opacity (alpha) values are expressed in hexadecimal notation. The order of expression is *aabbggrr*, where *aa*=alpha (00 to ff); *bb*=blue (00 to ff); *gg*=green (00 to ff); *rr*=red (00 to ff). For alpha, 00 is fully transparent, and ff is fully opaque.

<textColor>

Foreground color for text.

<text>

Text displayed in the balloon. You can add entities to the <text> tag using the following format to refer to a child element of Feature: $[name], $[description], $[address], $[id], $[Snippet], $[geDirections] (*driving directions*). The Earth browser looks in the current Feature for the corresponding string entity and substitutes that information in the balloon. To prevent the driving directions links from appearing in a balloon, include the <text> element with some content, or with $[description] to substitute the basic Feature <description>. Also see <ExtendedData> for information on how to create custom entity substitutions in a balloon (and in Chapter 8, see the section Entity Replacement for Extended Data Elements).

<displayMode>

If <displayMode> is default, the Earth browser uses the information supplied in <text> to create a balloon. If <displayMode> is hide, the Earth browser does not display the balloon. (In Google Earth, clicking the list view icon for a placemark whose balloon's <displayMode> is hide causes Google Earth to fly to the placemark.)

Contained By

<Style>

‹Camera›

```
<Camera id="ID">
    <longitude>0.0</longitude>          <!-- kml:angle180 -->
    <latitude>0.0</latitude>            <!-- kml:angle90 -->
    <altitude>0.0</altitude>            <!-- double -->
    <heading>0.0</heading>              <!-- kml:angle360 -->
    <tilt>0.0</tilt>                    <!-- kml:anglepos180 -->
    <roll>0.0</roll>                    <!-- kml:angle180 -->
    <altitudeMode>clampToGround</altitudeMode>
                                        <!-- kml:altitudeModeEnum -->
</Camera>
```

Description

Defines the virtual camera that views the scene. This element defines the position of the camera relative to the Earth's surface as well as the viewing direction of the camera. The camera position is defined by <longitude>, <latitude>, <altitude>, and <altitudeMode>. The viewing direction of the camera is defined by <heading>, <tilt>, and <roll>.

<Camera> provides full six-degrees-of-freedom control over the view, so you can position the camera in space and then rotate it around the x, y, and z axes. Most important, you can tilt the camera view so that you're looking above the horizon into the sky.

The order of rotation is important. By default, the camera is looking straight down the −Z axis toward the Earth. Before rotations are performed, the camera is translated along the Z axis to <altitude>. The order of transformations is as follows:

1. <altitude>   Translate along the z axis to <altitude>.

2. <heading>   Rotate around the z axis.

3. <tilt>   Rotate around the x axis.

4. <roll>   Rotate around the z axis (again).

Note that each time a rotation is applied, two of the camera axes change their orientation.

Elements Specific to Camera

<longitude>

> Longitude of the virtual camera (eye point). Angular distance in degrees, relative to the Prime Meridian. Values west of the Meridian range from −180 degrees to 0 degrees. Values east of the Meridian range from 0 degrees to 180 degrees.

<latitude>

> Latitude of the virtual camera. Degrees north or south of the Equator (0 degrees). Values range from −90 degrees to 90 degrees.

<altitude>

> Distance of the camera from the Earth's surface, in meters. See <altitudeMode> for how this value is interpreted.

<heading>

> Direction (azimuth) of the camera, in degrees. Default=0 (true North). Values range from 0 degrees to 360 degrees.

<tilt>

> Rotation, in degrees, of the camera around the x axis. A value of 0 indicates that the view is aimed straight down toward the Earth (the most common case). A value of 90 degrees for <tilt> indicates that the view is aimed toward the horizon. Values greater than 90 indicate that the view is pointed up into the sky.

<roll>

> Rotation, in degrees, of the camera around the z axis. Values range from −180 degrees to +180 degrees.

<altitudeMode>

Specifies how the <altitude> specified for the camera is interpreted. Possible values are as follows:

`clampToGround` (default)

Indicates to ignore the <altitude> specification and place the camera position on the ground.

`relativeToGround`

Interprets the <altitude> as a value in meters above the ground.

`absolute`

Interprets the <altitude> as a value in meters above sea level.

Contained By

Any element derived from Feature; <NetworkLinkControl>

A parent element cannot contain both a <Camera> and <LookAt> at the same time.

ColorStyle

```
<!-- ColorStyle id="ID"  -->
  <color>ffffffff</color>              <!-- kml:color -->
  <colorMode>normal</colorMode>        <!-- kml:colorModeEnum -->
<!-- /ColorStyle -->
```

Description

This is an abstract element and cannot be used in a KML file. It provides elements that are inherited by the styles derived from this element (<IconStyle>, <LabelStyle>, <LineStyle>, and <PolyStyle>).

Elements Specific to ColorStyle

<color>

Color and opacity (alpha) values are expressed in hexadecimal notation. The order of expression is *aabbggrr*, where *aa*=alpha (00 to ff); *bb*=blue (00 to ff); *gg*=green (00 to ff); *rr*=red (00 to ff). For alpha, 00 is fully transparent, and ff is fully opaque.

<colorMode>

Values for <colorMode> are `normal` (no effect) and `random`. A value of random applies a random linear scale to the base <color> as follows.

- To achieve a truly random selection of opaque colors, specify a base <color> of white (ffffffff).
- If you specify a single color component (for example, a value of ff0000ff for red), random color values for that one component (red) will be selected. In this case, the values would range from 00 (no red contribution to the color) to ff (full red).
- If you specify values for two or for all three color components, a random linear scale is applied to each color component, with results ranging from black to the maximum values specified for each component.
- The opacity of a color comes from the alpha component of <color> and is never randomized.

Container

```
<!-- Container  -->                      <!-- Document,Folder -->
  <!-- inherited from Feature element; see <Feature> -->
  <name>...</name>                       <!-- string -->
  <visibility>1</visibility>             <!-- boolean -->
  <open>0</open>                         <!-- boolean -->
  <address>...</address>                 <!-- string -->
  <AddressDetails xmlns="urn:oasis:names:tc:ciq:xsdschema:xAL:2.0">...
       </AddressDetails>                 <!-- string -->
  <phoneNumber>...</phoneNumber>         <!-- string -->
  <Snippet maxLines="2">...</Snippet>   <!-- string -->
  <description>...</description>         <!-- string -->
  <AbstractView>...</AbstractView>      <!-- LookAt or Camera -->
  <TimePrimitive>...</TimePrimitive>    <!-- TimeSpan or TimeStamp -->
  <styleUrl>...</styleUrl>              <!-- anyURI -->
  <StyleSelector>...</StyleSelector>    <!-- Style or StyleMap -->
  <Region>...</Region>
  <atom:author>...<atom:author>
     <!-- xmlns:atom="http://www.w3.org/2005/Atom" -->
  <atom:link />

  <!-- specific to Container -->
  <!-- 0 or more Features -->
<!-- /Container -->
```

Description

Container is an abstract element and cannot be used in a KML file. It provides elements that are inherited by the derived elements (<Document> and <Folder>). A Container element holds one or more Features and allows the creation of nested hierarchies.

‹Document›

```
<Document id="ID">
  <!-- inherited from Feature element -->
  <name>...</name>                        <!-- string -->
  <visibility>1</visibility>              <!-- boolean -->
  <open>0</open>                          <!-- boolean -->
  <atom:author>...<atom:author>           <!-- xmlns:atom -->
  <atom:link />                           <!-- xmlns:atom -->
  <address>...</address>                  <!-- string -->
  <xal:AddressDetails>...</xal:AddressDetails>  <!-- xmlns:xal -->
  <phoneNumber>...</phoneNumber>          <!-- string -->
  <Snippet maxLines="2">...</Snippet>    <!-- string -->
  <description>...</description>          <!-- string -->
  <AbstractView>...</AbstractView>        <!-- Camera or LookAt -->
  <TimePrimitive>...</TimePrimitive>      <!-- TimeSpan or TimeStamp -->
  <styleUrl>...</styleUrl>                <!-- anyURI -->
  <StyleSelector>...</StyleSelector>      <!-- Style or StyleMap -->
  <Region>...</Region>
  <ExtendedData>...</ExtendedData>

  <!-- specific to Document -->
  <!-- 0 or more Schema elements -->
  <!-- 0 or more Feature elements -->
</Document>
```

Description

A <Document> is a container for Features, shared Styles, and Schemas. This element is required if your KML file uses shared styles. See Chapter 4, Styles and Icons, for information on shared styles. A <Document> is the only element that can contain shared styles, and it is the only element that can contain schemas. A KML file can contain multiple <Document> elements.

Note that shared styles do not affect the Features in the <Document> unless the Feature explicitly references the style in a <styleUrl> element. For a <Style> to apply to a <Document>, the Document itself must explicitly reference the <styleUrl>.

- 0 or more elements derived from Feature
- 0 or more elements derived from <Schema>

‹ExtendedData›

```
<ExtendedData>
  <Data name="string">
    <displayName>...</displayName>     <!-- string -->
    <value>...</value>                 <!-- string -->
  </Data>
  <SchemaData schemaUrl="anyURI">
    <SimpleData name=""> ... </SimpleData>   <!-- string -->
  </SchemaData>
  <namespace_prefix:other>...</namespace_prefix:other>
</ExtendedData>
```

The <ExtendedData> element offers three techniques for adding custom data to a KML Feature. These techniques are

- Referring to XML elements defined in other namespaces by referencing the external namespace within the KML file using the *<namespace_prefix>* element (basic)
- Adding untyped data/value pairs using the <Data> element (basic)
- Declaring new typed fields using the <Schema> element and then instancing them using the <SchemaData> element (advanced)

These techniques can be combined within a single KML file or Feature for different pieces of data. For more information, see Chapter 8, Dealing with Large Data Sets.

<Data name ="string">

> Creates an untyped name/value pair. The name can have two versions: name and displayName. The name attribute is used to identify the data pair within the KML file. The <displayName> element is used when a properly formatted name, with spaces and HTML formatting, is displayed in an Earth browser. In the

<text> element of <BalloonStyle>, the notation $[name:displayName] is replaced with the value of <displayName>. If you substitute the value of the name attribute of the <Data> element in this format (for example, $[holeYardage]), the attribute value is replaced with its <value>. By default, the Feature's balloon displays the name/value pairs associated with it.

<displayName>

An optional formatted version of name, to be used for display purposes.

<value>

Value of the data pair.

<SchemaData schemaUrl="anyURI"**>**

This element is used in conjunction with <Schema> to add typed custom data to a KML Feature. The Schema element (identified by the schemaUrl attribute) declares the custom data type. The actual data objects ("instances" of the custom data) are defined using the SchemaData element.

The <schemaURL> can be a full URL, a reference to a Schema ID defined in an external KML file, or a reference to a Schema ID defined in the same KML file.

The <Schema> element is always a child of <Document>. The <ExtendedData> element is a child of the Feature that contains the custom data.

<SimpleData name="string">

This element assigns a value to the custom data field identified by the name attribute. The type and name of this custom data field are declared in the <Schema> element.

<namespace_prefix:other>

This element allows you to add untyped custom data. Be sure to reference the namespace prefix in the <kml> element of your file or as an attribute of the <ExtendedData> element and to prefix the name of each data element with the namespace prefix. Custom data added in this manner is preserved in the KML file but is not used by the Earth browser in any way. It is always saved along with the file.

Contained By

Any element derived from Feature.

See Also

<Schema>

```
<!-- Feature id="ID" -->             <!-- Document,Folder,NetworkLink,
                                          Placemark,GroundOverlay,
                                          PhotoOverlay,ScreenOverlay -->
    <name>...</name>                  <!-- string -->
    <visibility>1</visibility>        <!-- boolean -->
    <open>0</open>                    <!-- boolean -->
    <atom:author>...<atom:author>     <!-- xmlns:atom -->
    <atom:link />                     <!-- xmlns:atom -->
    <address>...</address>            <!-- string -->
    <xal:AddressDetails>...</xal:AddressDetails>  <!-- xmlns:xal -->
    <phoneNumber>...</phoneNumber>    <!-- string -->
    <Snippet maxLines="2">...</Snippet>  <!-- string -->
    <description>...</description>    <!-- string -->
    <AbstractView>...</AbstractView>  <!-- Camera or LookAt -->
    <TimePrimitive>...</TimePrimitive>  <!-- TimeStamp or TimeSpan -->
    <styleUrl>...</styleUrl>          <!-- anyURI -->
    <StyleSelector>...</StyleSelector>  <!-- Style or StyleMap -->
    <Region>...</Region>
    <ExtendedData>...</ExtendedData>
<-- /Feature -->
```

Description

This is an abstract element and cannot be used in a KML file. It provides elements that are inherited by the derived elements, which collectively are referred to as Features (Container, <Document>, <Folder>, <NetworkLink>, <Placemark>, Overlay, <GroundOverlay>, <PhotoOverlay>, <ScreenOverlay>).

> **Note**
>
> <Snippet> has been deprecated in KML 2.2 in favor of <snippet>. At the time of publication, however, Google Earth does not support the lowercase version <snippet>. For this reason, this reference continues to use the uppercase version of <Snippet>.

Elements Specific to Feature

<name>

User-defined text displayed in the 3D viewer as the label for the object (for example, for a placemark, folder, or network link).

<visibility>

Specifies whether the feature is drawn in the 3D viewer when it is initially loaded. For a feature to be visible, the <visibility> tag of all its ancestors must also be set to 1.

<open>

Specifies whether a document or folder appears closed or open when first loaded into the Places panel. 0=collapsed (the default), 1=expanded. See also <ListStyle>. This element applies only to <Document>, <Folder>, and <NetworkLink>.

<atom:author>

This element is defined in the Atom Syndication format. The complete specification is found at *http://atompub.org*. Include the namespace for this element in any KML file that uses it:

```
xmlns:atom="http://www.w3.org/2005/Atom"
```

(see Chapter 3). This information is displayed in geo search results, both in Earth browsers and in other geographic applications such as Google Maps.

<atom:link href="">

Specifies the URL of the website containing this KML or KMZ file. Be sure to include the namespace for this element in any KML file that uses it:

```
xmlns:atom="http://www.w3.org/2005/Atom".
```

<address>

A string value representing an unstructured address written as a standard street, city, state address, and/or as a postal code. You can use the <address> tag to specify the location of a point instead of using latitude and longitude coordinates. (However, if a <Point> is provided, it takes precedence over the <address>.)

<xal:AddressDetails>

A structured address, formatted as OASIS xAL 2.0, or eXtensible Address Language, an international standard for address formatting. Be sure to include the namespace for this element in any KML file that uses it:

```
xmlns:xal="urn:oasis:names:tc:ciq:xsdschema:xAL:2.0".
```

<phoneNumber>

A string value representing a telephone number. The number should be formatted according to IETF RFC 3966.

<Snippet maxLines="">

A short description of the Feature. If supplied, this text is used in the list view instead of the <description>. This tag does not support HTML markup.

<Snippet> has a `maxLines` attribute, an integer that specifies the maximum number of lines to display. (See the previous note on <Snippet>.)

<description>

User-supplied text that appears in the description balloon. See Chapter 2, Placemarks and Balloons. The <description> element supports plain text as well as a subset of HTML formatting elements, including tables. It does not support other web-based technology, such as dynamic page markup (PHP, JSP, ASP), scripting languages (VBScript, JavaScript), nor application languages (Java, Python). It does support video.

When using HTML to create a hyperlink around a specific word, or when including images in the HTML, you must use HTML entity references or the CDATA element to escape angle brackets, apostrophes, and other special characters. The CDATA element tells the XML parser to ignore special characters used within the brackets.

The HTML anchor element <a> contains an `href` attribute that specifies a URL. If the `href` is a KML file and has a *.kml* or *.kmz* file extension, the Earth browser loads that file directly when the user clicks it. If the URL ends with an extension not known to the Earth browser (for example, .html), the URL is sent to the web browser.

The `href` can be a fragment URL (that is, a URL with a # sign followed by a KML identifier). When the user clicks a link that includes a fragment URL, by default the browser flies to the Feature whose ID matches the fragment. If the Feature has a <LookAt> or <Camera> element, the Feature is viewed from the specified viewpoint.

The behavior can be further specified by appending one of the following three strings to the fragment URL:

`;flyto` (default)
   Fly to the Feature.

`;balloon`
   Open the Feature's balloon but do not fly to the Feature.

`;balloonFlyto`
   Open the Feature's balloon and fly to the Feature.

The `type` attribute is used within the <a> element when the `href` does not end in *.kml* or *.kmz*, but the reference needs to be interpreted in the context of KML (for example, a *.php* script that produces KML). Specify the following:

```
type="application/vnd.google-earth.kml+xml"
```

AbstractView

Defines a viewpoint associated with any element derived from Feature. See <Camera> and <LookAt>.

TimePrimitive

Associates this Feature with a period of time (<TimeSpan>) or a point in time (<TimeStamp>).

<styleUrl>

URL of a <Style> or <StyleMap> defined in a Document. If the style is in the same file, use a # reference. If the style is defined in an external file, use a full URL along with # referencing. See Chapter 4, Styles and Icons.

StyleSelector

Specifies one or more <Style> and <StyleMap> elements used to customize the appearance of any element derived from Feature or of the Geometry in a <Placemark>. See <BalloonStyle>, <ListStyle>, StyleSelector, and the styles derived from ColorStyle. Also see Chapter 4, Styles and Icons.

<Region>

Features and geometry associated with a region are drawn only when the region is active. See <Region>.

<ExtendedData>

Allows you to add custom data to a KML file. See <Extended Data>.

Contained By

<kml>, <Folder>

<Folder>

```
<Folder id="ID">
  <!-- inherited from Feature element -->
  <name>...</name>                          <!-- string -->
  <visibility>1</visibility>                <!-- boolean -->
  <open>0</open>                            <!-- boolean -->
  <atom:author>...<atom:author>             <!-- xmlns:atom -->
  <atom:link />                             <!-- xmlns:atom -->
  <address>...</address>                    <!-- string -->
  <xal:AddressDetails>...</xal:AddressDetails>  <!-- xmlns:xal -->
```

```
<phoneNumber>...</phoneNumber>          <!-- string -->
<Snippet maxLines="2">...</Snippet>     <!-- string -->
<description>...</description>          <!-- string -->
<AbstractView>...</AbstractView>        <!-- Camera or LookAt -->
<TimePrimitive>...</TimePrimitive>      <!-- TimeSpan or TimeStamp -->
<styleUrl>...</styleUrl>                <!-- anyURI -->
<StyleSelector>...</StyleSelector>      <!-- Style or StyleMap -->
<Region>...</Region>
<ExtendedData>...</ExtendedData>

<!-- specific to Folder -->
<!-- 0 or more Feature elements -->
</Folder>
```

Description

A folder is used to arrange other Features hierarchically (<Document>, <Folder>, <Placemark>, <NetworkLink>, or Overlays). A Feature is visible only if it and all its ancestors are visible.

Contained By

<kml>, <Folder>

Contains

0 or more elements derived from Feature.

Geometry

```
<!-- Geometry id="ID" -->       <!-- Point,LineString,LinearRing,
                                     Polygon,MultiGeometry,Model -->

<!-- /Geometry -->
```

Description

This is an abstract element and cannot be used directly in a KML file. It provides a placeholder object for all derived Geometry objects.

‹GroundOverlay›

```
<GroundOverlay id="ID">
  <!-- inherited from Feature element -->
  <name>...</name>                             <!-- string -->
  <visibility>1</visibility>                   <!-- boolean -->
  <open>0</open>                               <!-- boolean -->
  <atom:author>...<atom:author>                <!-- xmlns:atom -->
  <atom:link />                                <!-- xmlns:atom -->
  <address>...</address>                       <!-- string -->
  <xal:AddressDetails>...</xal:AddressDetails>  <!-- xmlns:xal -->
  <phoneNumber>...</phoneNumber>               <!-- string -->
  <Snippet maxLines="2">...</Snippet>          <!-- string -->
  <description>...</description>               <!-- string -->
  <AbstractView>...</AbstractView>             <!-- Camera or LookAt -->
  <TimePrimitive>...</TimePrimitive>           <!-- TimeSpan or TimeStamp -->
  <styleUrl>...</styleUrl>                     <!-- anyURI -->
  <StyleSelector>...</StyleSelector>           <!-- Style or StyleMap -->
  <Region>...</Region>
  <ExtendedData>...</ExtendedData>

  <!-- inherited from Overlay element -->
  <color>ffffffff</color>                          <!-- kml:color -->
  <drawOrder>0</drawOrder>                          <!-- int -->
  <Icon>...</Icon>

  <!-- specific to GroundOverlay -->
  <altitude>0.0</altitude>                          <!-- double -->
  <altitudeMode>clampToGround</altitudeMode>
     <!-- kml:altitudeModeEnum: clampToGround or absolute -->
  <LatLonBox>
    <north>180.0</north>                        <! kml:angle90 -->
    <south>-180.0</south>                       <! kml:angle90 -->
    <east>180.0</east>                          <! kml:angle180 -->
    <west>-180.0</west>                         <! kml:angle180 -->
    <rotation>0.0</rotation>                     <! kml:angle180 -->
  </LatLonBox>
</GroundOverlay>
```

Description

This element draws an image overlay draped onto the terrain. The <href> child of
<Icon> specifies the image to be used as the overlay. This file can be either on a local file

system or on a web server. If this element is omitted or contains no <href>, a rectangle is drawn using the color and size defined by the ground overlay. See Chapter 5, Overlays.

Elements Specific to <GroundOverlay>

<altitude>

Specifies the distance above the Earth's surface, in meters, and is interpreted according to <altitudeMode>.

<altitudeMode>

Specifies how the <altitude>is interpreted. Possible values are

`clampToGround` (default)

Indicates to ignore the altitude specification and drape the overlay over the terrain.

`absolute`

Sets the altitude of the overlay relative to sea level, regardless of the actual elevation of the terrain beneath the element.

<LatLonBox>

Specifies a 2D bounding box used to align the ground overlay.

<north>

Specifies the latitude of the north edge of the bounding box.

<south>

Specifies the latitude of the south edge of the bounding box.

<east>

Specifies the longitude of the east edge of the bounding box.

<west>

Specifies the longitude of the west edge of the bounding box.

<rotation>

Specifies a rotation of the overlay about its center, in degrees. Rotations are specified in a counterclockwise direction.

Contained By

<Document>, <Folder>

‹Icon›

```
<Icon id="ID">
  <href>...</href>                        <!-- string -->
  <refreshMode>onChange</refreshMode>
     <!-- kml:refreshModeEnum: onChange, onInterval, or onExpire -->
  <refreshInterval>4.0</refreshInterval>  <!-- double -->
  <viewRefreshMode>never</viewRefreshMode>
     <!-- kml:viewRefreshModeEnum: never, onStop, onRequest, onRegion -->
  <viewRefreshTime>4.0</viewRefreshTime>  <!-- double -->
  <viewBoundScale>1.0</viewBoundScale>     <!-- double -->
  <viewFormat>...</viewFormat>            <!-- string -->
  <httpQuery>...</httpQuery>              <!-- string -->
</Icon>
```

Description

Defines an image associated with an Icon style or overlay. <Icon> has the same child elements as <Link>. The <href> child element specifies the image to be used as the overlay or as the icon for the Placemark. This image can either be on a local file system or on a remote web server.

Elements Specific to ‹Icon›

<href>
> Specifies an HTTP address or a local file specification used to load an icon.

<refreshMode>
> For a description of <refreshMode> and the other elements listed below, see <Link>.

<refreshInterval>
<viewRefreshMode>
<viewRefreshTime>
<viewBoundScale>
<viewFormat>
<httpQuery>

Contained By

<GroundOverlay>, <PhotoOverlay>, <ScreenOverlay>, <IconStyle>

‹IconStyle›

```
<IconStyle id="ID">
  <!-- inherited from ColorStyle -->
  <color>ffffffff</color>                    <!-- kml:color -->
  <colorMode>normal</colorMode>
      <!-- kml:colorModeEnum:normal or random -->

  <!-- specific to IconStyle -->
  <scale>1.0</scale>                         <!-- double -->
  <heading>0.0</heading>                     <!-- kml:angle360 -->
  <Icon>
    <href>...</href>
  </Icon>
  <hotSpot x="0.5"  y="0.5"
    xunits="fraction" yunits="fraction"/>    <!-- kml:vec2 -->
</IconStyle>
```

Description

Specifies how icons for point placemarks are drawn, both in the list view and in the 3D viewer of Google Earth. The <Icon> element specifies the icon image. The <scale> element specifies the x, y scaling of the icon. The color specified in the <color> element of <IconStyle> is blended with the color of the <Icon>. See Chapter 4, Styles and Icons.

If a <ListStyle> element specifies an icon in its <ItemIcon> child, that icon takes precedence in the list view over the <Icon> specified in <IconStyle>.

Elements Specific to ‹IconStyle›

<scale>
Resizes the icon.

<heading>
Direction (that is, North, South, East, West), in degrees. Default=0 (North).

<Icon>
A custom icon. In <IconStyle>, the only child element of <Icon> is <href>.

  <href>
An HTTP address or a local file specification for the icon.

<hotSpot x="" y="" xunits="" yunits=""/>
Specifies the position within the Icon that is "anchored" to the <Point> specified in the Placemark. The x and y values can be specified in three different ways: as

pixels ("`pixels`"), as fractions of the icon ("`fraction`"), or as inset pixels
("`insetPixels`"), which is an offset in pixels from the upper-right corner of
the icon. The x and y positions can be specified in different ways—for example, x
can be in pixels, and y can be a fraction. The origin of the coordinate system is in
the lower-left corner of the icon.

x

Either the number of pixels, a fractional component of the icon, or a pixel inset
indicating the x component of a point on the icon.

y

Either the number of pixels, a fractional component of the icon, or a pixel inset
indicating the y component of a point on the icon.

xunits

Units in which the x value is specified. A value of `fraction` indicates the x
value is a fraction of the icon. A value of `pixels` indicates the x value in
pixels. A value of `insetPixels` indicates the indent from the right edge
of the icon.

yunits

Units in which the y value is specified. A value of `fraction` indicates the y
value is a fraction of the icon. A value of `pixels` indicates the y value in
pixels. A value of `insetPixels` indicates the indent from the top edge
of the icon.

Contained By

<Style>

<kml>   Section 7.1 of OGC KML Specification 07-147

```
<kml xmlns="http://earth.google.com/kml/2.2" hint="target=sky">
  <NetworkLinkControl>
  <!-- 0 or 1 Feature -->
</kml>
```

Description

The root element of a KML file. This element is required. It follows the xml declaration
at the beginning of the file. The `hint` attribute is used as a signal to Google Earth to
display the file as celestial data (see Appendix B). (Include this attribute only for sky data.)

The <kml> element should also include the namespace for any external XML schemas that are referenced within the file.

Contains

- 0 or 1 Feature
- 0 or 1 <NetworkLinkControl>

‹LabelStyle›

```
<LabelStyle id="ID">
  <!-- inherited from ColorStyle -->
  <color>ffffffff</color>              <!-- kml:color -->
  <colorMode>normal</colorMode>
     <!-- kml:colorModeEnum: normal or random -->

  <!-- specific to LabelStyle -->
  <scale>1.0</scale>                   <!-- double -->
</LabelStyle>
```

Description

Specifies how the <name> of a Feature is drawn in the 3D viewer. A custom color, color mode, and scale for the label (name) can be specified. See Chapter 4, Styles and Icons.

Element Specific to ‹LabelStyle›

<scale>
    A multiplier used to resize the label.

Contained By

<Style>

‹LinearRing›

```
<LinearRing id="ID">
  <extrude>0</extrude>                         <!-- boolean -->
  <tessellate>0</tessellate>                   <!-- boolean -->
  <altitudeMode>clampToGround</altitudeMode>
     <!-- kml:altitudeModeEnum: clampToGround,
        relativeToGround, or absolute -->
```

```
<coordinates>...</coordinates>              <!-- lon,lat[,alt] tuples -->
</LinearRing>
```

Description

Defines a closed line string, typically the outer boundary of a Polygon. Optionally, a LinearRing can also be used as the inner boundary of a Polygon to create holes in the Polygon. A Polygon can contain multiple <LinearRing> elements used as inner boundaries. See Chapter 3, Geometry.

Elements Specific to <LinearRing>

<extrude>

> Specifies whether to connect the LinearRing to the ground. To extrude this geometry, the <altitudeMode> must be either `relativeToGround` or `absolute`, and the altitude component within the <coordinates> element must be greater than 0 (that is, in the air). Only the vertices of the LinearRing are extruded, not the center of the geometry. The vertices are extruded toward the center of the Earth's sphere.

<tessellate>

> Specifies whether to allow the LinearRing to follow the terrain (curvature of the Earth). To enable tessellation, the value for <altitudeMode> must be `clampToGround`. Very large LinearRings should enable tessellation so that they follow the curvature of the Earth (otherwise, they may go underground and be hidden).

<altitudeMode>

> Specifies how altitude components in the <coordinates> element are interpreted. Possible values are `clampToGround`, `relativeToGround`, and `absolute`. See Chapter 3, Geometry, for a discussion of these modes.

<coordinates>

> Four or more tuples, each consisting of floating point values for longitude, latitude, and altitude. The altitude component is optional. Do not include spaces within a tuple. The last coordinate must be the same as the first coordinate. Coordinates are expressed in decimal degrees only.

Contained By

<innerBoundaryIs>, <outerBoundaryIs>, <MultiGeometry>, <Placemark>

‹LineString›

```
<LineString id="ID">
  <extrude>0</extrude>                      <!-- boolean -->
  <tessellate>0</tessellate>                <!-- boolean -->
  <altitudeMode>clampToGround</altitudeMode>
    <!-- kml:altitudeModeEnum: clampToGround,
         relativeToGround, or absolute -->
  <coordinates>...</coordinates>            <!-- lon,lat[,alt] -->
</LineString>
```

Description

Defines a connected set of line segments. Use <LineStyle> to specify the color, color mode, and width of the line. When a linestring is extruded, the line is extended to the ground, forming a polygon that looks somewhat like a wall or fence. For extruded linestrings, the line itself uses the current <LineStyle>, and the extrusion uses the current <PolyStyle>. A <LineString> is commonly referred to as a "path."

Elements Specific to ‹LineString›

<extrude>

Specifies whether to connect the linestring to the ground. To extrude a linestring, the value for <altitudeMode> must be either `relativeToGround` or `absolute`, and the altitude component within the <coordinates> element must be greater than 0 (that is, in the air). The vertices in the LineString are extruded toward the center of the Earth's sphere.

<tessellate>

Specifies whether to allow the linestring to follow the terrain. To enable tessellation, the value for <altitudeMode> must be `clampToGround`. Very large linestrings should enable tessellation so that they follow the curvature of the Earth (otherwise, they may go underground and be hidden).

<altitudeMode>

Specifies how altitude components in the <coordinates> element are interpreted. Possible values are `clampToGround`, `relativeToGround`, and `absolute`. See Chapter 3, Geometry, for a discussion of these modes.

<coordinates>

Two or more coordinate tuples, each consisting of floating point values for longitude, latitude, and altitude. The altitude component is optional. Insert a space between tuples. Do not include spaces within a tuple.

Contained By

<MultiGeometry>, <Placemark>

‹LineStyle›

```
<LineStyle id="ID">
  <!-- inherited from ColorStyle -->
  <color>ffffffff</color>                   <!-- kml:color -->
  <colorMode>normal</colorMode>
    <!-- colorModeEnum: normal or random -->

  <!-- specific to LineStyle -->
  <width>1.0</width>                        <!-- double -->
</LineStyle>
```

Description

Specifies the drawing style (color, color mode, and line width) for all line geometry. Line geometry includes the outlines of outlined polygons and the extruded "tether" of placemark icons (if extrusion is enabled). See Chapter 4, Styles and Icons.

Element Specific to ‹LineStyle›

<width>
  Width of the line, in pixels.

Contained By

<Style>

‹Link› Section 13.1 of OGC KML Specification 07-147

```
<Link id="ID">
  <href>...</href>                                  <!-- string -->
  <refreshMode>onChange</refreshMode>
    <!-- refreshModeEnum: onChange, onInterval, or onExpire -->
  <refreshInterval>4.0</refreshInterval>        <!-- double -->
  <viewRefreshMode>never</viewRefreshMode>
    <!-- viewRefreshModeEnum: never, onStop, onRequest, onRegion -->
  <viewRefreshTime>4.0</viewRefreshTime>        <!-- double -->
  <viewBoundScale>1.0</viewBoundScale>          <!-- double -->
```

```
<viewFormat>BBOX=[bboxWest],[bboxSouth],[bboxEast],[bboxNorth]
   </viewFormat>                              <!-- string -->
<httpQuery>...</httpQuery>                     <!-- string -->
</Link>
```

Description

The <Link> element specifies the location of any of the following:

- KML files fetched by network links
- Image files used in any Overlay (<Icon> has same fields as <Link>)
- Model files used in the <Model> element

The file is conditionally loaded and refreshed, depending on the refresh parameters supplied here. Two different sets of refresh parameters can be specified: One set is based on time (<refreshMode> and <refreshInterval>), and one is based on the current "camera" view (<viewRefreshMode> and <viewRefreshTime>). In addition, Link specifies whether to scale the bounding box parameters that are sent to the server (<viewBoundScale>) and provides a set of optional viewing parameters that can be sent to the server (<viewFormat>) as well as a set of optional parameters containing version and language information.

When a file is fetched, the URL that is sent to the server is composed of three pieces of information (see example in Chapter 6, Network Links):

- The *href* (hypertext reference) that specifies the file to load
- An *arbitrary format string* that is created from (a) parameters that you specify in the <viewFormat> element or (b) bounding box parameters (this is the default and is used if no <viewFormat> element is included in the file)
- A *second format string* that is specified in the <httpQuery> element

If the file specified in <href> is a local file, the <viewFormat> and <httpQuery> elements are not used.

Elements Specific to ‹Link› (and also ‹Icon›)

<href>

Specifies a URL (either an HTTP address or a local file specification). When the parent of <Link> is a NetworkLink, <href> is a KML file. When the parent of <Link> is a Model, <href> is a COLLADA file. When the parent of <Link> is an Overlay, <href> is an image. Relative URLs can be used in this tag and are evaluated relative to the enclosing KML file.

<refreshMode>

Specifies a time-based refresh mode, which can be one of the following:

`onChange`

Refresh when the file is loaded and whenever the Link parameters change (the default).

`onInterval`

Refresh every *n* seconds (specified in <refreshInterval>).

`onExpire`

Refresh the file when the expiration time is reached. If a fetched file has a <NetworkLinkControl>, the <expires> time takes precedence over expiration times specified in HTTP headers. If no <expires> time is specified, the HTTP `max-age` header is used (if present). If `max-age` is not present, the Expires HTTP header is used (if present). (See Section RFC2616 of the Hypertext Transfer Protocol—HTTP 1.1 for details on HTTP header fields.)

<refreshInterval>

Indicates to refresh the file every *n* seconds.

<viewRefreshMode>

Specifies how the link is refreshed when the view changes. Can be one of the following:

`never` (default)

Ignore changes in the view. Also ignore <viewFormat> parameters, if any.

`onStop`

Refresh the file *n* seconds after movement stops, where *n* is specified in <viewRefreshTime>.

`onRequest`

Refresh the file only when the user explicitly requests it. (For example, in Google Earth, the user right-clicks and selects Refresh in the Context menu.)

`onRegion`

Refresh the file when the <Region> becomes active. See <Region>.

<viewRefreshTime>

After camera movement stops, specifies the number of seconds to wait before refreshing the view. (See <viewRefreshMode> and `onStop` above.)

<viewBoundScale>

Scales the BBOX parameters before sending them to the server. A value less than 1 specifies to use less than the full view (screen). A value greater than 1 specifies to fetch an area that extends beyond the edges of the current view.

<viewFormat>

Specifies the format of the query string that is appended to the Link's <href> before the file is fetched. (If the <href> specifies a local file, this element is ignored.)

If you specify a <viewRefreshMode> of onStop and do not include the <viewFormat> tag in the file, the following information is automatically appended to the query string:

BBOX=[bboxWest],[bboxSouth],[bboxEast],[bboxNorth]

This information matches the Web Map Service (WMS) bounding box specification.

If you specify an empty <viewFormat> tag, no information is appended to the query string.

You can also specify a custom set of viewing parameters to add to the query string. If you supply a format string, it is used *instead of* the BBOX information. If you also want the BBOX information, you need to add those parameters along with the custom parameters. You can use any of the following parameters in your format string (and the Earth browser will substitute the appropriate current value at the time it creates the query string):

[lookatLon], [lookatLat]
   Longitude and latitude of the point that <LookAt> is viewing

[lookatRange], [lookatTilt], [lookatHeading]
   Values used by the <LookAt> element (see descriptions of <range>, <tilt>, and <heading> in <LookAt>)

[lookatTerrainLon], [lookatTerrainLat], [lookatTerrainAlt]
   Point on the terrain in degrees/meters that <LookAt> is viewing

[cameraLon], [cameraLat], [cameraAlt]
   Degrees/meters of the eyepoint for the camera

[horizFov], [vertFov]
   Horizontal, vertical field of view for the camera

[horizPixels], [vertPixels]
   Size in pixels of the 3D viewer

[terrainEnabled]
   Indicates whether the 3D viewer is showing terrain

\<httpQuery\>

Appends information to the query string based on the parameters specified. (The Earth browser substitutes the appropriate current value at the time it creates the query string.) The following parameters are supported:

```
[clientVersion]
[kmlVersion]
[clientName]
[language]
```

Contained By

\<Model\>, \<NetworkLink\>

See Also

\<NetworkLinkControl\>, \<Region\>

‹ListStyle›

```
<ListStyle id="ID">
  <listItemType>check</listItemType> <!-- kml:listItemTypeEnum:check,
                                          checkOffOnly,checkHideChildren,
                                          radioFolder -->
  <bgColor>ffffffff</bgColor>         <!-- kml:color -->
  <ItemIcon>                          <!-- 0 or more ItemIcon elements -->
    <state>open</state>
      <!-- kml:itemIconModeEnum:open, closed, error, fetching0,
           fetching1, or fetching2 -->
    <href>...</href>                  <!-- string -->
  </ItemIcon>
    <maxSnippetLines> 2 </maxSnippetLines>
</ListStyle>
```

Description

Specifies how a Feature is displayed in the list view. The list view is a hierarchy of Containers and children.

Elements Specific to ‹ListStyle›

\<listItemType\>

Specifies how a Feature is displayed in the list view. Possible values are

check (default)

The Feature's visibility is tied to its item's checkbox.

`radioFolder`

When specified for a Container, only one of the Container's items is visible at a time.

`checkOffOnly`

When specified for a Container or network link, prevents all items from being made visible at once—that is, the user can turn everything in the Container or network link off but cannot turn everything on at the same time. This setting is useful for Containers or network links containing large amounts of data.

`checkHideChildren`

Use a normal checkbox for visibility but do not display the Container or network link's children in the list view. A checkbox allows the user to toggle visibility of the child objects in the viewer.

<bgColor>

Background color for the v<Snippet>. Color and opacity values are expressed in hexadecimal notation. The range of values for any one color is 0 to 255 (00 to ff). For alpha, 00 is fully transparent, and ff is fully opaque. The order of expression is aabbggrr, where aa=alpha (00 to ff); bb=blue (00 to ff); gg=green (00 to ff); and rr=red (00 to ff).

<ItemIcon>

Icon used in the list view that reflects the state of a <Folder> or <Link> fetch. Icons associated with the `open` and `closed` modes are used for folders and network links. Icons associated with the `error` and `fetching0`, `fetching1`, and `fetching2` modes are used for network links. See Chapter 4, Styles and Icons.

<state>

Specifies the current state of the <Folder> or <NetworkLink>. Possible values are `open`, `closed`, `error`, `fetching0`, `fetching1`, and `fetching2`. These values can be combined by inserting a space between two values (no comma).

<href>

Specifies the URL of the image used in the list view for the Feature.

<maxSnippetLines>

Maximum number of lines to display for the snippet in the list view.

Contained By

<Style>

‹LookAt›

```
<LookAt id="ID">
  <longitude>0.0</longitude>        <!-- kml:angle180 -->
  <latitude>0.0</latitude>          <!-- kml:angle90 -->
  <altitude>0.0</altitude>          <!-- double -->
  <heading>0.0</heading>            <!-- kml:angle360 -->
  <tilt>0.0</tilt>                  <!-- kml:anglepos180 -->
  <range>0.0</range>               <!-- double -->
  <altitudeMode>clampToGround</altitudeMode>
      <!--kml:altitudeModeEnum:clampToGround, relativeToGround,
          absolute -->
</LookAt>
```

Description

Defines a viewpoint that is associated with any element derived from Feature. The
‹LookAt› element positions the viewpoint in relation to the object that is being
viewed. In Google Earth, the view "flies to" this ‹LookAt› viewpoint when the user
double-clicks an item in the list view or double-clicks an icon in the 3D viewer. See
Chapter 2, Placemarks and Balloons.

Elements Specific to ‹LookAt›

‹longitude›

> Longitude of the point the viewpoint is looking at. Angular distance in degrees,
> relative to the Prime Meridian. Values West of the Meridian range from −180
> degrees to 0 degrees. Values East of the Meridian range from 0 degrees to 180
> degrees.

‹latitude›

> Latitude of the point the viewpoint is looking at. Degrees North or South of the
> Equator (0 degrees). Values range from −90 degrees to 90 degrees.

‹altitude›

> Distance from the Earth's surface, in meters. See ‹altitudeMode› for how this
> value is interpreted.

‹heading›

> Direction (that is, North, South, East, West), in degrees. Default=0 (North).
> Values range from 0 degrees to 360 degrees.

<tilt>

Angle between the direction of the LookAt position and the normal to the surface of the Earth. Values range from 0 degrees to 90 degrees. Values for <tilt> cannot be negative. A <tilt> value of 0 degrees indicates viewing from directly above. A <tilt> value of 90 degrees indicates viewing along the horizon.

<range>

Distance in meters from the point specified by <longitude>, <latitude>, and <altitude> to the LookAt position.

<altitudeMode>

Specifies how altitude components in the <coordinates> element are interpreted. Possible values are `clampToGround`, `relativeToGround`, and `absolute`. See Chapter 3, Geometry, for a discussion of these modes.

Contained By

Any element derived from Feature; <NetworkLinkControl>

⟨Model⟩

```
<Model id="ID">
  <altitudeMode>clampToGround</altitudeMode>
    <!--kml:altitudeModeEnum: clampToGround,relativeToGround,
        or absolute -->
  <Location>
    <longitude>0.0</longitude> <!-- kml:angle180 -->
    <latitude>0.0</latitude>    <!-- kml:angle90 -->
    <altitude>0.0</altitude>    <!-- double -->
  </Location>
  <Orientation>
    <heading>0.0</heading>      <!-- kml:angle360 -->
    <tilt>0.0</tilt>            <!-- kml:anglepos180 -->
    <roll>0.0</roll>            <!-- kml:angle180 -->
  </Orientation>
  <Scale>
    <x>1.0</x>                  <!-- double -->
    <y>1.0</y>                  <!-- double -->
    <z>1.0</z>                  <!-- double -->
  </Scale>
  <Link>...</Link>
```

```
  <ResourceMap>
    <Alias>
      <targetHref>...</targetHref>     <!-- anyURI -->
      <sourceHref>...</sourceHref>     <!-- anyURI -->
    </Alias>
  </ResourceMap>
</Model>
```

Description

A 3D object described in a COLLADA file (referenced in the <Link> tag). COLLADA files have a *.dae* file extension. Models are created in their own coordinate space and then located, positioned, and scaled in the Earth browser. See Chapter 3, Geometry.

Elements Specific to ‹Model›

<altitudeMode>

>   Specifies how altitude components in the <coordinates> element are interpreted. Possible values are `clampToGround`, `relativeToGround`, and `absolute`. See Chapter 3, Geometry, for a discussion of these modes.

<Location>

>   Specifies the exact coordinates of the Model's origin in <longitude>, <latitude>, and <altitude>. Latitude and longitude measurements are standard lat-lon projections with WGS84 datum. Altitude is distance above the Earth's surface, in meters, and is interpreted according to <altitudeMode>.

>   <longitude>
>   >   Longitude of the Model's origin.

>   <latitude>
>   >   Latitude of the Model's origin.

>   <altitude>
>   >   Altitude of the Model's origin.

<Orientation>

>   Describes rotation of a 3D model's coordinate system to position the object relative to the Earth.

>   <heading>
>   >   Rotation about the z axis (normal to the Earth's surface). A value of 0 (the default) equals North. A positive rotation is clockwise around the z axis and specified in degrees from 0 to ±360.

Rotation about the *x* axis. A positive rotation is clockwise around the *x* axis and specified in degrees from 0 to +180.

<roll>

Rotation about the *y* axis. A positive rotation is clockwise around the *y* axis and specified in degrees from 0 to ±180.

<Scale>

Scales a model along the *x*, *y*, and *z* axes in the Model's coordinate space.

<x>

Scale factor along the *x* axis.

<y>

Scale factor along the *y* axis.

<z>

Scale factor along the *z* axis.

<Link>

See <Link> element.

<ResourceMap>

Specifies 0 or more <Alias> elements, each of which is a mapping for the texture file path from the original COLLADA file to the KML or KMZ file that contains the Model. This element allows you to move and rename texture files without having to update the original COLLADA file that references those textures. One <ResourceMap> element can contain multiple mappings from different (source) COLLADA files into the same (target) KMZ file.

<Alias>

Contains a mapping from a <sourceHref> to a <targetHref>:

<targetHref>

Specifies the texture file to be fetched by the Earth browser. This reference can be a relative reference to an image file within the *.kmz* archive, or it can be an absolute reference to the file (for example, a URL).

<sourceHref>

Is the path specified for the texture file in the COLLADA *.dae* file.

Contained By

<MultiGeometry>, <Placemark>

‹MultiGeometry›

```
<MultiGeometry id="ID">
  <!-- 0 or more Geometry elements -->
</MultiGeometry>
```

Description

A container for zero or more geometry elements associated with the same feature.

Contained By

<MultiGeometry>, <Placemark>

Contains

0 or more Geometry elements

‹NetworkLink›

```
<NetworkLink id="ID">
  <!-- inherited from Feature element -->
  <name>...</name>                       <!-- string -->
  <visibility>1</visibility>             <!-- boolean -->
  <open>0</open>                         <!-- boolean -->
  <atom:author>...<atom:author>          <!-- xmlns:atom -->
  <atom:link />                           <!-- xmlns:atom -->
  <address>...</address>                 <!-- string -->
  <xal:AddressDetails>...</xal:AddressDetails>  <!-- xmlns:xal -->
  <phoneNumber>...</phoneNumber>         <!-- string -->
  <Snippet maxLines="2">...</Snippet>   <!-- string -->
  <description>...</description>         <!-- string -->
  <AbstractView>...</AbstractView>       <!-- Camera or LookAt -->
  <TimePrimitive>...</TimePrimitive>     <!-- TimeSpan or TimeStamp -->
  <styleUrl>...</styleUrl>               <!-- anyURI -->
  <StyleSelector>...</StyleSelector>     <!-- Style or StyleMap -->
  <Region>...</Region>
  <ExtendedData>...</ExtendedData>

  <!-- specific to NetworkLink -->
  <refreshVisibility>0</refreshVisibility> <!-- boolean -->
  <flyToView>0</flyToView>                 <!-- boolean -->
  <Link>...</Link>
</NetworkLink>
```

Description

References a KML file or KMZ archive on a local or remote network. Within the <Link> element, you can define the refresh options for updating the file. See Chapter 6, Network Links, and Chapter 8, Dealing with Large Data Sets.

Elements Specific to <NetworkLink>

<refreshVisibility>

> A value of 0 leaves the visibility of features within the control of the Earth browser user. A value of 1 resets the visibility of features each time the NetworkLink is refreshed.

<flyToView>

> A value of 0 specifies to ignore the AbstractView. A value of 1 causes the Earth browser to fly to the view of the <LookAt> or <Camera> specified in the <NetworkLinkControl> of the fetched KML file. See Chapter 6 for details.

<Link>

> Specifies the location of the KML or KMZ file. See <Link> element.

Contained By

Any element derived from Container

<NetworkLinkControl>

```
<NetworkLinkControl>
  <minRefreshPeriod>0.0</minRefreshPeriod>              <!-- double -->
  <maxSessionLength>-1.0</maxSessionLength>             <!-- double -->
  <cookie>...</cookie>                                  <!-- string -->
  <message>...</message>                                <!-- string -->
  <linkName>...</linkName>                              <!-- string -->
  <linkDescription>...</linkDescription>               <!-- string -->
  <linkSnippet maxLines="2">...</linkSnippet>          <!-- string -->
  <expires>...</expires>                                <!-- kml:dateTime -->
  <Update>...</Update>                     <!-- Change,Create,Delete -->
  <AbstractView>...</AbstractView>         <!-- LookAt or Camera -->
</NetworkLinkControl>
```

Description

Controls the behavior of files fetched by a <NetworkLink>. When a KML files fetches a <NetworkLink>, it also processes any <NetworkLinkControl> element it finds in the fetched KML file. The <linkName>, <linkDescription>, and <linkSnippet> elements operate on the file that contains the original <NetworkLink> (see Chapter 6, Network Links).

Elements Specific to <NetworkLinkControl>

<minRefreshPeriod>

> Specified in seconds, <minRefreshPeriod> is the minimum allowed time between fetches of the file. This parameter allows servers to throttle fetches of a particular file and to tailor refresh rates to the expected rate of change to the data.

<maxSessionLength>

> Specified in seconds, <maxSessionLength> is the maximum amount of time for which the client <NetworkLink> can remain connected. The default value of −1 indicates not to terminate the connection explicitly.

<cookie>

> Use this element to append a string to the URL query on the next refresh of the network link. You can use this data in a script to provide more intelligent handling on the server side, including version querying and conditional file delivery. See Chapter 6, Network Links.

<message>

> You can deliver a pop-up message, such as usage guidelines for your network link. The message appears when the network link is first loaded into the Earth browser, or when it is changed in the <NetworkLinkControl>.

<linkName>

> You can control the name of the network link from the server, so that changes made to the name on the client side are overridden by the server.

<linkDescription>

> You can control the description of the network link from the server, so that changes made to the description on the client side are overridden by the server.

<linkSnippet maxLines="2"**>**

> You can control the snippet for the network link from the server, so that changes made to the snippet on the client side are overridden by the server. <linkSnippet> has a maxLines attribute, an integer that specifies the maximum number of lines to display.

<expires>

You can specify a date/time at which the link should be refreshed. This specification takes effect only if the <refreshMode> in the <Link> of the fetching <NetworkLink> has a value of onExpire. See the <refreshMode> child of <Link>.

<Update>

With <Update>, you can specify any number of <Change>, <Create>, and <Delete> tags for a .kml file or .kmz archive that has previously been loaded with a network link. The child elements of <Update> are executed in the order they appear. See also Chapter 7, Dynamic KML.

<targetHref>

Specifies the KML to update. This file must be on the same server as the file that contains the Update KML file.

<Change>

Modifies the values in a KML element that has already been loaded with a <NetworkLink>. The child of the <Change> element can be any Object element. This object element must have an id defined for it in the original KML file. Within the Change element, the child to be modified must include a targetID attribute that references the original element's id. In the modified element, only the values listed in <Change> are replaced; all other values remain untouched. When <Change> is applied to a set of coordinates, the new coordinates replace the current coordinates.

<Create>

Adds an element to KML that has already been loaded with a <NetworkLink>. The child of the <Create> element is *always* a Container element (that is, either a <Document> or a <Folder>). This Container element must have an id defined for it in the original KML file. Within the Create element, the child to be created must include a targetID attribute that references the original element's id. After the update occurs, this new element becomes part of the original file. To perform subsequent updates on this element, use the URI of the original KML file.

<Delete>

Removes an element from a file that has already been loaded with a <NetworkLink>. The child of the <Delete> element is *always* a Feature element (<NetworkLink>, <Placemark>, <GroundOverlay>, <PhotoOverlay>, <ScreenOverlay>, <Document>, <Folder>). This object must have an id defined for it in the original KML file. Within the Delete element, the child to be deleted must include a `targetID` attribute that references the original element's `id`.

\<AbstractView\>

If the \<flyToView\> element in the calling \<NetworkLink\> has a value of 1, the view flies to the \<Camera\> or \<LookAt\> specified here.

Contained By

\<kml\>

See Also

\<NetworkLink\>

Object

```
<!-- abstract element; do not create -->
<!-- Object id="ID" targetId="NCName" -->
<!-- /Object> -->
```

Description

This is an abstract base class and cannot be used directly in a KML file. It provides the `id` attribute, which allows unique identification of a KML element, and the `targetId` attribute, which is used to reference objects that have already been loaded into the Earth browser and are the target of an Update operation. The `id` attribute must be assigned if the \<Update\> mechanism is to be used.

Overlay

```
<!-- Overlay  -->                     <!-- GroundOverlay, PhotoOverlay,
                                            ScreenOverlay -->

  <!-- inherited from Feature element -->
  <name>...</name>                        <!-- string -->
  <visibility>1</visibility>              <!-- boolean -->
  <open>0</open>                          <!-- boolean -->
  <atom:author>...<atom:author>           <!-- xmlns:atom -->
  <atom:link />                           <!-- xmlns:atom -->
  <address>...</address>                  <!-- string -->
  <xal:AddressDetails>...</xal:AddressDetails>  <!-- xmlns:xal -->
  <phoneNumber>...</phoneNumber>          <!-- string -->
```

```
<Snippet maxLines="2">...</Snippet>       <!-- string -->
<description>...</description>            <!-- string -->
<AbstractView>...</AbstractView>          <!-- Camera or LookAt -->
<TimePrimitive>...</TimePrimitive>        <!-- TimeSpan or TimeStamp -->
<styleUrl>...</styleUrl>                  <!-- anyURI -->
<StyleSelector>...</StyleSelector>        <!-- Style or StyleMap -->
<Region>...</Region>
<ExtendedData>...</ExtendedData>

<!-- specific to Overlay -->
<color>ffffffff</color>                          <!-- kml:color -->
<drawOrder>0</drawOrder>                          <!-- int -->
<Icon>
  <href>...</href>
  <refreshMode>onChange</refreshMode>
      <!-- kml:refreshModeEnum: onChange, onInterval, or onExpire -->
  <refreshInterval>4.0</refreshInterval>   <!-- float -->
  <viewRefreshMode>never</viewRefreshMode>
      <!-- kml:viewRefreshModeEnum: never, onStop, onRequest,
          onRegion -->
  <viewRefreshTime>4</viewRefreshTime>    <!-- float -->
  <viewBoundScale>1</viewBoundScale>      <!-- float -->
  <viewFormat>...</viewFormat>            <!-- string -->
  <httpQuery>...</httpQuery>              <!-- string -->
</Icon>
<!-- /Overlay -->
```

Description

This is an abstract element and cannot be used directly in a KML file. Overlay is the
base type for image overlays drawn on the planet surface or on the screen. <Icon> specifies the image to use and can be configured to reload images based on a timer or by
camera changes. This element also includes specifications for stacking order of multiple
overlays and for adding color and transparency values to the base image.

Elements Specific to Overlay

<color>

> Color values are expressed in hexadecimal notation, including opacity (alpha)
> values. The order of expression is alpha, blue, green, red (aabbggrr). The range of
> values for any one color is 0 to 255 (00 to ff). For opacity, 00 is fully transparent,
> and ff is fully opaque.

\<drawOrder\>

Specifies the stacking order for the images in overlapping overlays. The draw order is with respect to the camera and has nothing to do with the altitude of the overlays. The overlay with the largest \<drawOrder\> is drawn last (that is, closest to the camera).

\<Icon\>

Specifies the image associated with the Overlay. See \<Link\>.

\<href\>

Specifies the location of the image to be used as the Overlay. This location can be either on a local file system or on a web server. If this element is omitted or contains no \<href\>, a rectangle is drawn using the color and size defined by the ground or screen overlay.

\<refreshMode\>

For a description of \<refreshMode\> and the other elements listed below, see \<Link\>.

\<refreshInterval\>
\<viewRefreshMode\>
\<viewRefreshTime\>
\<viewBoundScale\>
\<viewFormat\>
\<httpQuery\>

⟨PhotoOverlay⟩

```
<PhotoOverlay>
  <!-- inherited from Feature element -->
  <name>...</name>                              <!-- string -->
  <visibility>1</visibility>                    <!-- boolean -->
  <open>0</open>                                <!-- boolean -->
  <atom:author>...<atom:author>                 <!-- xmlns:atom -->
  <atom:link />                                 <!-- xmlns:atom -->
  <address>...</address>                        <!-- string -->
  <xal:AddressDetails>...</xal:AddressDetails>  <!-- xmlns:xal -->
  <phoneNumber>...</phoneNumber>                <!-- string -->
  <Snippet maxLines="2">...</Snippet>           <!-- string -->
  <description>...</description>                 <!-- string -->
  <AbstractView>...</AbstractView>              <!-- Camera or LookAt -->
  <TimePrimitive>...</TimePrimitive>            <!-- TimeSpan or TimeStamp -->
  <styleUrl>...</styleUrl>                      <!-- anyURI -->
  <StyleSelector>...</StyleSelector>            <!-- Style or StyleMap -->
```

```
<Region>...</Region>
<ExtendedData>...</ExtendedData>

<!-- inherited from Overlay element -->
<color>ffffffff</color>                    <!-- kml:color -->
<drawOrder>0</drawOrder>                    <!-- int -->
<Icon>
  <href>...</href>                         <!-- anyURI -->
  ...
</Icon>

<!-- specific to PhotoOverlay -->
<rotation>0.0</rotation>                    <!-- kml:angle180 -->
<ViewVolume>
  <leftFov>0.0</leftFov>                    <!-- kml:angle180 -->
  <rightFov>0.0</rightFov>                  <!-- kml:angle180 -->
  <bottomFov>0.0</bottomFov>                <!-- kml:angle90 -->
  <topFov>0.0</topFov>                      <!-- kml:angle90 -->
  <near>0.0</near>                          <!-- double -->
</ViewVolume>
<ImagePyramid>
  <tileSize>256</tileSize>             <!-- int -->
  <maxWidth>0</maxWidth>               <!-- int -->
  <maxHeight>0</maxHeight>             <!-- int -->
  <gridOrigin>lowerLeft</gridOrigin>   <!-- lowerLeft or upperLeft -->
</ImagePyramid>
<Point>...</Point>
<shape>rectangle</shape>              <!-- rectangle,cylinder,sphere -->
</PhotoOverlay>
```

Description

The <PhotoOverlay> element allows you to geographically locate a photograph on the Earth and to specify viewing parameters for this photo. The PhotoOverlay can be a simple 2D rectangle, a partial or full cylinder, or a sphere (for spherical panoramas). The overlay is placed at the specified location and oriented toward the viewpoint.

Because <PhotoOverlay> is derived from Feature, it can contain one of the two elements derived from AbstractView—either <Camera> or <LookAt>. The <Camera> (or <LookAt>) specifies a viewpoint and a viewing direction (also referred to as a *view vector*). The PhotoOverlay is positioned in relation to the viewpoint. Specifically, the plane of a 2D rectangular image is orthogonal (at right angles) to the view vector. The normal of this plane—that is, its front, which is the part with the photo—is oriented toward the viewpoint.

The URL for the <PhotoOverlay> image is specified in the <Icon> element. The <Icon> element must contain an <href> element that specifies the image file to use for the <PhotoOverlay>. In the case of a very large image, the <href> is a special URL that indexes into a pyramid of images of varying resolutions. See Chapter 5, Overlays.

Elements Specific to <PhotoOverlay>

<rotation>

Adjusts how the photo is placed inside the field of view. This element is useful if your photo has been rotated and deviates slightly from a desired horizontal view.

<ViewVolume>

Defines how much of the current scene is visible. Specifying the field of view is analogous to specifying the lens opening in a physical camera. A small field of view, like that of a telephoto lens, focuses on a small part of the scene. A large field of view, like that of a wide-angle lens, focuses on a large part of the scene.

<leftFov>

Angle, in degrees, between the camera's viewing direction and the left side of the view volume.

<rightFov>

Angle, in degrees, between the camera's viewing direction and the right side of the view volume.

<bottomFov>

Angle, in degrees, between the camera's viewing direction and the bottom side of the view volume.

<topFov>

Angle, in degrees, between the camera's viewing direction and the top side of the view volume.

<near>

Measurement in meters along the viewing direction from the camera viewpoint to the <PhotoOverlay> shape.

<ImagePyramid>

For very large images, you'll need to construct an image pyramid, which is a hierarchical set of images, each of which is an increasingly lower resolution version of the original image. Each image in the pyramid is subdivided into tiles, so that only the portions in view need to be loaded. The Earth browser calculates the current viewpoint and loads the tiles that are appropriate to the user's distance from the image.

When you specify an image pyramid, you also modify the <href> in the <Icon> element to include specifications for which tiles to load. See Chapter 5, Overlays.

<tileSize>

Size of the tiles, in pixels. Tiles must be square, and <tileSize> must be a power of 2. A tile size of 256 (the default) or 512 is recommended. The original image is divided into tiles of this size, at varying resolutions.

<maxWidth>

Width in pixels of the original image.

<maxHeight>

Height in pixels of the original image.

<gridOrigin>

Specifies where to begin numbering the tiles in each layer of the pyramid. A value of lowerLeft specifies that row 1, column 1 of each layer is in the bottom-left corner of the grid.

<Point>

This <Point> element functions in the same way as the <Point> inside a <Placemark> element. It draws an icon to mark the position of the photo overlay. The icon drawn is specified by the <styleUrl> and StyleSelector fields, just as it is for <Placemark>.

<coordinates>

Location where the icon is drawn for this photo overlay.

<shape>

The photo overlay is projected onto the <shape>. The <shape> can be one of the following:

`rectangle` (default)
  For an ordinary photo

`cylinder`
  For panoramas, which can be either partial or full cylinders

`sphere`
  For spherical panoramas

<Folder>, <Document>, or <kml>

‹Placemark›

```
<Placemark id="ID">
  <!-- inherited from Feature element -->
  <name>...</name>                        <!-- string -->
  <visibility>1</visibility>              <!-- boolean -->
  <open>0</open>                          <!-- boolean -->
  <atom:author>...<atom:author>           <!-- xmlns:atom -->
  <atom:link />                           <!-- xmlns:atom -->
  <address>...</address>                  <!-- string -->
  <xal:AddressDetails>...</xal:AddressDetails>  <!-- xmlns:xal -->
  <phoneNumber>...</phoneNumber>          <!-- string -->
  <Snippet maxLines="2">...</Snippet>     <!-- string -->
  <description>...</description>          <!-- string -->
  <AbstractView>...</AbstractView>        <!-- Camera or LookAt -->
  <TimePrimitive>...</TimePrimitive>      <!-- TimeSpan or TimeStamp -->
  <styleUrl>...</styleUrl>                <!-- anyURI -->
  <StyleSelector>...</StyleSelector>      <!-- Style or StyleMap -->
  <Region>...</Region>
  <ExtendedData>...</ExtendedData>

  <!-- specific to Placemark element -->
  <Geometry>...</Geometry>
        <!-- Point,LineString,LinearRing,Polygon,MultiGeometry,Model -->
</Placemark>
```

Description

A <Placemark> is a Feature with associated Geometry. In Google Earth, a placemark appears as an item in the list view. A <Placemark> with a <Point> has an icon associated with it that marks a point on the Earth in the 3D viewer.

Note that a <Placemark> is the only place to put Geometry elements in KML.

In the Google Earth 3D viewer, a point placemark is the only object you can click or roll over. Other Geometry objects do not have an icon in the 3D viewer. To give the user something to click in the 3D viewer, you would need to create a MultiGeometry object that contains both a <Point> and the other Geometry object. See also <Icon>.

Contained By

<Document>, <Folder>

Contains

0 or 1 <Geometry> elements (Multiple Geometry elements can be asssociated with a placemark using the <MultiGeometry> element.)

‹Point›

```
<Point id="ID">
  <!-- specific to Point -->
  <extrude>0</extrude>                      <!-- boolean -->
  <altitudeMode>clampToGround</altitudeMode>
    <!-- kml:altitudeModeEnum: clampToGround, relativeToGround,
         or absolute -->
  <coordinates>...</coordinates>            <!-- lon,lat[,alt] -->
</Point>
```

Description

A geographic location defined by longitude, latitude, and (optional) altitude. If the altitude value is not specified, it is assumed to be 0. When a <Point> is contained by a <Placemark>, the point itself determines the position of the placemark's name and icon. When a point is extruded, it is connected to the ground with a line. This "tether" uses the current <LineStyle>.

Elements Specific to ‹Point›

<extrude>

Specifies whether to connect the point to the ground with a line. To extrude a point, the value for <altitudeMode> must be either relativeToGround or absolute, and the altitude component within the <coordinates> element must be greater than 0 (that is, in the air). The point is extruded toward the center of the Earth's sphere.

<altitudeMode>

Specifies how altitude components in the <coordinates> element are interpreted. Possible values are clampToGround, relativeToGround, and absolute. See Chapter 3, Geometry, for a discussion of these modes.

<coordinates>

A single tuple consisting of floating point values for longitude, latitude, and altitude (in that order). Longitude and latitude values are in degrees. Altitude values (optional) are in meters above sea level. The default altitude value is 0. Altitude values are ignored if the <altitudeMode> is clampToGround. Do not include spaces between the three values that describe a coordinate.

longitude   −180 and ≤ 180

latitude   −90 and ≤ 90

Contained By

<MultiGeometry>, <Placemark>

‹Polygon›

```
<Polygon id="ID">
  <extrude>0</extrude>                          <!-- boolean -->
  <tessellate>0</tessellate>                    <!-- boolean -->
  <altitudeMode>clampToGround</altitudeMode>
    <!-- kml:altitudeModeEnum: clampToGround, relativeToGround,
         or absolute -->
  <outerBoundaryIs>
    <LinearRing>
      <coordinates>...</coordinates>            <!-- lon,lat[,alt] -->
    </LinearRing>
  </outerBoundaryIs>
  <innerBoundaryIs>        <!-- can include multiple inner boundaries -->
    <LinearRing>
      <coordinates>...</coordinates>            <!-- lon,lat[,alt] -->
    </LinearRing>
  </innerBoundaryIs>
</Polygon>
```

Description

A <Polygon> is defined by an outer boundary and 0 or more inner boundaries. The boundaries, in turn, are defined by linear rings. When a polygon is extruded, its boundaries are connected to the ground to form additional polygons, which give the appearance of a building or a box. Extruded polygons use <PolyStyle> for their color, color mode, and fill.

Elements Specific to ‹Polygon›

<extrude>

> Specifies whether to connect the polygon to the ground. To extrude a polygon, the value for <altitudeMode> must be either relativeToGround or absolute, and the altitude component within the <coordinates> element must be greater than 0 (that is, in the air). Only the vertices are extruded, not the geometry itself (for example, a rectangle turns into a box with five faces). The vertices of the polygon are extruded toward the center of the Earth's sphere.

<tessellate>

> Specifies whether to allow the polygon to follow the terrain. To enable tessellation, the polygon must have an <altitudeMode> of clampToGround. Very large polygons should enable tessellation so that they follow the curvature of the Earth (otherwise, they may go underground and be hidden).

<altitudeMode>

> Specifies how altitude components in the <coordinates> element are interpreted. Possible values are clampToGround, relativeToGround, and absolute. See Chapter 3, Geometry, for a discussion of these modes.

<outerBoundaryIs>

> Contains a <LinearRing> element.

> <LinearRing>
>> See <LinearRing>.

<innerBoundaryIs>

> Contains a <LinearRing> element. A <Polygon> can contain multiple <inner-BoundaryIs> elements, which create multiple cut-outs inside the polygon.

> <LinearRing>
>> <See LinearRing>.

Contained By

<MultiGeometry>, <Placemark>

‹PolyStyle›

```
<PolyStyle id="ID">
  <!-- inherited from ColorStyle -->
  <color>ffffffff</color>                <!-- kml:color -->
  <colorMode>normal</colorMode>
    <!-- kml:colorModeEnum: normal or random -->

  <!-- specific to PolyStyle -->
  <fill>1</fill>                         <!-- boolean -->
  <outline>1</outline>                   <!-- boolean -->
</PolyStyle>
```

Description

Specifies the drawing style for all polygons, including polygon extrusions (which look like the walls of buildings) and line extrusions (which look like solid fences).

Elements Specific to ‹PolyStyle›

‹fill›

Specifies whether to fill the polygon.

‹outline›

Specifies whether to outline the polygon. Polygon outlines use the current ‹LineStyle›.

Contained By

‹Style›

‹Region›

```
<Region id="ID">
  <LatLonAltBox id="ID">
    <north>180.0</north>                   <!-- kml:angle180 -->
    <south>-180.0</south>                  <!-- kml:angle180 -->
    <east>180.0</east>                     <!-- kml:angle180 -->
    <west>-180.0</west>                    <!-- kml:angle180 -->
    <minAltitude>0.0</minAltitude>         <!-- double -->
    <maxAltitude>0.0</maxAltitude>         <!-- double -->
    <altitudeMode>clampToGround</altitudeMode>
      <!-- kml:altitudeModeEnum: clampToGround,
           relativeToGround, or absolute -->
```

```
  </LatLonAltBox>
  <Lod id="ID">
    <minLodPixels>0.0</minLodPixels>          <!-- double -->
    <maxLodPixels>-1.0</maxLodPixels>         <!-- double -->
    <minFadeExtent>0.0</minFadeExtent>        <!-- double -->
    <maxFadeExtent>0.0</maxFadeExtent>        <!-- double -->
  </Lod>
</Region>
```

Description

A <Region> contains a bounding box (<LatLonAltBox>) that describes an area of interest defined by geographic coordinates and altitudes. In addition, a <Region> contains an LOD (level of detail) extent (<Lod>) that defines a validity range of the associated Region in terms of projected screen size. A region is said to be "active" when the bounding box is within the user's view and the LOD requirements are met. Geometries and overlays associated with a region are drawn only when the region is active. When the <viewRefreshMode> is onRegion, the <Link> or <Icon> is loaded only when the region is active. In a Container or <NetworkLink> hierarchy, a Feature is affected by its child <Region>, if present; if a Feature does not contain a <Region>, it uses the <Region> that is the closest ancestor in the hierarchy. See Chapter 8, Dealing with Large Data Sets.

Elements Specific to <Region>

<LatLonAltBox>

> A bounding box that describes an area of interest defined by geographic coordinates and altitudes. Default values and required fields are as follows:

> <north>
>> Specifies the latitude of the north edge of the bounding box, in decimal degrees from 0 to ±90.

> <south>
>> Specifies the latitude of the south edge of the bounding box, in decimal degrees from 0 to ±90.

> <east>
>> Specifies the longitude of the east edge of the bounding box, in decimal degrees from 0 to ±180.

> <west>
>> Specifies the longitude of the west edge of the bounding box, in decimal degrees from 0 to ±180.

<minAltitude>

> Specified in meters above sea level (and is affected by the <altitudeMode> specification).

<maxAltitude>

> Specified in meters above sea level (and is affected by the <altitudeMode> specification).

<altitudeMode>

> Specifies how altitude components in the <minAltitude> and <maxAltitude> elements are interpreted. Possible values are `clampToGround`, `relativeToGround`, and `absolute`. See Chapter 3, Geometry, for a discussion of these modes.

<Lod>

> Lod is an abbreviation for Level of Detail. <Lod> describes the size of the projected region on the screen that is required for the region to be considered "active." Also specifies the size of the pixel ramp used for fading between transparent and opaque.

<minLodPixels>

> Measurement in screen pixels that represents the minimum limit of the visibility range for a given Region. The Earth browser calculates the size of the Region when projected onto screen space. Then it computes the square root of the Region's area. (If, for example, the Region is square and the viewpoint is directly above the Region, and the Region is not tilted, this measurement is equal to the width of the projected Region.) If this measurement falls within the limits defined by <minLodPixels> and <maxLodPixels> (and if the <LatLonAltBox> is in view), the Region is active.

<maxLodPixels>

> Measurement in screen pixels that represents the maximum limit of the visibility range for a given Region. A value of −1, the default, indicates "active to infinite size."

<minFadeExtent>

> Distance over which the geometry fades between fully opaque and fully transparent. This ramp value, expressed in screen pixels, is applied at the minimum end of the LOD (visibility) limits.

<maxFadeExtent>
> Distance over which the geometry fades between fully opaque and fully transparent. This ramp value, expressed in screen pixels, is applied at the maximum end of the LOD (visibility) limits.

Contained By

Any element derived from Feature

‹Schema›

```
<Schema name="string" id="ID">
  <SimpleField type="string" name="string">
    <displayName>...</displayName>                <!-- string -->
  </SimpleField>
</Schema>
```

Description

Specifies a custom KML schema that is used to add custom data to KML Features. The id attribute is required and must be unique within the KML file. See Chapter 8, Dealing with Large Data Sets.

Elements Specific to ‹Schema›

<SimpleField type="string" name="string">
> The declaration of the custom field, which must specify both the type and the name of this field. If either the type or the name is omitted, the field is ignored. The type can be one of the following: string, int, uint, short, ushort, float, double, bool.

<displayName>
> The name, if any, to be used when the field name is displayed in the Earth browser. Use the [CDATA] element to escape standard HTML markup.

Contained By

<Document>

See Also

<ExtendedData>

‹ScreenOverlay›

```
<ScreenOverlay id="ID">
  <!-- inherited from Feature element -->
  <name>...</name>                            <!-- string -->
  <visibility>1</visibility>                  <!-- boolean -->
  <open>0</open>                              <!-- boolean -->
  <atom:author>...<atom:author>               <!-- xmlns:atom -->
  <atom:link />                               <!-- xmlns:atom -->
  <address>...</address>                      <!-- string -->
  <xal:AddressDetails>...</xal:AddressDetails>  <!-- xmlns:xal -->
  <phoneNumber>...</phoneNumber>              <!-- string -->
  <Snippet maxLines="2">...</Snippet>        <!-- string -->
  <description>...</description>              <!-- string -->
  <AbstractView>...</AbstractView>           <!-- Camera or LookAt -->
  <TimePrimitive>...</TimePrimitive>         <!-- TimeSpan or TimeStamp -->
  <styleUrl>...</styleUrl>                   <!-- anyURI -->
  <StyleSelector>...</StyleSelector>         <!-- Style or StyleMap -->
  <Region>...</Region>
  <ExtendedData>...</ExtendedData>

  <!-- inherited from Overlay element -->
  <color>ffffffff</color>                    <!-- kml:color -->
  <drawOrder>0</drawOrder>                   <!-- int -->
  <Icon>...</Icon>

  <!-- specific to ScreenOverlay -->
  <overlayXY x="double" y="double" xunits="fraction" yunits="fraction"/>
      <!-- vec2 -->
      <!-- xunits and yunits can be one of:
           fraction, pixels, or insetPixels -->
  <screenXY x="double" y="double" xunits="fraction" yunits="fraction"/>
      <!-- vec2 -->
  <rotationXY x="double" y="double" xunits="fraction" yunits"fraction"/>
      <!-- vec2 -->
  <size x="double" y="double" xunits="fraction" yunits="fraction"/>
      <!-- vec2 -->
  <rotation>0.0</rotation>                    <!-- angle180 -->
</ScreenOverlay>
```

Description

This element draws an image overlay fixed to the screen. Sample uses for screen overlays are compasses, logos, and heads-up displays. Screen overlay sizing is determined by the

<size> element. Positioning of the overlay is handled by mapping a point in the image specified by <overlayXY> to a point on the screen specified by <screenXY>. Then the image is rotated by <rotation> degrees about a point relative to the screen specified by <rotationXY>.

The <href> child of <Icon> specifies the image to use as the overlay. This file can be either on a local file system or on a web server. If this element is omitted or contains no <href>, a rectangle is drawn using the color and size defined by the screen overlay.

Elements Specific to <ScreenOverlay>

<overlayXY x="double" y="double" xunits="fraction" yunits="fraction"/>
Specifies a point on (or outside of) the overlay image that is mapped to the screen coordinate (<screenXY>). The origin of the coordinate system is in the lower-left corner of the image. See Chapter 5, "Overlays," for a detailed description of xunits and yunits.

<screenXY x="double" y="double" xunits="fraction" yunits="fraction"/>
Specifies a point relative to the screen origin that the overlay image is mapped to. The origin of the coordinate system is in the lower-left corner of the screen.

<rotationXY x="double" y="double" xunits="fraction" yunits"fraction"/>
Point relative to the screen about which the screen overlay is rotated.

<size x="double" y="double" xunits="fraction" yunits="fraction"/>
Specifies the size of the image for the screen overlay, as follows:

- A value of −1 indicates to use the native dimension.
- A value of 0 indicates to maintain the aspect ratio.
- A value of n sets the value of the dimension.

<rotation>
Indicates the angle of rotation of the parent object. A value of 0 means no rotation. The value is an angle in degrees counterclockwise starting from north. Use ±180 to indicate the rotation of the parent object from 0. The center of the <rotation>, if not (.5,.5), is specified in <rotationXY>.

Contained By

<Document>, <Folder>

‹Style›

```
<Style id="ID">
  <IconStyle>...</IconStyle>
  <LabelStyle>...</LabelStyle>
  <LineStyle>...</LineStyle>
  <PolyStyle>...</PolyStyle>
  <BalloonStyle>...</BalloonStyle>
  <ListStyle>...</ListStyle>
</Style>
```

Description

A <Style> defines an addressable style group that can be referenced by <StyleMap> and Features. Styles affect how Geometry is presented in the 3D viewer and how Features appear in the Places panel of the list view. Shared styles are collected in a <Document> and must have an id defined for them so that they can be referenced by the individual Features that use them.

Use an id to refer to the style from a <styleUrl>.

Contained By

Any element derived from Feature.

Contains

<IconStyle>, <LabelStyle>, <LineStyle>, <PolyStyle>, <BalloonStyle>, <ListStyle>

‹StyleMap›

```
<StyleMap id="ID">
  <Pair id="ID">
    <key>normal</key>
        <!-- kml:styleStateEnum:  normal or highlight -->
    <styleUrl>...</styleUrl> or <Style>...</Style>
  </Pair>
</StyleMap>
```

Description

A <StyleMap> maps between two different styles. Typically, a <StyleMap> element is used to provide separate normal and highlighted styles for a placemark, so that the highlighted version appears when the user mouses over the icon in the Earth browser. See Chapter 4, Styles and Icons.

Elements Specific to <StyleMap>

<Pair>

Defines a key/value pair that maps a mode (normal or highlight) to the predefined <styleUrl>. <Pair> contains two elements (both are required):

<key>

Identifies the mode, which is either `normal` or `highlight`

<styleUrl>

References the style. For referenced style elements that are local to the KML document, a simple # referencing is used. For styles that are contained in external files, use a full URL along with # referencing.

Contained By

Any element derived from Feature.

StyleSelector

```
<!-- StyleSelector id="ID" -->          <!-- Style or StyleMap -->
<!-- /StyleSelector -->
```

Description

This is an abstract element and cannot be used directly in a KML file. It is the base element for the <Style> and <StyleMap> elements. See Chapter 4, Styles and Icons.

See Also

<Style>, <StyleMap>

TimePrimitive

```
<!-- TimePrimitive id="ID" -->          <!-- TimeSpan,TimeStamp -->
<!-- /TimePrimitive -->
```

Description

This is an abstract element and cannot be used directly in a KML file. It is the base element for the <TimeSpan> and <TimeStamp> elements.

<TimeSpan>, <TimeStamp>

‹TimeSpan›

```
<TimeSpan id="ID">
  <begin>...</begin>        <!-- kml:dateTime -->
  <end>...</end>            <!-- kml:dateTime -->
</TimeSpan>
```

Description

Represents an extent in time bounded by begin and end `dateTimes`.

If <begin> or <end> is missing, then that span of the period is unbounded.

The `dateTime` is defined according to XML Schema time (see *XML Schema Part 2: Datatypes Second Edition*). The value can be expressed as **yyyy-mm-dd**T**hh:mm:ss**zzzzzz, where T is the separator between the date and the time, and the time zone is either Z (for UTC) or *zzzzzz*, which represents ±*hh:mm* in relation to UTC. Additionally, the value can be expressed as a date only. See Chapter 7, Dynamic KML.

Elements Specific to ‹TimeSpan›

<begin>
Specifies the beginning instant of a time period. If absent, the beginning of the period is unbounded.

<end>
Specifies the ending instant of a time period. If absent, the end of the period is unbounded.

Contained By

Any element derived from Feature.

‹TimeStamp›

```
<TimeStamp id=ID>
  <when>...</when>          <!-- kml:dateTime -->
</TimeStamp>
```

Description

Represents a single moment in time. The `dateTime` is specified in XML time (see *XML Schema Part 2: Datatypes Second Edition*). The precision of the TimeStamp is dictated by the `dateTime` value in the <when> element. See Chapter 7, Dynamic KML.

Elements Specific to <TimeStamp>

<when>

> Specifies a single moment in time. The value is a `dateTime`, which can be one of the following:
>
> - dateTime (*YYYY-MM-DDThh:mm:ssZ*) gives second resolution.
> - date (*YYYY-MM-DD*) gives day resolution.
> - gYearMonth (*YYYY-MM*) gives month resolution.
> - gYear (*YYYY*) gives year resolution.

Contained By

Any element derived from Feature.

Appendix B

Sky Data in KML

You can create KML files that display objects in the sky, such as stars, constellations, planets, the Earth's moon, and galaxies. This appendix explains how to create a KML file to display celestial data in an Earth browser that supports Sky data, such as Google Earth or Microsoft's WorldWide Telescope. Specifically, you'll need to do the following:

- Add a hint attribute to the <kml> element at the beginning of the KML file to indicate that the file contains sky data, not Earth data
- Convert celestial coordinates to Earth-based KML coordinates

Sky Mode

The Google Earth user can control when to switch to Sky mode, using the View > Switch to Sky menu option or the Sky button in the user interface. When the user switches to Sky mode, Google Earth transitions to show images of the sky photographed from telescopes around the world and in outer space. The view of the sky is as if the user is standing at the center of the Earth's sphere, looking outward toward the heavens. This model allows users to explore the sky above their heads as well as parts of the celestial sphere that would normally be seen only from the other side of the Earth.

Coordinates

Celestial coordinates are described in terms of right ascension (RA) and declination (DEC). Right ascension, which corresponds to longitude, represents a distance from the point in the sky where the sun crosses the celestial equator at the vernal equinox. Right ascension is measured from 0 to 24 hours, with one hour of RA equal to the amount the sky rotates above a given point on the Earth's surface in one hour of time. Zero hours of RA is at the point of the vernal equinox, with RA increasing eastward from that point.

Declination is analogous to latitude, with 0 degrees declination located at the celestial equator. Declination values range from −90° directly above the South Pole to +90° directly above the North Pole.

The idea behind the RA/DEC coordinate system is that the coordinates map directly into the apparent motion of the stars due to the rotation of the Earth. If you're at a latitude of 20.0 on the Earth, the zenith point on the sky above you will also be at DEC=20.0. That zenith point will move around the sky at a constant DEC until it reaches the same point on the sky at the end of the sidereal day.

Figure B-1 shows Google Sky with grid lines for right ascension and declination turned on.

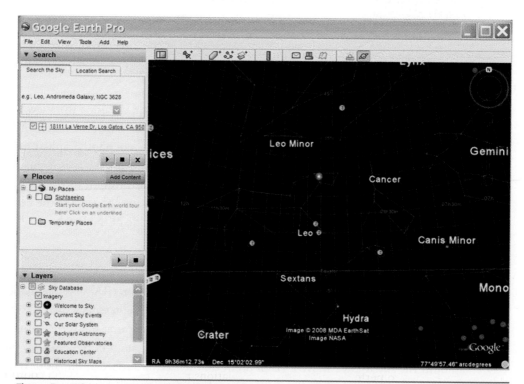

Figure B-1 When sky data is shown in an Earth browser, right ascension corresponds to longitude, and declination corresponds to latitude.

Supported Elements

Check the documentation for your Earth browser to determine which KML elements it supports. For example, the following elements are supported in Sky mode for Google Earth, Release 4.3:

- Placemark
- Ground Overlay
- LineString
- Polygon
- MultiGeometry
- LinearRing
- Point
- Style elements
- Container elements

Note, however, that <tilt> and <roll> are currently ignored in these elements.

The "hint" Attribute

If your KML file contains Sky data, be sure to add the hint attribute to the <kml> element at the beginning of the file:

```
<kml xmlns="http://www.opengis.net/kml/2.2" hint="target=sky">
```

When a file with the "target=sky" hint is loaded, Google Earth prompts the user to switch to Sky view if it is not already in this mode.

Converting Celestial Coordinates for Display in Google Earth

You'll need to perform some simple calculations to convert right ascension coordinates (Hours/Minutes/Seconds) into degrees of longitude so that the data displays correctly in Google Earth (Sky mode).

Convert Right Ascension Coordinates

To convert right ascension coordinates from values in a range from 0 to 24 to values in the range from −180 degrees to +180 degrees, use this formula, where hour, minute, and second are the original right ascension values of the data:

```
(hour + minute/60 + second/3600)*15 - 180
```

Convert Declination Coordinates

Declination coordinates correspond directly to latitude values, ranging from −90 degrees South of the celestial equator to +90 degrees North of the celestial equator.

Calculating Range for the LookAt Element

When you use the <LookAt> element with sky data, you will need to perform the following calculations to determine the range. The basic formula is as follows (also see Figure B-2):

```
r = R*(k*sin(β/2) - cos(β/2) + 1)
```

where

    r is the range, specified in the <LookAt> element.

    R is the radius of the celestial sphere (or, in this case, the Earth, since we're effectively inside it looking out at the sky), which is equal to 6.378×10^6.

    k is equal to $1/\tan(\alpha/2)$, or 1.1917536.

    α is the angular extent of the view in Google Earth when the camera is pulled back to the center of the celestial sphere (Earth).

    β is the desired arc seconds of your sky image.

Here are some sample ranges:

- Large spiral galaxy (Sunflower Galaxy): 20–30 km
- Large globular cluster (M15): 20–30 km
- Andromeda Galaxy: 200 km
- Planetary Nebula (Owl Nebula): 5–10 km
- Large Nebula (Trifid Nebula): 10–30 km

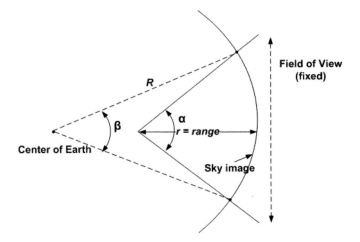

Figure B-2 When Sky data is viewed using KML, the field of view is fixed because the virtual viewpoint is at the center of the Earth, viewing the inside of the Earth's surface, with the celestial data projected onto this surface.

- Single Hubble Pointing (Seyfert's Sextet): 2–5 km
- Open star cluster (Praesepe): 30–60 km
- Smaller spiral galaxy: 5–10 km
- Large Magellanic Cloud: 400–500 km

Placemark Example

CrabNebula.kml is an example of creating a KML file that shows the Crab Nebula in Google Earth.

CrabNebula.kml

```
<?xml version="1.0" encoding="UTF-8"?>
<kml xmlns="http://www.opengis.net/kml/2.2" hint="target=sky">
<Document>
  <Style id="CrabNebula">
    <BalloonStyle>
      <text><center><b>$[name]</b></center><br/>$[description]</text>
    </BalloonStyle>
  </Style>
```

```
<Placemark>
  <name>Crab Nebula</name>
  <description>
    <![CDATA[
      This is the Crab Nebula. It is the remnant of a supernovae that
      was observed on Earth in 1054 CE. You can find out more about
      the Crab Nebula by looking at the information in the default
      layers, specifically:
      <ul>
        <li> <b>Backyard Astronomy</b>
        <li> <b>Hubble Showcase</b>
        <li> <b>Life of a Star</b>
      </ul>
      Enjoy exploring Sky!
    ]]>
  </description>
  <LookAt>
    <longitude>-96.366783</longitude>
    <latitude>22.014467</latitude>
    <altitude>0</altitude>
    <range>10000</range>
    <tilt>0</tilt>
    <heading>0</heading>
  </LookAt>
  <styleUrl>#CrabNebula</styleUrl>
  <Point>
    <coordinates>-96.366783,22.014467,0</coordinates>
  </Point>
</Placemark>
</Document>
</kml>
```

Figure B-3 shows how this file appears in Google Earth.

Adding an Overlay to Sky in KML

There are two basic techniques for creating an image overlay for sky data in Google Earth:

- Use the graphical user interface in Google Earth to match up the image overlay with the base imagery supplied by Google Earth. This method works well for relatively

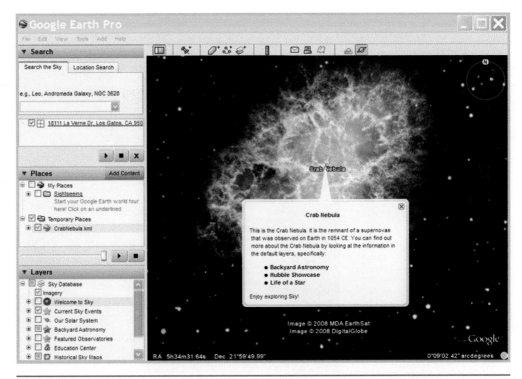

Figure B-3 Showing celestial data in Google Earth requires a simple recalculation of the ‹LookAt› element to control the view. Creating balloons in Sky mode is identical to creating them in "Earth" mode.

small areas of imagery. Be sure to save the file in Google Earth while you are still in Sky mode.

- Use a software utility such as **wcs2kml**, an open-source software package that reprojects data from world coordinate system (WCS) coordinates to KML. This method is commonly used for larger images and is easier than performing the mathematical calculations for converting between coordinate systems. The source file uses FITS (Flexible Image Transfer System) coordinates, which is the file format commonly used by astronomers.

The following example creates an image overlay using an image captured by the Hubble Space Telescope.

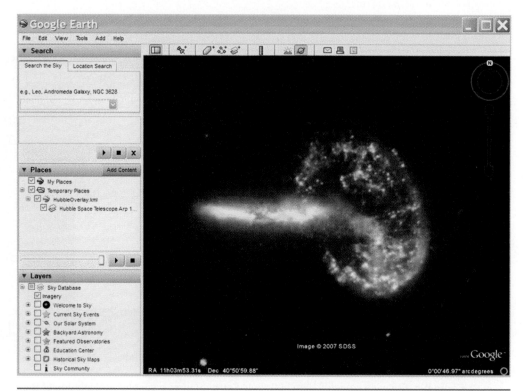

Figure B-4 Overlay image of Arp 148, the result of a collision between two galaxies located approximately 500 million light years away. www.spacetelescope.org/images/archive/top100/. Image from NASA, ESA, the Hubble Heritage Team (STScI/AURA)-ESA/Hubble Collaboration and A. Evans (University of Virginia, Charlottesville/NRAO/Stony Brook University), K. Noll (STScI), and J. Westphal (Caltech). Used with permission.

HubbleOverlay.kml

```
<?xml version="1.0" encoding="UTF-8"?>
<kml xmlns="http://www.opengis.net/kml/2.2" hint="target=sky">
<Document>
  <GroundOverlay>
    <name>Hubble Space Telescope Arp 148 Overlay</name>
    <LookAt>
      <longitude>-14.0270365795</longitude>
      <latitude>40.8499721419</latitude>
      <heading>0.00</heading>
      <range>2240.10965285</range>
      <altitudeMode>absolute</altitudeMode>
    </LookAt>
```

```
        <LatLonBox>
            <north>40.85706883329747</north>
            <south>40.84287545048161</south>
            <west>-14.03641921662847</west>
            <east>-14.01765394233431</east>
            <rotation>0</rotation>
        </LatLonBox>
        <Icon>
            <href>warped_image.png</href>
        </Icon>
    </GroundOverlay>
</Document>
</kml>
```

Index

A

absolute, as value, 33, 48, 224, 279
absolute file references, 152, 153
abstract elements, 40, 74, 262
AbstractView, 174, 265, 276 , 300
<address>, 274
AdvancedTemplate.kml, 30–31
Alaska Volcano Observatory examples, 5, 147, 158, 160–164
<Alias>, 68, 295
<altitude>, 32, 46, 48, 49, 118, 125–126, 267, 279, 292, 294
<altitudeMode>, 32, 33, 46, 48, 49, 118, 125–126, 224, 268, 279, 284, 285, 293, 294, 307, 309, 312
altitudeModeEnum type, 264
aMyPlacemark.kml, 184
angle180 type, 264
angle360 type, 264
angle90 type, 264
anglepos180 type, 264
animated ground overlays, 208
animated placemarks, 204
animation, using time elements, 195
Apache server, 151
aPlacemark.kml, 186, 188
arbitrary XML data, 245, 247
Ashbridge, Michael, xvii
astronomical coordinates
    conversion of, 324
    in KML, 8, 321–322
Atom Syndication Format, 70, 274
<atom:author>, 274
<atom:link href= >, 274
attributes, 81

AugustineWebcam.kml, 157–158
AugustineWebcamRevised.kml, 175–176
author elements, 70
AvianFluExcerpt.kml, 196, 204–208

B

background color, of balloon, 24
;balloon anchor, 38
;balloonFlyto anchor, 38
balloons, 11
    adding color elements to, 24–29
    adding hyperlinks to, 21
    adding images to, 21–22
    adding text to, 19–20
    adding typographical features to, 20
    default, 16, 18, 88
    templates for, 22–24, 30–31
<BalloonStyle>, 16, 17, 72, 87–88, 265
    using as template, 250
BalloonStyle.kml, 88–91
BalloonStyleTemplate.kml, 250–251
BalloonTemplate.kml, 22–24
BasicNetworkLink.kml, 175
<begin>, 200, 318
<bgColor>, 88, 91, 265, 291
boldface, 20
bOnePlacemark.kml, 184
boolean type, 264
Boolean values, defined, 77
bOriginalPlacemark.kml, 186
bOriginalPlacemarks.kml, 188–189
<bottomFov>, 135, 304
bounding box, 165, 216–217

O

OASIS xAL 2.0, 274
Object abstract base class, 300
object model, 171
ogckml22.xsd, 263
Ogle Earth, 4
Oklahoma example, 78
onChange value, 155, 159
onExpire value, 156, 159, 173
onInterval value, 155, 159
onRegion value, 156, 222
onRequest value, 156
onStop value, 156
<open>, 40, 274
Open Geospatial Consortium (OpenGIS), xiii,
    2, 264
order, importance of, 12, 262
<Orientation>, 66, 294
<outline>, 58, 310
<outerBoundaryIs>, 309
Overlay, 300–302
   syntax of, 114
overlays, 110
   common features of, 114–116
   creating, 112
   refreshing, 116
   types of, 110–111
<overlayXY>, 131, 315
overrides, server, 174

P

<Pair>, 317
PaleoGlobeExcerpt.kml, 209–211
paragraph spacing, 20
parent elements, 12, 262
paths, 48
<phoneNumber>, 274
<PhotoOverlay>, 133, 302–306
   features of, 134–136
   syntax for, 133–134
   use of, 133
PhotoOverlay.kml, 142–143
photo overlays, 111–112
   creating, 137
pixels units, 129

Pizzas.kml, 167, 168
<Placemark>, 11, 16, 306–307
   dividing into <Region>s, 233–234
   Geometry elements in, 18
   with <Point> child, 18
placemarks, 9, 40
   animation of, 200–208
   children of, 39
   flying to, 38
   syntax of, 39
<Point>, 11, 12, 46, 81, 134, 305, 307–308
   in placemarks, 18, 101
poly styles, 46, 58
<Polygon>, 18, 46, 56, 308–309
polygons, 55
   at altitude, 126
   highlighting, 104
   holes in, 59–60
   inner boundary of, 59
   outer boundary of, 56
   simple, 56
PolygonWithInnerAndOuterBoundaries.kml,
   60–61
<PolyStyle>, 56–58, 72, 77–78, 310
PolyStyle.kml, 77–79
PuffModel.kml, 161–163

Q

query string, 165

R

radioFolder value, 92, 291
random color, 75
<range>, 33, 293
rectangle, 134, 305
   field of view for, 136
refresh, 146–149, 159–160
   view–based, 167–170
<refreshInterval>, 156, 288
<refreshMode>, 155–156, 288
refreshModeEnum type, 264
<refreshVisibility>, 154, 297
<Region>, 214, 276, 310–313
   bounding box of, 216–217

W

wcs2kml, 327
Web Map Service, 165
<west>, 124, 224, 279, 311
<when>, 200, 319
WineRegions.kmz, 230–235
world coordinate system (WCS), 327

X

<x>, 295
x value, 282
<xal:AddressDetails>, 274
xunits value, 282

Y

<y>, 295
y value, 282
yunits value, 282

Z

<z>, 295
Zip archives, 41
Zulu time, 198

Google™ Web Toolkit Applications

Ryan Dewsbury | ISBN-13: 978-0-321-50196-7

Get the edge you need to deliver exceptional user experiences with this guidebook that provides developers with core information and instructions for creating rich web applications. Whether you're a developer who needs to build high-performance front-end applications, or to integrate with external web services, this resource from expert GWT developer Ryan Dewsbury delivers the in-depth coverage you'll need.

Google™ Web Toolkit Solutions

David Geary | ISBN-13: 978-0-132-34481-4

Focuses on the more advanced aspects of GWT and obstacles developers face. Each solution in this practical, hands-on book is more than a recipe. The sample programs are carefully explained in detail to help you quickly master advanced GWT techniques.

Google™ Web Toolkit Solutions (Digital Short Cut): Cool & Useful Stuff

David Geary | ISBN-13: 978-0-131-58465-5

This digital Short Cut explores and discusses a few of the advanced aspects of the GWT using two applications: an address book and a Yahoo! trip viewer—both of which use remote procedure calls to access information on the server or an online web service.

Googling Security

Greg Conti | ISBN-13: 978-0-321-27854-8

Google knows a lot more about each of us than we realize...more than we might want them to! This is the first book to reveal how Google's vast information stockpiles can be used against individuals or companies—and what you can do about it!

978-0-321-50196-7   978-0-132-34481-4

 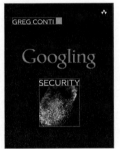

978-0-131-58465-5   978-0-321-51866-8

For more information and to read sample material, please visit informit.com.

Titles are also available at safari.informit.com.

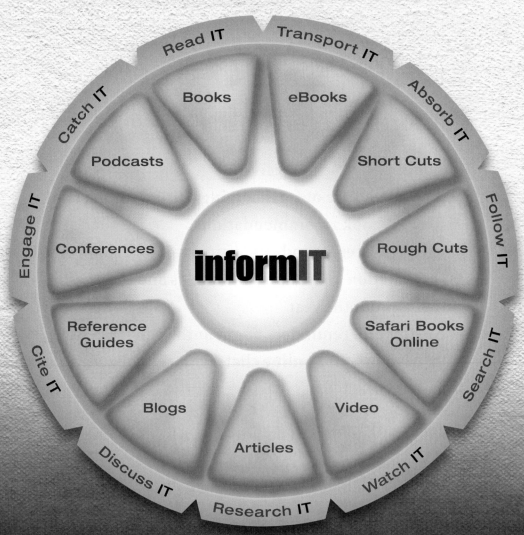

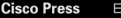

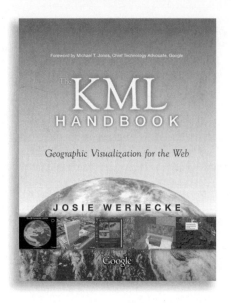

FREE Online Edition

Your purchase of **The KML Handbook** includes access to a free online edition for 45 days through the Safari Books Online subscription service. Nearly every Addison-Wesley Professional book is available online through Safari Books Online, along with more than 5,000 other technical books and videos from publishers such as, Cisco Press, Exam Cram, IBM Press, O'Reilly, Prentice Hall, Que, and Sams.

SAFARI BOOKS ONLINE allows you to search for a specific answer, cut and paste code, download chapters, and stay current with emerging technologies.

Activate your FREE Online Edition at www.informit.com/safarifree

> **STEP 1:** Enter the coupon code: SUQXTYG.

> **STEP 2:** New Safari users, complete the brief registration form.
> Safari subscribers, just log in.

If you have difficulty registering on Safari or accessing the online edition, please e-mail customer-service@safaribooksonline.com